JAMES M. WILLIAMS

CIVIL WAR GENERAL
and
INDIAN FIGHTER

★ ★

JAMES M. WILLIAMS

★ ★

Leader of the 1st Kansas Colored Volunteer Infantry
and the 8th U. S. Cavalry

by

ROBERT W. LULL

Number 12: War and the Southwest Series

University of North Texas Press
Denton, Texas

10   9   8   7   6   5   4   3   2   1

Permissions:
University of North Texas Press
1155 Union Circle #311336
Denton, TX 76203-5017

The paper used in this book meets the minimum requirements of the American National Standard for Permanence of Paper for Printed Library Materials, z39.48.1984. Binding materials have been chosen for durability.

Library of Congress Cataloging-in-Publication Data

Lull, Robert W., 1944–
 Civil War General and Indian Fighter James M. Williams: Leader of the 1st Kansas Colored Volunteer Infantry and the 8th U. S. Cavalry / by Robert W. Lull. — 1st ed.
   p. cm. — (War and the Southwest series ; no. 12)
 Includes bibliographical references.
 ISBN 978-1-57441-502-5 (cloth : alk. paper) — ISBN 978-1-57441-512-4 (e-book)
 1. Williams, James M. (James Monroe), 1833–1907. 2. United States. Army. Kansas Colored Infantry Regiment, 1st (1863–1864)—Biography. 3. United States. Army. Cavalry, 8th—Biography. 4. Generals—United States—Biography. 5. United States—History—Civil War, 1861–1865—Campaigns. 6. Indians of North America—Wars—1866–1895. I. Title. II. Series: War and the Southwest series ; no. 12.
 E467.1.W73L85 2013
 355.0092—dc23
 [B]
                    2012050962

Civil War General and Indian Fighter James M. Williams: Leader of the 1st Kansas Colored Volunteer Infantry and the 8th U. S. Cavalry is Number Twelve in the War and the Southwest Series.

Dedication

For Penny; her patience was tested, and she met the challenge.

The Man in the Arena

"It is not the critic who counts: not the man who points out
how the strong man stumbles
or where the doer of deeds could have done better.
The credit belongs to the man who is actually in the arena,
whose face is marred by dust and sweat and blood, who strives valiantly,
who errs and comes up short again and again,
because there is no effort without error or shortcoming,
but who knows the great enthusiasms, the great devotions,
who spends himself for a worthy cause;
who, at the best, knows, in the end, the triumph of high achievement,
and who, at the worst, if he fails, at least he fails while daring greatly,
so that his place shall never be with those cold and timid souls
who knew neither victory nor defeat."

Theodore Roosevelt
April 23, 1910

Contents

Illustrations

Preface

A Story Never Told

James Monroe Williams (1833–1907) had the privilege of being part of some of the most exciting years in American History. His contributions helped maintain the momentum of American history wherever he went. He not only lived it; he made some of that history, and helped to transform the character of his country.

In his childhood, Williams was a participant in the Great Migration, moving west with the frontier. As a young man, he led Kansas Jayhawkers on raids into Missouri during the bloody antebellum conflict over slavery. Williams entered the Civil War commanding a cavalry company, and moved on to organize and command a regiment of black infantrymen before President Lincoln even authorized black men to serve in the army. Williams' First Kansas Colored Volunteer Infantry was the first black regiment to engage Confederate forces, and the first to win—establishing the black soldiers' credibility as fighters. Under Williams' command, they established an exceptional combat record in the Trans-Mississippi Theater of war. James Williams' leadership in recruiting, training, and commanding the First Kansas Colored Volunteer Infantry contributed significantly to the history of the Civil War in the often-overlooked Trans-Mississippi region. His regiment's achievements and sacrifices in the Civil War eclipsed those of many others, both white and black.

Because of Williams' established record of leadership and dependability, higher-level commanders formed a preferential reliance upon him and his regiment. Before war's end, he earned a brevet promotion to brigadier general and command of a brigade.

In the postwar southwest, Williams commanded cavalrymen charged with securing the southwestern frontier for the flood of settlers. He scored early victories in conflicts with Indians, restoring settler confidence in the military after several years of unrestricted depredations. His ventures against the Indians established successful tactics, achieving results where others had failed. His successful raids on the Apache and Hualapai earned strong praise from the relieved citizenry of Arizona, commendation from higher commanders, and later accolades from Congress.

When Williams left the army—debilitated by five wounds at the hands of Confederates and hostile Indians—he became a pioneer rancher and businessman in southern Colorado, again putting his imprint on history.

To date, no one has produced a single biography of this man. Yet, his historic actions merited numerous appearances in books, newspapers, magazines, and journals. Similarly, no one has published a complete history of the groundbreaking First Kansas Colored Volunteer Infantry, nor is there a comprehensive description of the Eighth US Cavalry and its role in taming the West. James Monroe Williams played a part in all of that.

This narrative is an examination of Williams' life, and the context within which he stepped forward to shape history. It provides new insight into the days of "Bleeding Kansas" and Kansas Jayhawkers. It offers an account of the creation of a regiment of black Americans who made history in the Trans-Mississippi Civil War. It illustrates the reality of life in the postwar, frontier army of Apacheria in Arizona and New Mexico. This story is overdue.

Acknowledgments

When I first became interested in James Monroe Williams several years ago, all I knew was that he had been a general in the Civil War. I then learned that his wife grew up on a plantation and owned slaves, so I presumed he had been a Confederate general. Then, I came across a *carte de visite* photograph of him. He was in a Yankee uniform! As a novice pursuing an interest in history, I had little idea how to research or where to look. Armed with the *carte de visite* photograph, I began my quest. The back of that card had a photographer's imprint from Leavenworth, Kansas, so I posted an inquiry about Williams to the web site for the Kansas City Civil War Roundtable. About a year later, I received a message from Chris Tabor of Butler, Missouri, who proved to be a treasure chest of information. He generously shared volumes of information with me, and on my subsequent visits to Missouri and Kansas, he took the time to guide me to key locales in Williams' history. He introduced me to Arnold Schofield, then a historian at the Fort Scott National Historic Site, and an encyclopedic source of knowledge about the First Kansas Colored Volunteer Infantry. Chris then took me to Blair Tarr of the Kansas State Historical Society and Curator of the Kansas Museum of History who, on his own time, shared artifacts and knowledge of James Williams' history. For all this, Chris Tabor is due special thanks for his information, perspiration, and inspiration. No one knows more about this subject than Chris.

Through Chris, I met Commissioner Donna Gregory of Bates County and Butler, Missouri. Donna is a dynamic leader who has been instrumental in preserving the heritage earned by the First Kansas Colored Volunteer

Infantry. At her side, Peggy Buhr, Curator of the Bates County Museum, has also been a tremendous help. They are a great team.

The internet provided an endless chain of information. It was nearly magical. Many kind and helpful folks provided unsolicited information leading to more information. Messages from third party connections popped up from time to time without anticipation. It was like stumbling upon gold nuggets.

Naturally, organized searches for information were bricks built upon the foundation provided by Chris. The National Archives, state historical societies, university archives, genealogical societies, county archives, and numerous other groups have also provided amazing volumes of information.

Prominent individual historians have patiently opened up pathways of thought and inspiration. Ed Bearss, a giant among America's Civil War historians, is due a great debt of gratitude for his information, continuing encouragement, and patience with the text. Likewise, Robert Utley, the extraordinary historian of the Indian Wars, graciously provided his support and information to this project. Charlotte Beagle, historian of Lowville, New York, gave freely of her knowledge, time, and support. Steven Warren, historian and television producer, filled in gaps, provided encouragement, and became an internet intermediary of great value. Neta Pope and Andrea Jaquez, researchers of Fort Bayard, New Mexico, provided inspiration, time, information, and continuing support. They, too, are a great team. Likewise, the staff members of the Kansas State Archives and Library were truly understanding and supportive, especially Nancy Sherbert. The library staffs of New Mexico State University, Western New Mexico University, and Baylor University all proved to be generous, interested, and gracious in their professional support.

I would like to thank Brett Woods, PhD, and Mark Bowles, PhD, of the American Military University, who provided essential encouragement, guidance, support, and patience. Steven Woodworth, PhD, of Texas Christian University provided encouragement, constructive criticism, and valuable suggestions. His recommendations led, ultimately, to publication. Charles Williams of Fort Worth, and Courtney Welch, PhD, of the University of North Texas, graciously shared joint information that provided structure to this study. Bob Alexander, an entertaining and prominent historian of the wild Southwest, has been a great source of information, as well as guidance on translating information into text. Bill Shaw of Colorado Springs, who bought and refurbished a house built by James Williams in Trinidad, Colorado, took time to research its history, and shared it with me, for which I am grateful. To Shirley Sisk, M. J. Norton, Joe Chase, Janis Franchi, and other genealogy buffs in Wisconsin, I owe my gratitude for a veritable barrage of information.

Significantly, Ron Chrisman, Director of the University of North Texas Press, proved to be an unending source of patient guidance, assisting in the complex task of negotiating the path to publication. Susan Thomas, who patiently edited the manuscript, making it much more readable, is also due my thanks, and the appreciation of those who read this story.

Introduction

Growing Up
in the North Country

As America wearily entered the fourth year of its cataclysmic civil war, James M. Williams commanded a brigade in the Union Army's Seventh Corps in Arkansas. On February 13, 1865, he became a brigadier general at the age of thirty-one.[1] He had come a long way from the distant days when he was the youngest of thirteen children on a farm in extreme northern New York. In the process of getting to that point, the events of his life thus far combined into an adventure characterizing that era of America's history. His story was America's story.

On September 12, 1833, Fannie Williams gave birth to James Monroe Williams and his twin sister, Mary. They joined their eleven brothers and sisters in an expansive farmhouse located in the remote North Country of New York.[2] Their farm was northwest of the tiny village of Lowville, in the sparsely populated landscape east of where Lake Ontario flows into the Saint Lawrence River, defining America's shared boundary with Canada.

Northern New York, near the Canadian border, was very much a frontier. Huge lake-effect snowstorms blocked the primitive roads and unpredictable dirt paths in the winter. Deep mud in the spring, and swarms of mosquitoes in the summer had similar effect. Much of the country was naturally wild growth, and uninhabited.

Lowville, and the Williams farm, is approximately twenty-seven miles east of present-day Watertown and Lake Ontario, nestled in a small valley bounded on three sides by large wooded hills. The valley served as passage for French troops and their Indian allies to campaign south against the British colonies in the 1750s and 1760s. It served a similar purpose for American troops moving north in the Revolution.

Lowville was the product of a land lottery in 1798—the lucky winner, Nicholas Low, promptly named the land after himself. It originally was part of an enormous 3.8 million-acre tract of land purchased by Alexander Macomb for eight cents an acre, subdivided it, and held a lottery to sell townships. Although Lowville became a village in 1800, a half-century would pass before its incorporation in 1854. Even then, its population had only reached around nine hundred. In the two centuries of its existence, it has grown to only thirty-five hundred residents.[3]

Early settlers constructed log houses.[4] Rustic was as good as it got. Nevertheless, some hardy souls saw the promise of the North Country and set about taming it. Among them was James Williams' family. His father, Absalom Williams, was one of the earliest settlers in what became the village of Lowville, arriving there around 1800.[5] Like many frontiersmen, Absalom Williams set about the serious work of carving productive land out of the wilderness. His farm eventually extended across a few hundred acres of Lewis County. Over time, he bought and sold parcels of land, adjusting his inventory to provide the most profitable mix.[6] By 1825, his livestock included horses, cattle, sheep, and hogs. The Williams family produced wool, flannel, and cotton linen.[7] Every member of the large family contributed to the enterprise. Typical of frontier settlers, they were hard working, independent, and productive.

Williams was born in the rural North Country, which clearly shaped him as a person. Patriotic pride came early in life; it was central to his family heritage, his public education, and community activities. As late as 1840, when Williams was a schoolboy, there were still thirty-eight Revolutionary War pensioners publicly honored in Lewis County. One of them was Williams' maternal grandfather, Salmon Root, who served in the Continental Army from April 1778 to June of 1783 as a corporal in Judd's Company of Colonel Zebulon Butler's Fourth Connecticut Regiment.[8] Periodic drills of militia regiments were frequent community affairs, with a few hours of drill followed by a picnic-type atmosphere, martial music and flags waving in the breeze. The North Country's local regiment mustered as early as 1805 with many men from Lewis County. With the advent of the War of 1812, the federal government issued a draft of one hundred thousand men from militias around the United States. This included 230 men from the North Country who served for just over three months at nearby Sackets Harbor. Another company of men from the Lowville area mustered, and successfully skirmished with British troops that October. More mobilization calls followed through late 1814, when the war ended.[9] Absalom Williams, James Williams' father, served in the War of 1812 as a private in New York's Fifth Brigade.[10]

These seasoned veterans were the center of attention on Independence Day and other occasions when the good citizens of Lowville gathered. Local politicians never dared to allow such public events to take place without embracing veterans of America's two wars of independence from Britain. The Williams family used such events to gather in Lowville and congregate with others from the community. Young James Williams and his pals restlessly listened to the long-winded commemorations of the aging veterans. Sometimes, the children found it difficult to comprehend how men that old could have accomplished such military feats of dashing bravery. Nevertheless, the exposure to such pomp and circumstance surely caught the children's attention, leaving a long-term impact.

Lowville today is an attractive small town of friendly, hard-working people of mostly French, German, and English background. They reflect values evolved in the North Country, and a sense of independence little different from that prevalent when James Williams was a child. Alexis De Tocqueville, the prominent writer and student of American democracy at about the time Williams was born, addressed the unique focus of America's small towns, "[T]he interests of the country are everywhere kept in view . . . and every citizen is as warmly attached to them as if they were his own. He takes pride in the glory of his nation; he boasts of its success, to which he conceives himself to have contributed."[11]

James Williams was born into an exciting and rapidly changing America—the era of Andrew Jackson. The United States was only a half-century past the Revolution, and less than two decades beyond re-asserting its independence in the War of 1812. Americans were confident in the future, and eagerly looking over the western horizon for whatever was next.

The vigorous growth of America was not without controversy. While democracy opened up grand vistas for whites, slavery isolated a significant part of society from those vistas. The Missouri Compromise of 1820 had only drawn a line separating free North and slave South; it left the issue itself to fester and weigh on the country's mind. The abolitionist movement took hold and grew stronger throughout the North.

Williams' childhood passed in an environment classically suited to form early conclusions about the idea of slavery. As a schoolchild early in America's history, he would have heard all about the Declaration of Independence and the concept that "All men are created equal." Likewise, slavery was a prime subject of discussion in any North Country community. The growing ideological rift between slave and free states was never far from the news. The Missouri Compromise was always a hot topic.

The northern states, including New York, had abolished slavery. New York began in 1781 with manumission of slaves who had served in the Continental Army, later following with similar legislation for those who served America in the War of 1812. The state assembly passed general legislation in 1799 initiating a gradual emancipation of New York slaves, freeing the last of its slaves on July 4, 1827.[12] Ownership of slaves was incomprehensible to northern farmers who believed individuals exerted their own efforts to reap their own rewards. In the Williams family, it is likely James Williams' grandfather, Salmon Root, reinforced the antislavery bias with his own experiences. In his revolutionary war regiment, the Fourth Connecticut, the Second Company consisted of fifty-two black men serving alongside the white men of the regiment.[13]

In 1844, after three decades in Lowville, the Williams family sold their land, packed their belongings into wagons, and emigrated west, caught up in America's great migration. The lure of western lands was strong. Lowville was growing and closing in on Williams' land. The Erie Canal, passing only forty-five miles from Lowville, was a likely a means of transporting the large Williams family to the west. Settlers were rapidly populating lands of the Old Northwest Territory, particularly Ohio, Michigan, Illinois, and Indiana. Although most of those pioneers settled along the Ohio River in the southern reaches of the Old Northwest, other hardy souls pursued the less-traveled northern route.[14]

The journey west was an adventure for young James. He was traveling into new lands, leaving behind less adventurous folks. Every hilltop brought forth a new view; every valley a dense forest, where excitement lurked behind every tree. This was the former "Northwest Territory." Only a few years earlier, Sauk war chief Blackhawk fought American soldiers across this terrain. Less than a century before, two other wars—the French and Indian War (Seven Years' War) and the American Revolution—ebbed and flowed across this landscape.

Ultimately, the Williams family, including eleven-year-old James Williams, trekked to Wisconsin Territory. They found a destination at Lafayette Township, in Walworth County. Their journey of 850 miles westward from Lowville was over.[15]

Once in Wisconsin, Absalom Williams and his oldest son Absalom, Jr., proceeded to acquire farmland in Walworth and Rock counties, obtaining 520 acres of land, of which 40 were in Walworth County, and 480 were in adjacent Rock County.[16] By then, Absalom was nearing seventy years of age. Consequently, Absalom, Jr. in his thirties took up the reins, as well as control of the land. He set up his own home in nearby Spring Prairie. The passing of years brought change to the family as the children grew up. By 1850, all but five of the Williams children reached adulthood, and moved on from Absalom's household. James and his twin sister, Mary, at seventeen years of age, were the youngest of those remaining.[17]

It was evident that as the youngest male in the family, James would have little future role in running or owning the family farm. He needed to find his own way. It was time to strike out on his own. In 1853, he went to Janesville, in nearby Rock County to study law.[18]

For a budding young attorney in Janesville, politics, especially in regards to slavery, were a major part of discussions. The Kansas-Nebraska Act of 1854 was, under guise of "popular sovereignty," abrogating the Missouri Compromise of 1820, carving out the territories of Kansas and Nebraska from the Louisiana Purchase, re-allocating the status of slavery in territories, and dramatically opening up the land to expanded opportunities for slavery.

Popular sovereignty was a classic example of the law of unintended consequences. Rather than being soothed with the realization that settlers would decide the slavery issue via the ballot box in their own soon-to-be states, hostilities between the opposing factions escalated. Thousands of proponents for and against slavery poured into Kansas Territory with undisguised intentions of swinging the vote. Missourians, fearing their slaves would have escape routes on three sides if Kansas became a free state, stormed across the border stuffing ballot boxes, harassing and intimidating Free-State supporters, burning them out of their homes, and creating havoc. Rabid abolitionists struck back, fueling the atmosphere of terror. Kansas became a violent and dangerous place.

The Whig Party collapsed, leaving Democrats from North and South eyeing each other suspiciously. The nascent Republican Party, evolving in Wisconsin, stepped in to fill the void, taking a stance against slavery. In context, it is readily apparent at this stage of Williams' life many factors were coalescing to form the man who would involve himself in America's future. His family history, exposure to mores of frontier communities in the North, and a formal education all combined to create the character of the man he became. He was intelligent, independent, informed, and principled. At an ideological stage of life, he was representative of many strong-willed young Americans; those who would make things happen.

In the mid-1850s, Kansas was the place to make history. Upon completing his studies and passing the bar exam in 1856, James Williams and his older brother Sam set out for Kansas to become part of the great adventure. In so doing, they joined the mass of northerners streaming across America in a crusade to keep Kansas Territory from becoming a slave state.[19] The road to James Williams' future, and that of America, stretched before him.

Chapter One

Bleeding Kansas, Border Ruffians, and Jayhawkers

James Williams and his brother Sam arrived at Leavenworth, Kansas in 1856. They found the town growing at an explosive rate, with opportunity, excitement and conflict everywhere. Leavenworth had all the trappings of a western boomtown, and then some.

The Kansas-Nebraska act, signed by President Pierce two years earlier in 1854, opened huge expanses of the western prairie to settlers. Pierce's signature prompted a major land rush and several years of bloody conflict. Prior to the act's implementation date, much of what would become Kansas was Indian land—off limits to white men.[1] When the Kansas-Nebraska Act became law, there were fewer than 800 whites in Kansas. When the first territorial census was completed the following year, Kansas population numbered 8,000 whites and 192 slaves.[2]

The political heat of popular sovereignty and the conflict over slavery drew the Williams brothers into the maelstrom like moths to a flame. They became part of the volatile mix of immigrants with competing agendas crowding by thousands into Kansas at Leavenworth. There were abolitionist activists, pro-slavery advocates, and ordinary folks all capitalizing on opportunities for new land. The sheer number of such individuals was sure to create a flashpoint.[3]

Most of the first people who swarmed across the border into northeast Kansas were from Missouri. They were friends of Missouri Senator David

Atchison, an outspoken pro-slavery advocate. Atchison, though a legislator from Missouri, felt no compunction about jumping into Kansas politics to ensure a pro-slavery outcome on the planned elections. He forewarned about 200 of his pals of the coming passage of the bill and had them ready to move. At the prime moment, he telegraphed them: "go over and take possession of the good land, it is yours."[4]

Atchison's cronies, especially the more fervent supporters of slavery, established two small communities in the northeast corner of Kansas. They named one town Atchison, for obvious reasons, and the other Kickapoo, after the Indians who had been there first. More moderate supporters of the pro-slavery cause laid out the nearby community of Leavenworth.

The next wave, which included both Williams brothers, consisted primarily of abolitionists and Free-State immigrants from the East and upper Midwest. Some piled off fleets of steamboats coming up the Missouri River to Leavenworth landing. Others traveled by covered wagons coming cross-country.[5]

Many of the new Kansans stormed into the territory in groups sponsored by abolitionist or pro-slavery organizations in their respective states, especially Massachusetts and South Carolina. Not all the migrants, however, came from those two political hotbeds. Strong feelings prevailed in other states as well, including Wisconsin. Several sponsored emigrant groups left Wisconsin in 1856, destined for Kansas. Among the sponsors were the Wisconsin Emigrant Aid Society and the Wisconsin Kansas Aid Society. The latter organization was reputed to be sending heavily armed men ready to fight. Other groups were more intent upon sending legitimate settlers of the abolitionist persuasion. James and Sam Williams likely were part of one of these groups, enthused by a series of fiery speeches by Jim Lane of Kansas throughout Wisconsin.[6]

As they settled into Leavenworth, James and his brother opened a business together—a book and stationery shop on Delaware Street, variably known as *J.M. Williams, Book Seller*, or as *Williams & Bro.* The store sold books, stationery, sheet music, wallpaper, and schoolbooks. James chose not to practice law. Sam, already an attorney, ultimately took up the practice. He became a justice of the peace and a land agent, establishing his office near his brother's store.[7]

Figure 1   Leavenworth, Kansas 1856

The Kansas-Nebraska Act of 1854 led to the creation of instant communities in the new Territory of Kansas. Prospects of land, livelihood and adventure drew thousands from around the country. By 1856, Leavenworth's population reached three thousand. LIBRARY OF CONGRESS IMAGE.

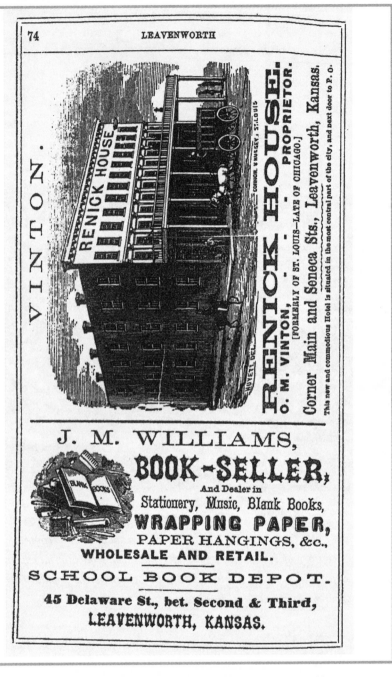

Figure 2   Advertisement for J.M. Williams, Bookseller

This advertisement for James and Sam Williams' business appeared in the Leavenworth City Directory *of 1858. City directories of the time equated to the telephone books of today—white and yellow pages.*

Williams arrived in Leavenworth in a period of escalating conflict between the two sides of the slavery issue. Arguments frequently led to gunplay and even death. Mobs from either side of the argument captured and tarred and feathered members of the opposition. Those hapless souls, newly initiated in sartorially feathered elegance, subsequently rode into exile on a wooden rail.[8] There was little or no room for neutrality; Williams, like everyone else, had to participate.

Preliminary elections were held to determine Kansas' future status as a slave or free state and to elect a territorial legislature. Missouri Border Ruffians in large numbers came across the border into Kansas, stuffed ballot boxes, threatened and intimidated legitimate voters, and stole the elections. The results yielded heavy pro-slavery outcomes, but there were suspiciously more than twice as many votes cast as there were eligible voters. A federally appointed governor ignored the obvious fraud, recognizing the pro-slavery legislature.[9]

Free-State supporters, enraged by the outcomes, established a shadow government in Topeka, while the recognized pro-slavery legislature ultimately settled in at Lecompton. The irrepressible Senator Atchison of Missouri continued his crusade to stir up conflict in Kansas by egging on the pro-slavery faction. In a un-statesman-like mien, Atchison exhorted his Kansas followers: "We will be compelled to shoot, burn and hang . . . the abolitionists."[10] The Missouri incursions and violent Kansas backlash set the stage for the coming national brutality of a Civil War.

On May 21, 1856, in what is known as the sacking of Lawrence, Atchison led a pro-slavery gang of several hundred Border Ruffians, apparently originating from Kickapoo, into the town of Lawrence—the stronghold of the Free-State movement. His role in the incident is controversial; some historians acknowledge his presence and/or role as a leader, others deny it, and still others quote him verbatim as below. Atchison's gang styled themselves as the "Kickapoo Rangers." Among their numbers was Sheriff Sam Jones from Leavenworth who had come to arrest two fugitives, which he did without incident. Atchison, with his own brand of devilment in mind, had a cannon brought up before the Free-State Hotel. The hotel was a two-story edifice serving as headquarters of the Emigrant Aid Society, the sponsoring agency for many of the Freestaters who had come from Massachusetts. It had also been the site of the constitutional convention of the Free-State shadow government. Atchison gave hotel residents a short time to evacuate the buildings, and proceeded to whip his Border Ruffians into frenzy with an impassioned speech:

> Boys, this day I am a Kickapoo Ranger, by God! This day we have entered Lawrence with Southern Rights inscribed upon our banner, and not one damned abolitionist dared to fire a gun.
>
> Now, boys, this is the happiest day of my life. We have entered that damned town, and taught the damned abolitionists a Southern lesson they will remember until the day they die. And now, boys, we will go in again . . . and test the strength of that damned Free-State Hotel, and teach the Emigrant Aid Company that Kansas shall be ours. . . . Your duty I know you will do. If one man or woman dare stand before you, blow them to hell with a chunk of cold lead.[11]

That said, Atchison lit off the fuse. With his accuracy somewhat diffused by ardent spirits, however, he overshot, shooting the cannonball clear over the top of the building—this in keeping with his moniker, "Staggering Davy," attributed to the *Boston Evening Telegraph*.[12] Thoughtful leaders of the Kickapoo Rangers then placed the cannon in the hands of those better able to display artillerist skills. These cannon-wielding sharpshooters fired thirty shots at the building, leaving equally as many holes in the stone structure, but minimal permanent damage. Frustrated, the dauntless Border Ruffians planted two barrels of gunpowder in the basement in an attempt to blow down the building. Again, the Free-State Hotel stood its ground—seriously wounded, but not leveled. Armed with anger and debris from looting the premises, the Missourians set fire to the structure from within. The inside of the building burned, and the remaining gaunt ruin was more a testimony of its survival than its destruction. The abolitionists rebuilt it.

The cannon in that event, later named Kickapoo Cannon, or "Old Kickapoo," has an illustrious history, especially worthy of telling because it includes James Williams. An amalgamation of several, sometimes-divergent stories follows. Colonel Alexander Doniphan captured the cannon at the Battle of Sacramento in Chihuahua, Mexico, in the course of his legendary campaign into Mexico in 1846–47 during the Mexican War. At that time, the cannon had no name, although a sister cannon captured at the same time picked up the moniker "Old Sacramento." Doniphan brought both cannons back from Mexico and stored them at the US Army arsenal in Liberty, Missouri. Missouri Border Ruffians subsequently stole The Cannon with No Name from the arsenal and took it to Weston, Missouri, and then to Kickapoo, Kansas. Ultimately, the Kickapoo Rangers took it with them in May 1856 and used it on the Free-State Hotel in Lawrence in the previously described raid, known as the Sacking of Lawrence. They returned triumphantly to Kickapoo with the cannon in tow, and from time to time would trot it out for public celebrations.

Now the cannon had a name—"Old Kickapoo." Much of the time, Kickapoo Rangers kept it carefully hidden to keep it from Freestaters, but alas, the Freestaters got wind of the hiding place. On one cold night in January 1858, fifty or sixty Freestaters, including James Williams, quietly slipped into Kickapoo and stole the cannon. The following day, "the Free-State boys of Leavenworth, with drums beating and flags flying - some of the victorious army on foot, some on horseback, paraded the streets, dragging glorious Old Kickapoo after them."[13] Over twenty years later, Williams reminisced over his role in the adventure with fervor, writing "As one of the parties who left Leavenworth that cold night and returned at daylight the next morning bearing the cannon with us . . . and . . . safely land[ing] it in freedom loving Lawrence . . . I hope Free Kansas may forever keep it as a memento of the triumph of the 'Free State Boys' over those who would blacken the soil with the curse of African Slavery."[14] His narrative on this incident makes clear Williams' thoughts on slavery, and places him firmly in the abolitionist camp.

Old Kickapoo, having achieved antebellum notoriety and enjoyed its few minutes of fame, slowly faded into obscurity. The only service the cannon provided in the Civil War was to intimidate a captain on a steamboat into lowering his Confederate flag and raising Old Glory.[15] After the war, local officials fired it ceremoniously on July 4, and kept it on a bluff over the Missouri River to fire salutes welcoming inbound steamboats. Later, its custodians relegated it to a coal mine where it was used to blast tunnels. Unfortunately (or possibly fortunately), someone overcharged it, and the back of the barrel split. Afterward, ungrateful denizens of the mine consigned the faithful old cannon to a junk heap. In 1884, someone recognized and rescued it. The Kansas State Historical Society paid a scrap dealer $114 for Old Kickapoo, which now rests in dignified display at their museum in Topeka.[16]

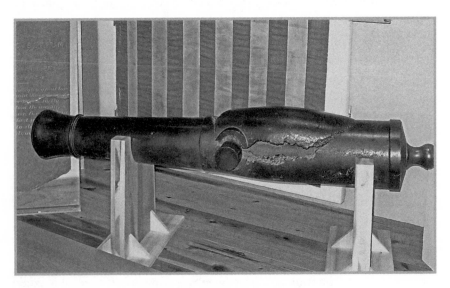

Figure 3   **Kickapoo Cannon**

The Kickapoo Cannon—an icon of the pre-Civil War conflict over slavery in Kansas—is now on display at the Museum of Kansas History in Topeka, Kansas. Note the split in the barrel, caused by overloading it in a coalmine after the war. Williams was proud to help capture it from the pro-slavery "Kickapoo Rangers." AUTHOR'S COLLECTION.

Williams did not allow his business or politics to eclipse the need for a personal life. He married Lydia Francis on July 5, 1856. Lydia, ten years his senior, was originally from Connecticut. Interestingly, she was also a twin. Sam also started a family. In spite of the growing violence in Kansas, James and his brother were determined to stay. The brothers bought homes next to each other and settled in.[17]

Having arrived two years into the boomtown festivities, Williams was anxious to catch up and take advantage of capitalist opportunities. Like many of the earliest residents of Leavenworth, he jumped into land speculation. He was involved in the purchase or sale of fourteen properties between 1857 and 1859. Some of those properties were in real estate developments in which Williams was a partner.[18]

With a further foray into domesticity, James and Lydia started a family. In 1858, he and Lydia had their first and only child—a daughter, Frances.

During the antebellum period, another attorney briefly had an office near James and Sam Williams. He was the future Major General William Tecumseh Sherman. He arrived at Leavenworth in September 1858 and entered into the practice of law as a partner in the firm of Sherman and Ewing. Their offices were on Main Street between Shawnee and Delaware, only a couple blocks from Williams' and his brother's business. Not being an attorney when he arrived, Sherman approached Judge Samuel Lecompte about training. Lecompte told Sherman training was unnecessary—he would grant Sherman a license immediately "on the grounds of general intelligence." Sherman did not see much future in the practice of law, so he applied for a job as superintendent of a new military college in Louisiana. He left his Leavenworth practice in the summer of 1859 and, after a stop in Ohio, took the job in Louisiana. That military college eventually became Louisiana State University.[19]

James Henry Lane, a leader in the Free-State movement and a lightning rod for controversy, would profoundly affect James Williams' future. Arriving in Kansas shortly before Williams, wielding a magnetic personality, he quickly became a prominent figure, attracting large numbers of people with similar interests. An attorney, he served as lieutenant governor of Indiana from 1849–1853 and, later, a United States representative for an undistinguished term . During the Mexican War, he was colonel of the Third Indiana

Volunteer Regiment, and served creditably at the Battle of Buena Vista, but
not without the type of controversy that would characterize the remainder of
his life. Back then, James Lane's regiment was in a brigade commanded by
Brigadier General Joseph Lane. These two men named Lane were not related,
and were "glad of it." They thoroughly despised each other. At one point in
the Mexican War, they had a verbal altercation on a parade ground in front
of troops and a number of fascinated bystanders. The "portly and dignified,"
but infuriated General Joseph Lane hauled off and took a swing at the tall,
lean Colonel James Lane. Colonel Lane blocked General Lane's punch and
delivered one of his own smack-dab in the General's chops. Nearby officers
broke up the melee, whereupon the general stormed off to his tent, yelling
that his miscreant subordinate best prepare himself for a duel. The general
returned with a rifle, and yelled " 'Ready!' " Fortunately, a number of the pro-
vost guard stepped in and broke up the altercation before some of Colonel
Lane's soldiers could shoot General Lane. To prevent further incidents, higher
headquarters worked out a solution that kept the two combatants away from
each other. James Lane's conduct in the coming years proved to be just as
combative and erratic.[20]

James Lane's appearance and demeanor were riveting, contributing
to his ability to hold sway over crowds with his impassioned oratory. His
narrow, almost gaunt face featured a prominent chin, straight nose, high
forehead, and heavy brows over intense eyes that bored into the souls of
observers. His hair flew away from his head and upward, almost appearing
to be aflame. His clothes appeared as if he dressed while distracted, loose and
uneven, surmounted by a commodious cape with military-styled soutache,
or embroidered braid. Chances are his style of dress, like his unkempt
appearance, was carefully calculated to add to his imposing visage, earning
him the appellation "Grim Chieftain." He radiated an intense energy, which
swept up his audience. Ian Spurgeon describes James Lane's hypnotic grasp
of an audience:

> If Lane's words electrified a crowd, they certainly seemed to electrify him
> as well. He could sway an audience like an orchestra director, exciting
> its senses and emotions. He ranged from low, guttural growls to high
> shrieks as he lectured fellow Americans on the most pressing matters of

the day, pointing a long bony finger toward the crowd for effect, and gazing at them with those powerful eyes. As his speech warmed up, Lane was known to partially undress himself, like a man preparing for a street fight. Off came his jacket, then tie; then he would roll up his shirt sleeves, all the while holding the audience with his eyes. A speech from lane was part political lecture, part evangelical sermon, and part theatrical production.[21]

In search of fame, Lane jumped into Kansas politics as a Democrat, but, to his dismay, no one noticed. Dissatisfied with the lack of attention, he shifted his energies to the Free-State Party and by 1855 became a delegate to its state convention. His position at that time was to tread softly on the issue of slavery, but he wanted blacks excluded from Kansas when it became a state. He soon achieved the recognition he sought and, by October, was elected president of the Free-State Party's constitutional convention.[22]

Lane's political colors continued to morph into extreme radicalism. He pushed the boundaries of polarization on the difference between the pro– and anti-slavery factions in Kansas, embracing the cause of abolition with a vengeance. While attending a formative meeting of the Free-State Party, he advocated the use of force in resisting the pro-slavery legislature in Lecompton.[23]

Kansas was a dangerous place. Harassment, intimidation, assault, house burning, and any other depredation in the name of one's stance on slavery, were commonplace. Armed conflict began late in the fall of 1855 with the killing of a Freestater by a pro-slavery man in what was actually a dispute over a land claim. A confrontation followed between Missouri Border Ruffians and Free-State supporters at Lawrence in what became the "Wakarusa War." Missourians in significant numbers (reported to be a thousand[24]) crossed the border, and converged on the Wakarusa River outside the Free-State town of Lawrence.[25]

The first Free-State militias were already formed by the time Lane and Williams arrived. The earliest of these was the Kansas Legion, soon followed by a number of similar paramilitary organizations. They received tangible support from northeastern states in the form of shipments of weapons and ammunition.[26]

Figure 4   **Senator James H. Lane of Kansas**

*Senator Lane—or General Lane, as he styled himself from time to time—was a
prominent figure in antebellum Kansas. He stirred the political pot wherever he
went, creating tempests that went down in history. His influence stretched from the
farmer behind the plow to the President of the United States. When his position of
influence became redundant, he killed himself.* LIBRARY OF CONGRESS PHOTOGRAPH.

In Lawrence, a militia of seven hundred men, dubbed the " 'Lawrence Legion' " quickly emerged with Lane extravagantly represented as a brigadier general. He promptly assumed the leadership role, directing the construction of redoubts and defensive positions.[27] Lane trained and drilled men as a cold winter storm settled in. In the meantime, a small delegation from Lawrence reached Governor William Shannon in Leavenworth and prevailed upon him to save the day. Shannon quickly rode to Lawrence and convinced the Missourians to go home. The Wakarusa war was over. It was the first organized confrontation of militias from Missouri and Kansas with each other, in a conflict that would last until 1865.[28]

The Lawrence Legion in the Wakarusa War was the first formally recognized Kansas military organization (albeit with questionable legitimacy) in which Lane held a leadership position. While Governor Shannon was in Lawrence, he saw that the opposing force was the Missourians, and recognized that his citizens could soon to be attacked by a militia from outside his territory. At one point in his discussions, a militiaman reported that the Missourians were moving to the attack. Lane, ever the opportunist, prevailed upon the governor to sign an authorization for the Lawrence Legion to repel attackers. When the attack did not take place, Governor Shannon demanded elimination of the written authorization. By then, however, enterprising journalists had obtained copies of it and communicated messages to Eastern newspapers. Lane's military role in Kansas was underway.[29]

In what amounted to a continuation of the Wakarusa War, Lane led a number of raids on pro-slavery "forts" around Kansas. About a hundred of his men attacked a blockhouse near Franklin, exchanging shots with the pro-slavery defenders for several hours and suffering some casualties. Daunted by their inability to achieve success with musket fire against thick wood walls and small loopholes from which defenders could shoot, they achieved victory by rolling a flaming wagon of hay against the blockhouse walls. The defenders fled, leaving behind a substantial cache of weapons, including the cannon "Old Sacramento." They took another blockhouse, Fort Titus, in the same fashion, with a flaming wagon, augmented by the firing of their newly acquired artillery piece.[30]

Many of these "forts" were actually homes converted to blockhouses by pro-slavery occupants. One such place, "Fort Saunders," was attacked in August 1856. It was a two-story structure capable of holding up to a hundred

defenders. Lane and a number of other anti-slavery leaders attacked the fortified house with four to five hundred men, reinforced by an equal number of
deceptive straw dummies. The pro-slavery defenders, deluded into believing
as many as twelve hundred men were attacking, fled, leaving behind an ample
booty of guns and powder. This scenario repeated itself many times over the
next five years.[31]

During this period, Williams and Lane came to know each other. Williams
probably participated in some armed attacks, and was definitely active in abolition and Free-State movements, as noted in the Kickapoo Cannon incident.
Whether he participated on his own initiative or under Lane's leadership is
open to question, but he very clearly served with Lane shortly thereafter.

In the latter half of the 1850s, frequent confrontations ensued with
increasingly larger forces opposing each other. Marauding armies of men
crisscrossed the land, attacking each other, burning homes, stealing animals
and property, and terrifying families. Some of these forces exceeded two thousand men. At one point, Atchison, the now former senator from Missouri, set
out with twenty-seven hundred men to wipe out Lane's Army.[32]

The violence continued to escalate. John Brown, another recent arrival
in Kansas, and a rabid abolitionist, responded to the Missourians' assault on
Lawrence with an attack on pro-slavery settlers. He and his sons on the night
of May 24, 1856 forced five men into a swale along Pottawatomie Creek in
Franklin County; murdered them, hacking them to death with swords. In
May of 1858, a group of border ruffians rounded up eleven Free-State settlers,
lined them up on the edge of a ravine near the Marais Des Cygnes River, and
gunned them down. Five of the settlers died.

It is not possible to exaggerate the breadth of violence that took place
along the Kansas-Missouri border in the antebellum period. Gangs of
marauders roamed across the land, "filling the air with profanity, intimidating pro-slavery settlers, shooting at those who were not sufficiently docile,
and plundering right and left." Free-State and pro-slavery factions alike terrorized the country.[33]

In the midst of these events, Williams took an increasingly more active
role in anti-slavery activity. On one occasion, Williams and his new acquain-
tance from down the street, William Tecumseh Sherman, were involved in
a scuffle with border ruffians. The Missouri ruffians chased down a fugitive

slave, intent on dragging him back into Missouri. Williams and Sherman jumped into the fray, fought off the pursuers, and rescued the runaway slave.[34]

James Montgomery of Kansas, who soon would be Williams' regimental commander, was a Free-State man, committed to abolition, and excelled at raiding pro-slavery supporters on both sides of the border.[35] Another prominent Free-State leader was Charles R. Jennison. His band of men, known as "Jennison's Jayhawkers," gave birth to the term "Jayhawking," which would come to describe any raiding or plundering by Freestaters.[36] Jennison earned a reputation with his taste for violence and mayhem. In describing these two leaders, Albert Castel writes that Jennison's "chief traits were brutality, unscrupulousness, and opportunism. Montgomery was probably a sincere anti-slavery fanatic, but with Jennison, fighting against slavery was mainly an excuse for banditry."[37]

A number of paramilitary anti-slavery units flooded into Kansas from midwestern and northeastern states. Well organized and heavily armed with new, state-of-the-art Sharps rifles and carbines, they sought out unlikely routes (through Iowa, for instance) into Kansas in order to avoid federal troops and Border Ruffians from Missouri. Lane led one such unit of 250 men into Kansas. Known as Lane's "Army of the North," this was another antecedent unit of what would later become "Lane's Brigade."[38]

It is highly probable that Williams participated in similar actions. No formal records exist for these units in the years before the Civil War broke out, nor for the actual formation of Lane's Brigade. Telling evidence of Williams' experience, however, is found in a description of an engagement his company was involved at Harrisonville, Missouri, a few years later, on July 24, 1861. This was very early in the formation of Lane's Brigade. Together, Williams and his company mustered into the brigade just twelve days prior to the engagement, becoming one of the first companies to do so. It was common practice at the time for an individual to recruit a unit and then hold elections for officers. Presumably, the elected commander would be the organizer.[39] The fact that Williams had a company ready to muster so quickly indicates it was already a functioning organization. At Harrisonville, Williams engaged the enemy immediately, aggressively deployed his troops, maneuvered them deliberately and in control, and overcame opposition (a description of the engagement follows in the next chapter). Historian Bryce Benedict quoted a soldier in Williams' company, writing to the *Leavenworth Conservative*, reporting the conduct of troops when taking a break at one point in their march: "The bugle sounded the assembly and the men fell 'into two rows, like the regulars' with unusual alacrity.'"[40] Williams' troops' teamwork and response to orders in combat indicate that Williams had been in command of this company much longer than twelve days. His men were well trained, and he was comfortable in command; clearly, he and his men had been in combat together before. This kind of preparation takes months, not days. A logical conclusion is that he had been participating in paramilitary operations of one kind or another well before the formal baptism of Lane's Brigade. It is also probable that he had done this in one or another of Lane's antecedent units.

Another legislative election took place in October 1857. This time, it proved to be a dramatic Free-State victory. The conflict subsided for a time, but simmered in the background. The years of 1859 and 1860 provided diversions taking precedence over politics. A drought of historic severity swept the territory, wiping out farmers by the thousands, leaving many struggling with the specter of starvation. Due to a drought—practically no rain for two years—over thirty thousand settlers left Kansas. Equally as many additional settlers stayed because they could not financially afford to leave. Only vast amounts of aid from eastern states kept the remaining settlers alive.[41]

The dawn of 1861 brought statehood to Kansas. On January 29, The *Leavenworth Conservative* heralded a symbolic firing of Old Kickapoo in salutation of statehood: "About noon, Old Kickapoo, in the presence of a joyous crowd, sent forth, in thunder tones, a greeting to the now sister State of Missouri." Celebrants loaded Old Kickapoo with copies of the laws from the discredited pro-slavery Lecompton legislature and blasted them across the river into Missouri.[42]

The only service the cannon provided in the Civil War was to intimidate a captain on a steamboat into lowering his Confederate flag and raising Old Glory. After the war, local officials fired it ceremoniously on July 4, and kept it on a bluff over the Missouri River to fire salutes welcoming inbound steamboats. Later, its custodians relegated it to service in a coal mine, where it was used to blast tunnels. Unfortunately (or possibly fortunately), someone overcharged it, and the back of the barrel split. Afterward, ungrateful denizens of the mine consigned the faithful old cannon to a junk heap. In 1884, someone recognized and rescued it. The Kansas State Historical Society paid a scrap dealer $114 for Old Kickapoo, which now rests in dignified display at their museum in Topeka. It is clear that Williams relished his active participation in Free-State activities, and had strong abolitionist feelings.

That same spring, southern states were seceding. The United States lost its unity. A terrifying Civil War exploded across the land. The Kansas legislature elected James Lane as United States senator in a tumultuous session in which those present changed their votes as many as six times. The session got so far out of hand that clerks charged with tracking the votes lost count. They then counted whichever votes suited their fancy.[43]

The new Senator Lane arrived in Washington in the midst of the chaos of Southern secession and the looming darkness of Civil War. He called upon President Abraham Lincoln, whom he had supported in the 1860 election. He found the White House disconcerted and unprotected from potential attack from Confederates across the Potomac River in Virginia. Recognizing a political opportunity, Lane rounded up enough Kansas men to form two companies, which he dubbed the "Kansas Frontier Guards." He bivouacked them in the East Room of the White House, and deployed them in defense of the President, earning Lincoln's gratitude.[44]

Lincoln's regard for Lane was such that he endorsed most of Lane's patronage requests without reading them. Ultimately, in June 1861, Lane secured an offer for a commission as brigadier general, and the authority to raise two regiments. These actions completely overrode the legitimate authority of Governor Robinson, the only person empowered to raise militia in the new state of Kansas. This reflected an ongoing feud between Lane and Robinson over previous years, with both seeking control of the Kansas government and the Republican Party of Kansas. Robinson, upon hearing about Lane's commission, immediately declared Lane's senate seat vacant, as he could not be a senator and serve in the military at the same time—that was a violation of Article I, Section 6 of the United States Constitution.[45] Lane neatly sidestepped Robinson's action on a technicality: he did not sign his acceptance of the commission. He then proceeded, however, to act the part and respond to the title of "General."[46] Lane was so proud of himself that he sent letters to Kansas newspapers notifying the public of his appointment as brigadier general of volunteers.[47]

Figure 5   General James Lane

James Lane decked out with impromptu apparatus he felt appropriate for a general's image. He was obviously ready for all contingencies, with a musket, bayonet, and saber. LIBRARY OF CONGRESS PHOTOGRAPH.

During Williams' five years there, Leavenworth proved to be the most exciting, politically supercharged, and dangerous atmosphere in the United States since the American Revolution. Despite the dangers, however, he unhesitatingly committed himself as an abolitionist, fully embracing the cause. James H. Lane emerged as the most influential abolitionist leader in Kansas during that period. He was a dynamic personality, a spellbinding speaker, a political opportunist, and an experienced military leader. He established a number of paramilitary units, leading raids on pro-slavery elements in Kansas and Missouri. Lane swept Williams up in his organization, giving him command over company-sized units in Jayhawking operations. By the outbreak of the Civil War, Williams was a veteran commander and an unreserved subscriber to the Federal cause. The border conflict was moving to a new level of violence.

Chapter Two

Williams, Lane's Brigade, and the Civil War

The Civil War in the Trans-Mississippi, or Frontier area of the United States, was generally an annoyance to the authorities in Washington and Richmond. Senior commanders and politicians were more focused on the huge formations of troops swarming across the eastern landscape, led by clusters of generals with impressive names. Casualties in the east defied imagination. Northern and Southern capitals were at stake. The Trans-Mississippi was far away, sparsely populated, and perceived to have little value in affecting the outcome of the conflict.

Across the Mississippi, in Kansas, Missouri, Indian Territory (now Oklahoma), and Arkansas, the largely unheralded war was savage. Troop populations were smaller, resources were limited, and there were many old scores to settle. Civilian populations did not escape violence; their lack of density made them more vulnerable. The same enemies fought each other repeatedly, with each engagement ratcheting up in fury. Their numbers may have been fewer, but the stakes were just as high to them as they were to the people of the eastern United States.

Until recently, even historians ignored the Civil War west of the Mississippi River. The big guns were in the East. Politicians were in the East. Most of the population was in the East. Foreign embassies were in the East. West of the Mississippi, sectional arguments over slavery exploded into killing and terror five turbulent years before the night of January 9, 1861, when cadets from the Citadel fired their cannon at the *Star of the West* while it sought to reinforce the garrison at Fort Sumter, South Carolina. The conflict consumed the people of the Kansas and Missouri, controlling their lives for an entire decade from the mid-1850s.

Late summer and early fall of 1861 was a violent time along the Missouri-Kansas border. In mid-August, Senator Lane arrived home from Washington, and spoke to a rally in Leavenworth, seeking recruits. Two days later, he travelled south to Fort Scott to take command of what formally became "Lane's Brigade," sometimes referred to as the "Kansas Brigade." The brigade consisted of the Third, Fourth, Fifth, Sixth, Seventh, and Eighth Kansas Volunteer Regiments.[1]

For a couple months, the regiments busily put themselves together. Lane's old friend James Montgomery commanded the Third Regiment and was second in command of the brigade.[2] Montgomery had already spent the first part of the summer raiding and plundering in Missouri.[3] William Weer commanded the Fourth Regiment. He was a man of questionable competence whose subordinates later mutinied against him in 1862. Fed up with his performance, higher command eventually court-martialed him and threw him out of the army in 1864.[4] Hamilton Johnson claimed a commission as Colonel of the Fifth Kansas Volunteer Regiment, quickly earning the reverence of his men. Colonel William R. Judson led the Sixth Kansas.[5] Colonel Charles R. Jennison of Jayhawker infamy accepted a commission as commander of the Seventh Regiment (Jennison's Jayhawkers).[6] Colonel Henry Wessel commanded the Eighth Kansas Volunteer Regiment.[7] The coalescence of Free-State militias into a single brigade bore the unmistakable stamp of Jim Lane's jayhawking background. In effect, the establishment of Lane's Brigade at the outset of the Civil War was the creation of formal structure for the continuation of Jayhawking. It changed little, but gave legitimacy to their mission.

James Williams' cavalry company mustered into the brigade on July 12, 1861, as a component of Montgomery's Third Regiment. The unit designation at this stage was not important; it changed frequently. His company was initially Company A, Third Regiment. Within a few months, his company had changed to "B," then transferred to the Fifth Regiment and became Company F, Fifth Regiment.[8] Due to the confusion of organizing several regiments at once, various companies were sometimes required to serve together. Such was the situation when Major Robert Van Horn, commanding two companies of the US Reserve Corps, ran into deep trouble en route to relieve two companies of Cass County Home Guards in Missouri. On July 18, he was near Harrisonville, Missouri, outnumbered, outflanked, and out of ideas. He sent messengers for reinforcements. Williams and John Ritchie of Weer's regiment, both company commanders, responded from their locations at Kansas City, as did Jennison from Mound City. They all converged on Van Horn's location at once, completing the rescue.[9]

That accomplished, Williams moved on toward Harrisonville on July 23. The next day, about five miles from Harrisonville, his lead element of eight men was approached by a group of thirty men who they assumed to be from Jennison's company, but they were sorely mistaken—a mistake easily made because neither side had uniforms that early in the conflict. The oncoming enemy group opened fire and, after some exchange, quickly fled the area, leaving one of Williams' men dead. That man, Sergeant William Hill, was the first man in Lane's Brigade killed in action.[10]

Undaunted, Williams continued his advance. After another brief skirmish, his scouts spotted a Confederate unit of about two hundred men. He immediately sought out a defensible position and prepared to fight, but was advised not to because he was so heavily outnumbered. As they were pulling back, reinforcements arrived, and Williams could restrain himself no longer. He led his men in a charge on the enemy, forcing them to withdraw.[11]

Continuing to close on Harrisonville, he encountered still another Confederate force of three hundred men. He gathered up Jennison's company with his own and charged a second time; again, the Confederates withdrew. Williams then stopped his company to allow his troopers and horses a break. Shortly, he took thirty men from his own company, and fourteen from Jennison's to a point where they found approximately two hundred more Confederates. Again, Williams attacked, and the soldiers of the pro-Confederate Missouri State Guard, painfully surprised, broke in disarray, leaving between seven and twenty-three dead on the field (mixed reports). One of Williams' men later reported, " 'our men with one accord rose and gave them the contents of their Sharp's [rifles,] and then came the fun. Such a stampede was never witnessed before!' " The Confederates attempted to reform their lines, and Williams attacked again. The enemy had enough, and fled the field.[12] Williams' predilection for aggressive action when confronted with enemy troops was obvious. He was not the kind to shy away from a fight.

Colonel Weer arrived on the scene shortly thereafter with more troops and assumed command of all those present. The next day, the federal column swept into Harrisonville unopposed and raised the Union flag. The Federal headquarters in Kansas City recalled Williams' and Ritchie's companies, who returned triumphantly on July 27 to a loud welcoming celebration.[13]

Late the next month, Union forces received word that a Confederate militia battalion under Colonel Thomas Cummins was at Ball's Mill, a gristmill near Little Osage, Missouri. They were having flour ground for the Confederate army. On August 27, Williams led a cavalry column of two companies from the brigade, a home guard company, and a single cannon manned by Sergeant Thomas Moonlight. His mission was to stop the Confederates from getting any more flour. The next day, shortly before arriving at the mill, Williams was riding out front of his scouts when he ran into a lead element from Cummins' battalion. Surprised opponents exchanged challenges, probably some curses, then shots. The initial barrage of Confederate fire shot Williams' horse from under him, but he leapt to his feet, returning fire with his revolver, and drove off the enemy. In short order, Williams and Cummins deployed their forces opposite each other in a large field. Shooting continued until Moonlight's cannon broke up the Confederate line. After that, Williams briefly gave chase before calling off the pursuit. Casualties had been comparatively light—one Unionist and two Confederates killed.[14]

Williams returned to the site of the mill and had the howitzer unlimbered and positioned to face the mill. The mill's owner, claiming to be a Union sympathizer needing protection from Confederate looters, begged Williams' men not to destroy his mill. Williams' response was "We don't load cannons for nothing; that mill has ground its last grist for the rebels – fire into her, boys!" The next day, Williams' troops completed the job, burning the mill and an adjoining bridge across the Osage River. Unbeknownst to them, the destruction of the bridge would later interfere with Confederate General Sterling Price in his 1861 retreat from Lexington, and force him to change the route of his incursion into Kansas in 1864. The directional change channeled Price into the jaws of the Union army, which led to his dramatic loss at the Battle of Mine Creek, one of the largest cavalry battles of the Civil War.[15]

Figure 6   Captain James M. Williams, 1861

This photograph of James Monroe Williams appears on a carte de visite *found in his granddaughter's records after her death. The back of the card is inscribed "A.C. Nichols, Photographist, 62 Delaware St., Leavenworth, Kansas." The photograph probably dates to 1861 or 1862.* AUTHOR'S COLLECTION.

Williams returned to Fort Scott on August 30. He was not empty-handed; he brought twenty-five contrabands (escaped slaves, in some cases involuntarily), two hundred head of cattle, fifty horses, and nearly forty sheep.[16] Old jayhawking habits were apparently hard to break. It is noteworthy, however, that there is no evidence of Williams participating in the kind of depredations that characterized the more infamous Jayhawkers, such as Jennison. There are no records of Williams' involvement in the murder of non-combatant civilians, torture, or similar abuses.

Although the brigade grew to around thirty-five hundred men by Mid-August 1861, mission requirements forced the dispersal of its units on multiple missions. This hampered its ability to conduct larger-scale operations or respond to significant threats from enemy forces.

The Union suffered a major setback at Wilson's Creek on August 10 near Springfield, Missouri. Confederates under command of Generals Benjamin McCulloch and Sterling Price killed Union commander, Brigadier General Nathaniel Lyon and defeated his command. General Price then dispatched Brigadier General James Rains and his Eighth Division of the Missouri State Guards to combat the increasing incursions into Missouri by troops from Kansas. When Rains determined that there were more Yankees than he could handle, Price veered in his direction to back him up. Residents of southeast Kansas recoiled in fear of a Confederate invasion, and there were few federal troops available to defend them.[17] What they did not know was that Price, McCulloch, and their Confederate and Arkansas state troops, having returned to their base in northwest Arkansas, were not in a position for a full-blown invasion of Kansas—they did not have nearly enough trained, equipped manpower. Cutting his losses, he determined to concentrate on the Union threat in his home state of Missouri. Just for the fun of it though—and maybe because he thought it would draw some of the Jayhawkers back into Kansas—he sent Brigadier General A.E. Steen and seven hundred mounted troopers toward Fort Scott, Kansas. On the way, Steen's lead element (about seventy-five men) came upon the mule herd of Colonel Weer's Fourth Kansas regiment. The Confederates captured sixty mules and two teamsters, killing a third teamster. Weer sent some of his cavalry after them, but when charged by General Steen's Confederates, Weer's Federals quickly withdrew.[18]

Williams plunged into the fray late, when Weer's cavalry was already running toward home. Williams attacked, stopping the Confederates in their tracks. In the meantime, Johnson brought his regiment out flanking the Confederates, convincing them it was their turn to withdraw.[19]

As these events transpired, Lane thought he saw an opportunity. He marshaled all his available troops, and recalled Jennison's regiment from a mission. Lane was going to attack the Confederates. On September 2, the Yankees caught up with the much larger force of Rebels east of the Missouri line at Drywood. Both sides elected to fight dismounted, which must have been an entertaining spectacle because they were fighting in a cornfield at a time and place where corn was as high as . . . the troopers were tall. The combatants wasted a lot of ammunition shooting high in attempts to clear the growth from across a cornfield. The contest devolved into an artillery duel between one gun on the Union side and a half-dozen Confederate cannon. At some point, James Montgomery decided to pull his Kansans out of the fray. Williams stepped in and covered the retreat. Given the size of the forces engaged, casualties were light. Union units reported five killed and six wounded. The Missourians lost either two or four killed, and sixteen to twenty-three wounded. Benedict reports two Confederates were wounded when their mules "foundered in a deep mud hole and [they] were trampled by their own cavalry."[20]

On September 17, Johnson's Fifth Regiment and Montgomery's Third Regiment converged on the small town of Morristown, Missouri in two columns. Confederate Colonel William Ervin of the Missouri State Guard and 250 troops defended Morristown. The two Union regiments planned a dawn attack. Montgomery's regiment was late in arriving, so Johnson, impatient with the wait, launched his attack. The Confederates, having positioned themselves in a trench, opened fire on the Yankees. A hail of nine bullets hit Colonel Johnson killing him instantly.[21] Another soldier took a fatal shot, and eleven more were wounded. Ultimately, Union troops took the town, but the loss of Johnson was devastating.[22]

Lieutenant Colonel John Ritchie assumed command of the Fifth Kansas Cavalry. Ritchie was a rabid abolitionist with a history of conflicts with the Lecompton pro-slavery crowd. He was a delegate to both the Leavenworth and Wyandotte Free-State constitutional conventions and a friend of John Brown's. He killed a US marshal who tried to arrest him, but his trial led to an acquittal. In addition to being an outspoken abolitionist, he was also a strong supporter of temperance and female suffrage. His extreme positions isolated him, and ultimately forced his departure from the regiment.[23]

About fifteen hundred men of Lane's Brigade undertook a controversial expedition on September 10, 1861. Their mission was to "clear out" the Osage River valley and, in the process, take the towns of Butler, Harrisonville, Osceola and Clinton, Missouri.[24] The real prize was Osceola, which lay farther into Missouri than Lane's troops had heretofore gone. Osceola was a thriving steamboat port on the Osage River. Estimates of its population at the time led to a guess of over two thousand.[25] Osceola was the Confederate army supply depot that supported General Price's siege of Lexington. Destruction of these stores would embarrass Price north into the Little Dixie region of central Missouri. Lane's objective for the expedition was clear, and it extended far beyond taking out a rebel supply depot. He announced, "We believe in a war of extermination. . . . There is no such thing as Union men in the border of Missouri. I want to see every foot of ground in Jackson, Cass, and Bates counties burned over – everything laid waste." He added, "Everything disloyal from a Shanghai rooster to a Durham cow must be cleaned out." To Lane, anyone not actively fighting as an abolitionist was disloyal.[26]

Upon reaching Osceola on September 22, the Yankees encountered light resistance from the Rebels. Most of the male population of the town was gone, serving elsewhere in the Missouri State Guard. A Missouri State Guard captain in command of about 150 remaining men bravely skirmished with Montgomery's Third Kansas troops as they advanced upon the town. The response from Montgomery's infantry and Moonlight's artillery quickly scattered the inexperienced Confederate militia. Skirmishes, organized and not, resulted in two Kansans dead, three wounded; seventeen Confederates dead, twenty-seven wounded.[27]

Union troops entered the town and destroyed most of it. They burned nearly all of the buildings within the town limits. There are, however, some conflicting reports as to the details of the event. One report included a description of a wager between Weer and Moonlight as to the accuracy of Moonlight's artillery. Moonlight won, at the expense of the courthouse. Another disagreement had to do with liquor found in town. Soldiers found 150 to 300 barrels of whiskey. Although one of Williams' soldiers reported that Montgomery ordered all of it destroyed, other accounts reported many Union soldiers first filling their stomachs and canteens, ending up as stumbling, falling-down drunks. The assertion continued that so many of these soldiers, about three hundred, were so inebriated that they had to depart on wagons because they could not walk. This claim is questionable, however, because all of the expedition's wagons were already overflowing with plunder. The reported plunder included gunpowder, several tons of lead for bullets with accompanying kegs of gunpowder, three thousand sacks of flour, fifty sacks of coffee, sugar, assorted foodstuff, camp equipment, and other general supplies. There is no doubt that Lane's troops plundered the town, but not to the extent that some authors have claimed. There were not near enough wheeled vehicles to transport all the asserted plunder, plus the acknowledged plunder, plus three hundred drunken soldiers, in addition to some unionists and a large number of slaves.

In spite of all the claims of Union outrages—pillaging, looting, drinking, freeing slaves, executing confederates—reports indicate that Lane ordered his men to desist from molesting women and children, and this seems to have been the case. There are accounts of soldiers helping occupants take furnishings out of their homes before burning them. Regimental commanders disputed over whether to burn the whole town, or just a cartridge factory. Some writers reported claims of three thousand people left homeless. The official population in 1860 was 267 whites. One author reported 283 blacks in town. Even estimates of up to two thousand inhabitants negate the credibility of such reports. Richard Sunderwirth, an author who lives in Osceola, notes that most of the estimated two–three thousand people lived outside the actual town limits.[28]

What is incontrovertible is that Lane's Brigade of Jayhawkers destroyed most of the town of Osceola. When the news got around, especially to Missouri's guerrilla forces, Osceola took on a "Remember the Alamo" sense of revenge. William Clark Quantrill, the infamous Confederate guerilla, visited Osceola after the raid, and used it as justification for his horrendous raid on Lawrence, Kansas on August 21, 1863, in which he burned the town, killing 150–200 men and boys.[29] Quantrill was specifically looking for Lane, whose home was in Lawrence. Quantrill bore an intense hatred for the man. Lane escaped, dressed only in his nightshirt.[30] Two years later, Quantrill lay dying of wounds in Kentucky. When queried about what he had in mind for Lane if he had not escaped, Quantrill responded: "I would have burned him at the stake."[31]

After Osceola, the brigade chased shadows, patrolled the countryside, and skirmished with the enemy. They linked up with Major General John C.

Frémont's army just in time for President Lincoln to fire him on November 2, bringing that operation to an abrupt close. That fall, President Lincoln determined that he did not have the logistical resources to support troops saturating the Missouri countryside, and communicated that observation to Major General David Hunter, Frémont's successor. Hunter ordered the establishment of three separate bases of operations by pulling his troops back to Sedalia and Rolla with Lane's Brigade posted on the western border of Missouri. In consequence, thousands of Union supporters were left unprotected and, in many cases, displaced. Confederate forces under General Price re-occupied much of southwestern Missouri.[32]

The scene of Civil War on the Kansas-Missouri border was ugly. Fighting was savage, having a tragic impact on civilians, with little gain realized by either side. Although there were significant military engagements, far more encounters were guerrilla warfare. The freebooting style of fighting of Lane's Brigade and disregard for those Missourians who were Yankee sympathizers drove a valuable source of support into the arms of the enemy. General Halleck, commander of the Army of the Missouri, reported to General George McClellan, then general-in-chief, that although the Confederates were losing ground in Missouri because of Union actions, control of the Union troops was loose. In a report on December 10, 1861, he noted the damage Lane's Brigade had done to the Union cause: "The course pursued by those under Lane and Jennison, has turned against us many thousands who were formerly Union men. A few more such raids . . . will make this State as unanimous against us as is Eastern Virginia."[33]

In a subsequent report to Secretary of War Edwin M. Stanton in March 1862, Halleck pursued the same line of thought about "robbers, who were organized under the auspices of Senator Lane." He went on:

> They wear the uniform of, and it is believed receive pay from, the United States. Their principal occupation of the last six months seems to have been the stealing of negroes, the robbing of houses, and the burning of barns, grain, and forage. The evidence of their crimes is unquestionable. They have not heretofore been under my orders. I will now keep them out of Missouri or have them shot.[34]

As Lane pulled his brigade back to the Fort Scott area in November, he granted married soldiers leaves of absence. The adjutant of the Fifth Kansas announced that the US paymaster would be paying the troops—an unfortunate mistake. The paymaster did not show up. Infuriated, Lane announced that he was going to Fort Leavenworth to bring the paymaster back. Neither Lane, nor the paymaster came back to Fort Scott, however. Lane never returned to the brigade; instead, he went to Washington to resume his duties as senator. Montgomery assumed command of the brigade, changing its designation to the "Army of the Western Border." Lane's Brigade ceased to exist.[35]

In late 1861, the War Department directed the reorganization of Kansas regiments. Major General David Hunter assumed command of the new Department of Kansas on November 25, 1861, which sealed the fate of the brigade. Hunter was less than impressed by the lax and scruffy organization he inherited as part of his new command. He immediately began restructuring most of the command into an effective, disciplined fighting force. Among all the changes, Williams' company transferred to the Third Regiment. At the close of 1861 the brigade went into winter quarters. Much shuffling followed: a number of units were consolidated, and officers from understrength units were mustered out. General Halleck, commanding the Department of the Missouri was tiring of complaints about Lane's Brigade and its incursions into Missouri. In a letter to Major General George McClellan dated December 19, 1861, he grumbled, "The conduct of the forces under Lane and Jennison has done more for the enemy in this state [Missouri] than could have been accomplished by twenty thousand of his own army."[36]

On February 28, 1862, Hunter abolished the brigade, leading to another realignment of its units. He made his opinion of the brigade very clear in a report to Major General Halleck on the status of Kansas regiments, and the brigade in particular. He described the remnants of Lane's command, "the Third and Fourth Kansas Infantry and Fifth and Sixth Kansas Cavalry, formerly known as 'Lane's Brigade'" as "a mere ragged, half-armed, diseased, and mutinous rabble."[37] The designation of the brigade did not transition to a new one with a number; it simply ceased to exist. Lane created it without regard to formality, charged off into the distance, and chose to follow his own guidance. Administrative niceties did not matter. It might be said that the whole episode of Lane's Brigade was questionable. After all, Lane protested that he never had been a general.

In March, Williams found his company in the Fifth Kansas Cavalry regiment in a new brigade under acting Brigadier General George Deitzler.

This new command included the First, Fifth, and Sixth Kansas, Thirteenth Wisconsin, and Captain John Rabb's Second Indiana Battery.[38] The Third Regiment ceased to exist, and is not included in the *Official History of Kansas Regiments during the War for the Suppression of the Great Rebellion*.[39] Lieutenant Colonel Powell Clayton, who recently joined the Fifth Regiment as executive officer, became its colonel in February of 1862. The regiment entered into a phase of heavy retraining in the spring of 1862, alternating with occasional missions.[40]

Events during that period greatly impacted Williams' life. Williams found the new chain of command to be onerous. For several years, he had labored under the command of officers such as Montgomery and Johnson who supported abolition as passionately as he did. Many members of the Union army, however, had other motives. The majority of Kansans supported preservation of the Union; few were radical abolitionists. Even in the radical leadership of Lane's Brigade, Colonel Jennison seemed to be more interested in violence and theft than abolition. Racial prejudice was widespread throughout the North, even amongst those who advocated abolition.[41] Williams concluded that the moral and political gap between himself and Colonel Clayton was sufficiently large that he could not serve under his command. The problem between Clayton and Williams had everything to do with abolition.

Williams submitted a letter of resignation to Colonel Clayton on May 8, 1862, requesting an immediate leave of absence while his resignation was processed. The letter read:

> My reason for tendering my resignation at this time is the total disagreement between myself and my superior officers in relation to the question of slavery. As a citizen of Kansas since the year 1856, I had learned to hate the institution of slavery and I was taught to believe that every effort that could consistently be made to crush the institution should be made. And believing as I do that this infamous institution lies at the bottom of the present unholy rebellion, I conceive it to be my duty as a patriot and soldier to strike the institution in every possible direction, hoping to wipe out the curse as well as the rebellion itself. With these views, I entered the service of the Government as a soldier under the command of Col J Montgomery and Genl J H Lane. I chose my companions then. Since that time it has pleased those in power to

dismiss from service these my old commanders and place me under the command of persons of very different sentiment. And I find myself now under the command of those whose orders I cannot obey and execute without doing violence to my feelings as a man.[42]

These were strong abolitionist sentiments. Williams was willing to sacrifice his commission as a matter of adherence to his principles. His commander, Colonel Clayton, forwarded the letter to General Halleck in St. Louis with what appears to be a tongue-in-cheek recommendation for approval, stating, "He says he cannot obey the orders of those who are placed over him without doing violence to his manhood; if that be so, he certainly acts wisely in resigning."[43] General Halleck accepted Williams' resignation May 15, 1862.[44] Williams' resignation proved to be only a temporary lull in his military career. Further opportunity for military service and leadership in the growing conflict was just around the corner.

Chapter Three

The First Kansas Colored Volunteer Infantry Regiment

While Lane's Brigade was being disbanded and Williams was resigning from the Fifth Kansas Cavalry, James Lane, back in the persona of United States Senator, was finagling to continue his behind-the-scenes involvement with elements of the military in Kansas. He became a godfather of sorts for some of his favored officers, such as James G. Blunt, former executive officer of the Third Regiment. Blunt later proved to be a good commander, progressed in rank, became a brigadier general, and then commander of the Department of Kansas. Supposedly, Lane engineered the appointments so that he could pull strings in the background.[1] The godfather relationship spread down the chain, and by June of 1862, General Blunt had orders published attaching Williams to him on special duty.[2]

The next month, Senator Lane had the War Department appoint him recruiting commissioner for Kansas, with the rank of brigadier general. His authority extended to the recruitment of "one or more brigades of volunteer infantry."[3] This gave him license to travel the length and breadth of Kansas, involving himself in military affairs.

Lane jumped into his new role with enthusiasm and, with his usual flair, proceeded to ignore the rules, or at least twist them to his ends. He appointed captains James Williams and Henry Seaman as recruiting commissioners on his behalf.[4] Captain Seaman had also been a company commander in the

Fifth Kansas Cavalry. He resigned at the same time as Williams, citing an almost identical dissatisfaction with the ideals of the regimental commander, Colonel Powell Clayton. His resignation letter described his "total difference of feeling" between himself and the command structure.[5]

Williams was responsible for recruiting in the northern part of Kansas, and Seaman in the southern half. Both were to recruit black men. These actions were consistent with Lane's grand plan, which he exposed to Congress in January of 1862 with a resolution allowing Kansas commanders in the field to muster in "such persons as may present themselves for that purpose." It was a thinly disguised plan to recruit blacks and Indians into federal regiments. It sparked a noisy debate in the Senate over black troops, which dissolved into the larger issue of whether or not Lane was entitled to his seat in Congress. The dispute was based upon a perceived conflict between his Congressional responsibilities and those of a general officer in the field. Further, there were assertions that Lane would be in violation of Article 1, Section 6 of the Constitution, which stipulates that "No Senator or Representative shall, during the Time for which he was elected, be appointed to any civil Office under the Authority of the United States . . . and no Person holding any Office under the United States, shall be a Member of either House during his Continuance in Office." Ultimately, Lane was allowed to play at both general and senator.[6]

Lane's orders as Recruiting Commissioner required him "to report frequently . . . the progress and prospects of the work." He did so. His first report, on August 5, blithely announced, "Recruiting opens up beautifully. Good for four regiments of whites and two of blacks."[7] A close review of this report surely would have produced consternation in the nation's capital, but as the War Department worked to get three hundred thousand men into the army, Lane's report was easily looked over as just one in a blizzard of messages flying around. Knowing that President Lincoln was not yet ready for blacks in the army, Lane covered his tracks by sending another message on August 6: "I am receiving negroes under the late act of Congress. Is there any objection? Answer by telegraph. Soon to have an army."[8]

Lane was referring to the Militia Act of July 17, 1862, authorizing the President to recruit and employ blacks in Federal service for construction of fortifications, camps, "or any military or naval service." The act also provided that "any man or boy of African descent" who was legally enslaved by any person who was fighting for the Confederacy would be "forever thereafter free." His mother, wife, and children would also be free under the provision of the act.[9]

That same day, Lane ordered his recruiting officers to read the new law and thoroughly explain it to black recruits, so that they all understood the impact of their actions.[10] There was huge potential in this law for recruits: originally passed in 1795, and amended in 1862, it promised freedom to former slaves in exchange for military service. In the meantime, Lane did not wait for any response to his message that would curtail his activities. He charged ahead, directing Williams and Seaman to quickly round up and recruit black men.

In order to cast the recruiting net as far as possible, a number of white officers received commissions from Williams and Seaman to recruit black companies. Those commissions extended to officers in Fort Scott, Osawatomie, Atchison, Lawrence, Topeka, and elsewhere. The new soldiers came from all over. There were free blacks, escaped slaves, mulattos, and even black Cherokees from Indian Territory.[11]

In a bold step, Williams extended pre-signed commissions, obtained from Senator Lane, to two black men: William D. Matthews and Patrick Minor. Matthews was born in Washington, DC around 1825, and immigrated to Kansas in 1854. He had been superintendent of contrabands for the Kansas Emancipation League since early in 1862. The League was an outgrowth of a school for fugitive blacks established a year earlier in Lawrence. Soon, Matthews had branches throughout Kansas, operating as stops on the Underground Railroad.[12] After the Civil War, Matthews became a prominent citizen of Leavenworth, and was National Grand Master of a prominent Masonic organization for black men.[13] Williams commissioned Matthews as a captain, placing him in command of Company D of what came to be the First Kansas Colored Volunteer Infantry Regiment. Williams and Matthews would become lifelong friends.

Lieutenant Patrick Minor was a native of Louisiana. He had obtained formal education in France and at Oberlin College Prep Department (1846–1848). Minor's mother was a slave, and his father a white planter who later married her. Minor was no ordinary field hand, but with his Louisiana roots and a background in higher education, he knew very well what was at stake for black soldiers.[14] Lieutenant Minor was placed second in command of Company D.

Figure 7   Captain William Matthews

William Matthews was a man of dignity. His actions repeatedly earned the respect of those around him. He and James Williams forged a lifelong friendship. His accomplishments as a company commander in the First Kansas Colored Volunteer Infantry earned accolades from other officers within and outside the regiment. Later, as executive officer and commander of the Independent Kansas Colored Battery, he earned continued respect. His accomplishments later in life were equally significant. KANSAS STATE HISTORICAL SOCIETY PHOTOGRAPH.

Commissioning those two men was a dramatic move on William's part. Even as pressure built to recruit black men in the Federal army, national consensus was that white men should command black troops. There was a concern that circumstances were bound to arise in which black officers might be in command of white men, generating unwanted conflict. On the other hand, one of the initial obstacles to recruitment was the resistance of black men to white officers. Potential black recruits were concerned that the white men placed in command over black troops would be of lesser caliber than those commanding all-white units—a concern which was later alleviated by the proven quality of their officers. Such concerns did not dissuade Williams, however. He commissioned these men based upon his principles and desires to provide quality leadership.[15]

General Halleck, now the General-in-Chief of the army, fired off a message to the Secretary of War on August 18, pointing out that the law authorized only President Lincoln to receive blacks into military service, and Lincoln had not delegated that authority to recruiting commissioners. Thus, "General Lane is without the authority of law."[16]

On August 23, the Secretary of War finally answered the message Lane had sent on the sixth. He echoed the message he had received from Halleck, telling Lane he was not authorized to recruit blacks.[17] By then, he was too late. Lane's recruiting commissioners, captains Williams and Seaman, were cheerfully recruiting large numbers of blacks. Lane did not have time to bother with the Secretary of War's message. He figured the rest of the world would eventually come around to his way of thinking. He was right.

Not all the recruits fit within the spirit of "volunteer." Most of them were escaped slaves, particularly from Missouri. There were questions about just how many of them had actually escaped, compared to the numbers granted unwelcome assistance from Jayhawkers, who captured them in raids into Missouri and took them back to Kansas, whether or not they wanted to go. There is no doubt that many of the Jayhawking raids into Missouri netted human loot as well as material booty. Chances are, some of the proud black men who put their "X" on the dotted line were stolen from their owners and given more than a little help in the enlistment process. Albert Castel, a notable Civil War historian, flatly remarked that "Lane's agents resorted to kidnapping as another means of filling the ranks of the Negro regiment."[18] That such could happen was no problem for Senator Lane, who had little interest in quibbling about the definition of "volunteer." He made his position clear in a homily delivered to a Leavenworth crowd: "The negroes are mistaken if they think white men can fight for them while they stay at home." Directing his comments to the blacks in the crowd, he went on: "We have been saying that you will fight, and if you don't fight, we will make you."[19]

One writer documented an event in which an upright citizen noted that a large number of escaped slaves voluntarily took up residence with Sac and Fox Indians, intending to keep a low profile. The concerned citizen, one Benjamin Van Horn, reported this fact to Senator Lane and General Blunt. Rewarded for his civic consciousness with a lieutenant's commission, Van Horn went amongst the Indians with missionary zeal, and returned with a ready-made company of eighty black men. For his efforts, he became commander of that company and part of the First Kansas Colored Volunteer Infantry. End results suggest that he might have gotten carried away in his zeal, however. As it turned out, a couple of his volunteers proved too young, and he was forced to drop them from the rolls.[20]

Sometimes, recruiting hit rough patches. The black soldier was not a universally popular idea in the North. In fact, this recruiting effort was the first one anywhere in the northern states. A noticeable part of the population was actively sympathetic with the secession. Prejudice against blacks was relatively common in the northern population, many of whom supported emancipation, but did not want blacks in their communities, even if black soldiers defended them. Some genuine Yankees were of the opinion that recruitment of blacks was a cause that would be disapproved at the War Department, concluding that much time was being wasted that could be better spent directly on the war. One of the obstacles Williams had to overcome was the public conviction that blacks would make poor soldiers. In spite of these obstacles, Williams and Seaman recruited over five hundred black men within sixty days.[21]

There were occasions when Williams collided head-on with various civil authorities over issues with his troops. Civil authorities arrested and jailed his soldiers in Leavenworth for minor infractions that would not merit a glance at white troops. Williams himself was arrested when he intervened, asserting his right of jurisdiction over his troops. Mostly, he ignored civil authority.

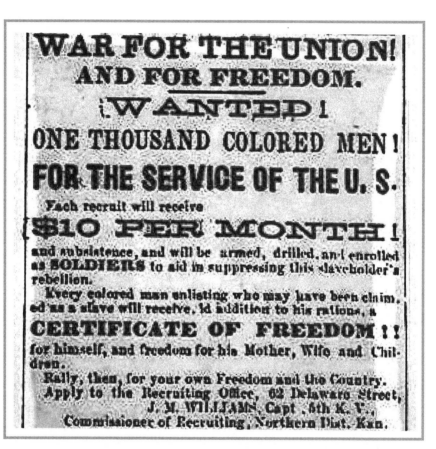

Figure 8   Advertisement for Colored Soldiers, Leavenworth 1862

James Williams posted this recruiting advertisement in the Leavenworth Daily Conservative *on August 6, 1862. Similar advertisements and broadside posters abounded throughout the country, attracting droves of recruits. Williams and Seaman were successful in filling their regiment.*

Nevertheless, constant harassment and the limelight proved to be a distraction from organizing and training the new soldiers. Seaman's recruits relocated from Mound City to Fort Lincoln in the Fort Scott area early in September. Lane ordered Williams and his recruits to follow a month later with a written directive: "I send you by the bearer, an order putting your troops into active service. . . . [E]nter into the discharge of your duties at once and prove to the country that you are soldiers."[22]

The recruits obtained uniforms and weapons. Many of their initial issue of uniforms consisted of surplus, out-of-date grey outfits—not always a good choice of color. While they did not initially fit the conventional image of the federal soldier, the standardized clothing provided a sense of unity. Eventually, they received more appropriate blue uniforms. The weapons were Belgian muskets with long bayonets procured early in the war for General Frémont's troops—they were found to be wanting. Nevertheless, training and drilling continued. The remarkable transition of escaped slaves into a cohesive regiment of combat soldiers progressed.[23]

In mid-October, Colonel N.P. Chipman, Chief of Staff to Major General Samuel Curtis (Commander of the Department of the Missouri), dropped in on Fort Lincoln to look over the black soldiers. James Williams showed him around, and proudly displayed his soldiers. They observed an afternoon dress parade. Chipman was impressed. In his report to General Curtis on October 16, he commented on the expertise of the black troops in the manual of arms, adding "the best company is the one officered by black men." His overall impression was, "I know I have seen very many Regts [Regiments] longer in the service than these which would appear badly beside them. . . . No one who could see these stalwart men, with their earnest faces, in battle line but would feel similarly."[24]

Although Williams was a central figure in the recruitment and organization of the regiment, there was ample politicking about who would be the commander when the regiment was finally up and running. Montgomery, who had been without a command since his Third regiment was absorbed into the Fifth Regiment, was one candidate. Jennison made no bones about the fact that he wanted the command, but Lane selected neither. Montgomery left Kansas for South Carolina and became commander of a black regiment there, where he performed very well. Jennison—probably not picked because of his lawless reputation—became angry and took off on his own. Before leaving, he led a raid on the recruits' encampment that scared many of the recruits into deserting. The officers in charge of the recruits rounded up most of them and returned them to camp.[25]

Lane's Selection of Williams to command the First Kansas Colored Volunteer Infantry not only aroused the hackles of more prominent men who wanted the nod from Lane, but it focused attention on Williams' allegiance to Lane without regard to Williams' record as a fighting leader. Albert Castel, author of "Civil War Kansas and the Negro," identified Williams as "an obscure character named James M. Williams—a man the Senator could easily control."[26]

Ethan Earle, a Boston emigrant to Kansas, who wrote of his involvement in the jayhawking days, also indicated that he expected to command a regiment of black soldiers, and had extensive interaction with James Lane on that subject. To his great indignation, Lane did not select him, a decision Earle said was even more frustrating after all the favors he had done for Lane. He also wrote that in addition to Williams and Seaman, Lane had promised the command to at least two other men.[27]

Earle went on to comment on Lane's choice in a way that indicated a certain disdain, "The appointment of Lieutenant Colonel Williams and Major Bowles [J.M. Bowles, Executive Officer] was another mistake to say the least. They were both taken from a cavalry regiment, [and] their only objective in the army was for promotion and plunder."[28] The opinion, once duly recorded, did not seem to dissuade Earle from joining the regiment. He quietly swallowed his pride and accepted a commission. He settled for command of a company in the First Kansas Colored Volunteer Infantry.

Few people actually sought commissions in black regiments. Most wanted to avoid a perceived stigma attached to service with black men. Many understood that service with black regiments meant duty in undesirable locations and supervision of labor gangs instead of line troops.[29]

There seemed to be two basic motivations that drove men to seek commissions in black regiments: altruism and ambition. Many of those who sought such commissions were strong supporters of the abolitionist movement. Early on, when the idea of black regiments was revolutionary and not yet an element of Federal strategy, the preponderance of white officers fit the abolitionist mold. Williams obviously fit into the abolitionist category, alongside the better-known Colonel Thomas Wentworth Higginson, who commanded the First South Carolina Volunteers (Colored), and Colonel Robert Gould Shaw of Fifty-Fourth Massachusetts Infantry fame. Williams began recruiting before either of the other two officers, and the First Kansas Colored was in combat eight months before the Fifty-Fourth Massachusetts. Such officers as these had a strong commitment to the abolition of slavery, and acted upon such principles.[30]

Many potential officers looked upon service with a black regiment as a stepping-stone to higher rank, greater privileges, and better pay. They found the winnowing-out process to be unexpectedly thorough. Candidates for such commissions faced rigorous War Department examining boards. Forty percent of those applicants who qualified to go before the examining boards failed. Only 25 percent of the applicants eventually earned commissions. The selection process ultimately provided the black regiments with well-qualified leaders such as James Williams, with sufficient combat experience and leadership skills.[31]

Lane pressed The First Kansas Colored Infantry into service before it completed the process of staffing, training, and mustering in as a functioning regiment. His orders transferring Williams and his men to Fort Lincoln also gave the units in training the mission to provide a presence along the Missouri-Kansas border. Their mission included physical protection of the border, as well as fortification of the towns of Barnesville and Fish Creek. High on their list of projects was actively driving bushwhackers from the border counties of Missouri. Lane carefully specified, "The persons, property and rights of the people of Missouri should be held sacred," but that "every infraction should be promptly and severely punished." Lane designated Major Benjamin S. Henning, the commander of Fort Scott as the coordinator for that sector of the border, and tasked the First Kansas to link with Colonel Charles Adams of the Twelfth Kansas Volunteers, who was responsible for the border north of the Osage. Within only a few days, Major Henning was compelled to deploy detachments. Confederate raids on communities along the border forced his hand. Several small groups of Confederates probed First Kansas defenses around Barnesville, prompting Henning to provide added coverage to that area and along Drywood Creek, where rebels had plundered settlers. Scouts soon discovered Confederate Major Thomas Livingston and two hundred men preparing to attack a wagon train escorted by Captain Earle. This intelligence compelled Henning to send reinforcements. The First Kansas was already becoming essential to the Federal mission.[32]

The soldiers of the First Kansas were soon equipped with newer and more reliable muskets than the original ones, which failed or misfired nearly 80 percent of the time. Their time spent on drilling, marksmanship, and maneuvering would come into play very soon, with only a couple of months spent thus far in recruitment, organization, equipping, and training the regiment of recruits.[33]

Chapter Four

They "Fought Like Tigers:" Island Mound, Misssouri

On October 26, 1863, Major Benjamin Henning at Fort Scott, Kansas, ordered elements of the First Kansas Colored Volunteer Infantry into Missouri, near the Bates County town of Butler, on a mission to clean out a supposed bushwhacker (enemy guerilla) headquarters.[1] Known locally as Hog Island, it was an island formed by a split in the Marais des Cygnes River.[2] Hog Island was about three miles long, and about a mile wide. The Marais des Cygnes flowed mostly on the north side, with only a narrow and muddy slough, or swamp, on the south. Thickets of dense undergrowth and swamp covered the island, making it easy for large numbers of enemy bushwhackers to hide.[3]

While James Williams was in Leavenworth on regimental business with Captain Matthews, Captain Henry Seaman inherited responsibility to command the mission. He took nearly 240 men from both his own and Captain Richard Ward's battalions of the regiment.[4] Ward's battalion included 160 men and 6 officers. Seaman's contingent included 64 men from the First Kansas, augmented by a small team of scouts from the Fifth Kansas Cavalry.[5]

The First Kansas troops arrived near Hog Island late in the afternoon of the twenty-seventh. Even though they quickly spotted some enemy cavalry at a distance, there was initially no direct contact or exchange of gunfire. Seaman moved his command onto a farm, two miles north of the Island, owned by Enoch Toothman—a notorious southern guerrilla. Toothman and one of his sons, Josephus, were away. Toothman's other son, John, a known bushwhacker, was captured earlier, and was biding his time in a prison camp at Fort Lincoln when the First Kansas deployed on the Toothman Farm. Toothman's wife, Christiana, and their two daughters were the only ones home on the farm.[6]

The Toothman farmhouse was on the forward crest of a hill atop a long open field of tall grass that sloped south and southwest nearly two miles in the direction of the Marais des Cygnes River, and Hog Island. Small hills, or mounds, in the long field provided terrain relief. On the east, a large hill, or mound, framed the left side of the field, sloping nearly all the distance as far up as the farmhouse. A distant tree line obscured the view at the base of the hill.[7]

Six scouts from the Fifth Kansas Cavalry, who accompanied the First Kansas, swept the area, reporting evidence that the enemy was much more than a loose band of bushwhackers. Intelligence gathered from local population, as well as Mrs. Toothman and her daughters, and by the cavalry escort's reconnaissance, reinforced these conclusions. It appeared that the enemy was a force of as many as seven hundred or more men under command of Confederate Colonel Vard Cockrell, and that other well-known guerilla leaders were present as well.[8] Only a couple months earlier Cockrell had commanded Confederate troops at the bloody Battle of Lone Jack, punctuating a successful recruiting campaign through western Missouri.[9] Years later, Confederate Brigadier General Sidney Jackman, who served under Cockrell at Lone Jack as a lieutenant colonel, continued to hold him in high esteem: "Col. Cockrell is a brave and good man and was as loyal to the South as any man who ever fought for her."[10] A subsequent report indicated that Cockrell was assembling various Confederate units into a single command for an attack upon Mound City, Kansas.[11]

Not wanting to back off, but recognizing the potential for disaster if they did not take deliberate action, Seaman established a headquarters in the Toothman farmhouse. The First Kansas troops established a fortified breastwork perimeter around the house and hunkered down for the night. They dubbed their ramshackle redoubt "Fort Africa."[12]

Seaman's infantrymen—heavily outnumbered and confronted by mounted Confederate cavalry—were at a decided disadvantage. He not only needed more troops, he needed them on horseback in order to maneuver against the mounted enemy. He dispatched messengers to Williams at Fort Lincoln, Fort Scott, and Paola, seeking cavalry reinforcements.[13]

The next day was uneventful, but continuous tension prevailed as the two enemy forces tested each other with brief skirmishes. The opposing forces were beyond the effective range of their various weapons, and windy conditions rendered most shots a waste of ammunition. The Kansans' strategy was to hold the rebels' attention with scattered skirmishes until reinforcements came to their rescue. The reinforcements, upon arriving at the scene, were to attack the Confederates from the south side of the river, and the First Kansas would conduct their assault from the north. But the needed reinforcements did not arrive. The blue-coated Yankees were in for another long night.[14]

Over the course of that night, tensions mounted in the makeshift redoubt at Toothman's Farm as the First Kansas soldiers realized that their first real combat was in the offing, with their lives and the reputations of black soldiers at stake. Their forward pickets spotted a large force of mounted men in the low area near the Marais des Cygnes River and Hog Island. The enemy came no closer, however, and none of the pickets wasted their ammunition on the shadowy targets.[15]

October 29 dawned upon tired, hungry soldiers, short of rations. Seaman took a chance leading out a forage party of fifty men, with Captain Luther Thrasher and Lieutenant Elkanah Huddleston (C.O., Company E). He sent two other officers, Captains Andrew Armstrong (C.O. Company H) and Andrew Crew (C.O. Company A), with sixty men as skirmishers, in an alternate direction to distract the Confederates' attention. The skirmishers succeeded in engaging the enemy, progressively pushing them back a couple miles. During the fighting, the First Kansas soldiers killed seven Confederates, and wounded an unknown number of others, without taking any casualties themselves. When Seaman's forage party returned, the skirmishers broke contact with the enemy and retired to defensive positions at Fort Africa.[16] The Federal officers who led the skirmishes reported that the Confederate force had apparently received substantial reinforcement the preceding night.[17]

By mid-day, the Confederates, impatiently wanting to force the Yankees' hand, had started a prairie fire—using the gusting wind to blow it toward the fortified position around the Toothman house. Union soldiers built a backfire to stop the bigger one, but the fire and smoke blocked their ability to see any Confederate movement. Seaman dispatched a team of eight soldiers under John Sixkiller to get past the smoke and observe the Confederate activity. Sixkiller was a Cherokee who brought his five slaves north from Indian Territory (now Oklahoma) to enlist. Sixkiller and his troops engaged the Confederate foes, forcing them south toward the river, but in the process, the Union troops strayed farther and farther away from their own defensive positions.

Seaman sent out Captain Henry Pierson (Seaman's Battalion) and Lieutenant Joseph Gardner (C.O. Company F) with a detachment of sixteen more men to aid Sixkiller and get his team back to the redoubt at Fort Africa.[18] Instead, Pierson and Gardner were drawn into the fight as it continued to drift away from the farmhouse, toward the river. Captain Crew and Lieutenant Huddleston set out together to assist Gardner. Hearing, but not seeing, a pronounced increase in the volume of gunfire, Seaman followed up by sending Captain Richard Ward, Lieutenant Patrick Minor (C.O. Company D, in Captain Matthews' absence), and Lieutenant Luther Dickerson (C.O. Company C), with more men to assist those already engaged.[19]

As the First Kansas soldiers neared the river in pursuit of the Confederates, a large contingent of approximately 130 mounted Confederates exploded from the trees at the far end of the mound east of the Gardner's Union soldiers. The Union soldiers—caught in the open and outnumbered by a force nearly five times their size—were now one and one-half mile from the safety of Fort Africa. They began to backpedal toward Fort Africa—a hopeless destination under such circumstances. Seaman organized a relief force under Captain Andrew Armstrong and deployed them to move around Gardner's right flank. He then led Lieutenant Thrasher's company to intercept the Confederate cavalry. Lieutenant Huddleston, who was with Gardner's unit, started two prairie fires to block the route of the Confederate cavalry, but even as the flames grew, the enemy cavalry surged on. Gardner then formed his infantrymen into firing ranks and unleashed a volley into the oncoming Confederate cavalry, emptying many of their saddles. With no time to reload, the contest quickly turned into furious, hand-to-hand fighting in the midst of the swirling maelstrom: fire, smoke, bayonets, knives, swords slashing and stabbing, and muskets used as clubs. Sixkiller and his men fought fiercely. Sixkiller killed at least four of the enemy before a half-dozen gunshot wounds finally felled him. Others First Kansas soldiers on the field distinguished themselves in the same way. The black soldiers fought fearlessly.

The Confederate cavalry poured through the ranks of the Union soldiers, cresting a hill behind them, only to be confronted by Armstrong's relief detachment. Along with troops from Lieutenants Thrasher, Minor, and Huddleston, Armstrong's soldiers quickly formed into firing ranks and unloaded a decimating volley into the Rebel cavalry. The Union men then pursued the cavalry back over the hill, firing into them even as they resumed the melee with Gardner's men. The fighting continued with the fierce grappling of the combatants spilling into the flames of the prairie fires. The combination of yelling and screaming soldiers, wounded horses, gunshots, and roaring fires created an unholy din. Confederate casualties were growing rapidly. Stunned by the tenacity of the black Yankees, the Confederates suddenly decided they had enough and withdrew precipitously.[20] It was over.

Dead and wounded soldiers, both Union and Confederate, lay commingled across the field of battle. The First Kansas lost eight men killed, and eleven wounded in the furious fighting:[21]

Killed in Action:

> Captain Andrew Crew, Company A
> Corporal Joseph Talbot, Company F
> Private John Sixkiller, Seaman's Battalion
> Private Samuel Davis, Company F
> Private Thomas Lane, Company F
> Private Marion Barger, Company F
> Private Allen Rhodes, Company F
> Private Henry Gash, Company F

Wounded in Action:

> Lieutenant Joseph Gardner, Company F
> Sergeant Edward Lowrey, Seaman's Battalion
> Sergeant Shelley Banning, Seaman's Battalion
> Corporal Andy Hytower, Seaman's Battalion
> Private Anderson Riley, Seaman's Battalion
> Corporal Jacob Edwards, Company E,
> Private Thomas Knight, Company F
> Private George Dudley, Company F
> Private Manuel Dobson, Company F
> Private Lazarus Johnson, Company F

Figure 9   First Kansas Colored at Island Mound, Missouri

This drawing,"A Negro Regiment in Action," appeared in Harper's Weekly *in March 1863. It depicted the engagement at Island Mound, Missouri in October 1862. The artist, Thomas Nast, was a popular journal artist of the last half of the nineteenth century. Although somewhat fanciful, the drawing conveys the ferocity of hand-to-hand combat that characterized the battle. The engagement at Island Mound was the first between a black Union unit and Confederates in the Civil War. It resulted in a victory for the First Kansas Colored Volunteer Infantry.*

Confederates, under a flag of truce, asked to remove their casualties from the battlefield. There was never any documented tally of their dead and wounded, but they were carried away in "several wagon loads." Captured Confederates reported at least thirty of their men killed.[22] Other reports indicated as many as forty Confederate soldiers slain.[23] No estimates were documented of the numbers of wounded rebels, but their casualties were significant.

On the next day, long-awaited reinforcements arrived under Williams' command. They included 150 more men from the First Kansas, an Ohio cavalry unit, and a section of artillery. On the day following, Williams led the reinforced command in pursuit of the retreating Confederates, but no further engagement resulted.[24] During their rapid retreat, however, the Confederates left valuable resources for the soldiers of the First Kansas Colored. The victorious soldiers rounded up a large number of Confederate horses, some wounded, and over a hundred head of cattle abandoned by the rebels at the Hog Island camp. The beef enhanced the soldiers' rations considerably. Two days later, the command returned to Fort Lincoln.[25]

The engagement, and subsequent victory, at Island Mound was enormously significant for a number of reasons. It was the first time black soldiers in the Union army fought organized Confederate troops. It was the first time a black man, Lieutenant Minor, lead troops in combat. Best of all, it was the first victory won by a black regiment. Such a victory demonstrated to the world that black men could, and would, fight well as soldiers. But most importantly, those men, most of whom had been slaves only weeks before, had proved to themselves and each other that they were soldiers—fighting men—and no longer needed to fear white southerners.

The organization and training provided by Williams and his officers proved effective. The soldiers functioned as a team, maneuvered professionally, and responded quickly to orders. This is all the more remarkable, as the soldiers had only been training for a few weeks. In fact, the regiment was so early in its organization and training process that it was not mustered into Federal service for more than two more months after the Battle of Island Mound.

There were many individual accounts of heroism. In his report, Captain Ward generally commented on the exceptional conduct of everyone involved in the fighting. He singled out five men for particular commendation: Captain

Crew (killed in action), Captain Armstrong, Sergeant Smithers (Company B), Private Scantling (Company B), and Private Prince (Company E).[26]

Perhaps the greatest recognition and commendation came from the enemy. Two days after the battle, the *New York Times* reported a statement from Bill Turman [Truman], one of the Confederate commanders: "the black devils fought like tigers . . . the white officers had got them so trained that not one would surrender."[27]

The consequences of this engagement extended far beyond its local sphere. It not only proved they could fight, but it demonstrated their value as a resource to the Union army. That these recruits were quick to learn soldier skills, maneuver as a fighting force, and achieve victory, gave them credibility, which helped erase public opposition to the recruitment and formation of black regiments.[28] The practical result was the incremental addition of new regiments that happened to be staffed by black men. These new regiments, with the First Kansas Colored Volunteer Infantry in the vanguard, notably reduced the workload demands of the existing regiments staffed by white men. Nevertheless, the practical benefits of the added regiments with black soldiers continued to be controversial. James Lane's actions —pushing the recruitment of black soldiers, personally commissioning Williams and Seaman as recruiters, and appointing Williams as commander—raised the ire of many who were opposed to black soldiers in the Union Army. But, as Ian Spurgeon wrote, Lane "did not follow public opinion on this issue; rather he led public opinion to a necessary political and military policy."[29]

A week later, Williams publicly congratulated his regiment for their victory at Island Mound in General Order Number 10. In it, he praised the performance of all those who participated, and cited by name the gallant conduct of those who died, and those whose exceptional performance on the field of battle merited special recognition.[30] Now, with their newly gained confidence, they had to get back to the business of building and training the regiment.

Chapter Five

The Regiment: "A Day of Great Rejoicing," and Grim Reality at Sherwood

The regiment continued to grow, but not without occasional bumps. In November 1862, Williams had a run-in with the law in Lecompton. Lecompton was not a community that would have extended a warm welcome to Williams. It had been the fraudulent capital of territorial Kansas established by the pro-slavery faction in the wake of the Kansas-Nebraska Act. Emotions in the community ran high against free black soldiers. Williams and Captain Matthews were there to apprehend some deserters. The mayor had Williams arrested on grounds that he had no right to arrest deserters. Lecompton authorities also asserted that the soldiers were not really in the army, as Lane did not have the authority to enlist them. Williams posted bond, reunited with Matthews, rounded up the soldiers, and escorted them out of town. Williams subsequently returned to town to retrieve one more soldier who was in jail on a trumped-up charge. Williams barged into the jail, intimidated the jailer into releasing the soldier, and returned to camp. Several days later, he wrote a letter to General Blunt letting him know what he had done.[1]

Under a blustery and overcast sky on January 1, 1863, the regiment celebrated Emancipation Day. It began with a full dress review, followed by a celebration in which the entire regiment sat at tables on the field arranged in company order (probably in anticipation of long-winded speeches). Captain Earle of Company F made the introductory statement. Lieutenant A.T. Scholes led a cheer for President Lincoln. The commander of Fort Leavenworth gave a speech in which he anticipated that in the near future "the official reports of some of our generals down south will electrify the land with the details of battle wherein colored men will be mentioned favorably as having fought and bled for their country." Colonel Williams was next on the agenda. Historian Noah Andre Trudeau noted that Williams waxed eloquent, "Speaking with all the flowery effusion expected of serious orators of that day." Williams expounded that the armed military service of black men "will be no mere struggle of conquest, but a struggle for their own freedom, a determined and, as I believe, irresistible struggle for the disenthralment of a people who have long suffered oppression and wrong at the hands of our enemies."[2]

Captain William D. Matthews, the black commander of Company D, briefly commented, "Today is a day of great rejoicing for us. As a thinking man I never doubted this day would come. . . . Now is our time to strike. Our own exertions and our own muscle must make us men. If we fight we shall be respected."[3]

After further speeches and singing, the formal part of the celebration ended with the regimental adjutant reading the second paragraph of Lincoln's Emancipation proclamation:

> That on the first day of January, in the year of our Lord one thousand eight hundred and sixty-three, all persons held as slaves within any State, or any designated part of a State, the people whereof shall be in rebellion against the United States, shall be then and thenceforward, and forever, free; and the Executive government of the United States, including the military and naval authority thereof, will recognize and maintain the freedom of such persons, and will do no act or acts to repress such persons, or any of them, in any efforts they make for their actual freedom.[4]

Not everyone in Kansas was enthusiastic about emancipation and black troops. The recent combat success of the regiment carried no weight. One of Williams' officers wrote to his wife on January 10, 1863, that following a review for General Blunt, the regiment marched into the town of Fort Scott and around the town square. As they marched, regulars stationed at Fort Scott assaulted them with demeaning remarks in front of the citizenry.[5]

On January 13, 1863, the First Kansas Colored Volunteer Infantry Regiment formally mustered into federal service with newly promoted Lieutenant Colonel James M. Williams as commander.[6] They did so with their reputation as a combat-experienced regiment already established. They were the first black regiment formed in a Union state mustered into the army.[7]

As the muster took place, the officers and men of the newly federalized regiment realized that the struggle for equality was not over. The Federal government denied Williams' friends, Captain Matthews and Lieutenant Minor, commissions because they were black, and the federal government at that time did not allow black officers. Twenty-one officers in the new regiment stepped forward in their support of commissioning Matthews, in written protest, that he was "among the most thorough and efficient officers in our organization: in every sense of the term, drilled, disciplined, and capable."[8] The War Department ruled against black officers on the premise that such circumstances would be untenable if black officers were to have to command white troops.[9] It was fine to do so in a Kansas regiment, but the First Kansas Colored Volunteer Infantry was now a federal regiment, and the War Department made the rules. Eventually, both Matthews and Minor would receive commissions, serving in the Independent Colored Kansas Battery.[10] Matthews and Minor would be the only officers present in the battery during the invasion of Confederate Major General Price's army into Kansas in 1864, and would lead it into combat. Lieutenant Minor would later die of disease, and Captain Matthews would continue to command the battery.[11]

While Williams was continuing to bring his regiment up to strength and enhance their battle readiness, political intrigues continued unabated. One of the men in his regiment was in touch with R.C. Anderson, an individual whom Governor Thomas Carney had wanted to commission as commander of the First Kansas Colored Infantry. Senator Lane stymied Carney by doing an end run, obtaining a War Department commission for Williams. Anderson's confidante in the regiment penned a letter to him on March 10, 1863:

Sir permit me to drop you a few lines and facts in regard to your appointment as Colonel of the Regiment. The majority of the officers here has
combined together against you and are using their influence against you
and in favor of Williams and if enny [any] man attempts to come in over
him that the[y] will shoot him[.]we herd a few days ago that you was on
your road here and would arrive that day[.] the[y] loaded their revolv-
ers and armed their selves and said that no damned Carney man could
come in the camp and instructed the guards to shoot the first man that
attempted to pass in[.]General Blunt is here and is working for Williams[.]
Lane has sent blank orders here with his name signed to them with orders
to Williams to fill them out and to muster no man that has been commissioned by Carney unless by order of Lane and you may plainly see that
Lane and Blunt will work against you[.] Williams started today for St.
Lewis [Louis] and expects to go to Washington and will obtain his commission threw [through] the Secratery of War by Lanes assistance that is a
great point for you to watch or you will be thrown out unless you are wide
awake and I would advise you to go to Washington at once with all speed
it is the only thing that will save you[.] Pomroy will doo all he can for you
I will doo all that is in my power for you but thare is a heavy combination
against me friend Sloat is working for you all he can[.]

Yours until Death
Asa Reynard[12]

Governor Carney followed up by sending correspondence to President
Lincoln with no apparent results. Lincoln wrote a note to Senator Lane on
April 27, 1863, seeking his help in settling the conflict over military authority. For some unknown reason, however, Carney ordered the message quashed
and not sent. Carney later traveled to Washington and, while there, called
upon the White House to see the President. Lincoln, or his staff, kept Carney
waiting, and they did not meet. In July, Governor Carney wrote a long letter to President Lincoln. In it, he demonstrated impotent frustration for his
archenemy Lane out-maneuvering him in securing commissions. Carney
expressed concern that Lincoln had ignored his recommendations for the
military command structure as it affected operations in Kansas. He also said,
"I gave you my reasons fully . . . when I wished Maj Genl Blunt's military

authority to be absolutely suspended in the State of Kansas." Carney asked
for revocation of any orders in which General Blunt had named officers for
Kansas. He went on to say, "I asked that Lt. Col. J.M. Williams commission
by the Secretary of War be dismissed the service, and the R.C. Anderson
commissioned by me on the 20th of Febry 1863 be made Col. of the 1st
Kansas Colored Regiment." Carney shaded his political motives for wanting
Anderson in command, by attacking Williams: "there is an attitude of defy-
ing the civil authorities (two indictments there being pending against him)."
He then cast the mantle of his frustration on Secretary of War Stanton, who
"done what I refused to do, and by so doing foisted upon the state an outlaw
in high military position."[13]

The indictments to which Carney was referring probably evolved from
Williams' arrest and the conflict over his military authority to apprehend
deserters from his regiment. There was never any action taken on the indictments. Williams was pleased with the attention, even honored by the level to
which Carney's frustration had risen.[14]

James Williams advanced from lieutenant colonel to colonel May 2,
1863. With his promotion came the duties of colonel commanding the First
Kansas Colored Volunteer Infantry regiment. He was thirty years old.[15]

Carney dated his last letter, noted above, July 19, 1863. His timing was
not good. In the interim, Williams had advanced to colonel, won battles
at Cabin Creek and Honey Springs in Indian Territory (July 17), and had
been wounded in the service of his country. Nothing further came from
Carney's pen.

Throughout the spring and into the summer, Williams had to deal with
a problem affecting all black regiments coming into the army–pay. There was
a growing dissatisfaction with a dichotomy of pay between white and black
soldiers. The army pay for a private soldier was thirteen dollars per month,
including a three-dollar clothing allowance if he were white. Black soldiers
were paid ten dollars per month, minus three for clothing, leaving just seven
dollars. The variance originated in the legislation that brought black men
into the military. The ten-dollar pay scale was included in the act that focused
upon recruitment of contraband laborers, not fighting soldiers. The fact that
the pay of a black sergeant was still ten dollars per month (net of seven dollars) further exacerbated the impact on soldiers.[16]

Grade	White	Colored
Sergeant Major	21	7
Quartermaster Sergeant	21	7
First Sergeant	20	7
Sergeant	17	7
Hospital Steward	30	7
Corporal	13	7
Private	13	7
Chaplain	100	7

This circumstance particularly offended black soldiers who fought, still suffering the pay inequity. Congress did not seem to be disposed to correct the issue. Adding to the perception in black regiments of ill intent by the federal government was the policy against commissioning black officers. The impact was a morale problem in black regiments throughout the army, resulting in some cases of mutiny, and executions of soldiers who refused to perform their duties until the pay issue was resolved.[17] In many black units, rather than put themselves open to punishment for refusing to perform their duties, the soldiers refused to accept any pay at all until the government fixed the problem.[18]

The pay problem was particularly onerous to the families of black soldiers. Even those soldiers who accepted the seven dollars in cash could not support a family on that amount. The ones who refused on principle to accept any pay until the issue resolved, put their families at risk of outright starvation. Much of the time, the families could not find employment, and prejudicial laws barred them from receiving public aid. Soldiers who had escaped slavery but had families still in the South, free or not, could not get money to them.[19]

Finally, in June 1864, Congress acted with legislation bringing equality in pay retroactive to 1862. However, there was a stipulation that any soldier eligible to receive the retroactive pay must have been free as of April 19, 1861. That prompted black soldiers to make false statements as to their freedom. Congress removed the stipulation in the fall of 1865, after the war was over.[20]

The morale problem created by pay issues contributed to the desertion rate. Sometimes having a starving family and being taken advantage of trumps motivation to serve the cause. Although the desertion rate in the First Kansas was comparatively low, it was a still a problem. The problem greatly magnified by April 1863 because once again, none of the men in the regiment received any pay–at all. Not even Williams and his officers were paid. Enraged, Williams penned a message to the commanding officer at Fort Scott: "My men have never yet received one cent of bounty or of pay although they have now been in the Service nearly ten months." In another letter to General Blunt, he complained that his men were "sorely troubled and grieved about the pay." Meanwhile, white soldiers in other units were paid. The black troops finally received their pay in July. There were few desertions after that, in spite of the fact that their pay was still less than white soldiers for another year.[21]

Williams published a general order on that first payday admonishing his soldiers to be responsible and frugal, reminding them that they were now free and earning pay for their service. He advised them to put their funds in safekeeping for support of their families and building of their homes.[22]

In May, the regiment transferred from Camp Lincoln to Baxter Springs in the southeast corner of the state. The First Kansas garrisoned the new post. Relocation of the regiment further south to Baxter Springs distanced its soldiers from the Kansas towns in which they could get in trouble or desert.[23]

Other more pressing problems presented themselves while the pay issues and political intrigue percolated. James Williams and his regiment were going to run headlong into the buzz saw of Confederate policy on treatment of black prisoners. Confederate regular and guerrilla activity was picking up. Early in May 1863, a detachment of sixty men from the Second Kansas Cavalry on a scout near Sherwood, Missouri (north of present-day Joplin) encountered a force of about 200 Confederates. They sent to Fort Scott for reinforcements, and Williams responded with two companies of infantry and an artillery section. Together, the Kansas units attacked the Confederates and routed them, capturing a few prisoners and fifty horses and mules. Confederate Major Thomas Livingston was operating throughout the area, and made reports of engagements with Union troops, but the dates do not exactly coincide. As can be expected, their reports of any such contact reflect favor on their own side.[24]

Given the level of guerrilla activity around Baxter Springs, Williams set about establishing his expectations to bring stability to the area. He published a challenge to his foes:

> I came here . . . to put a stop to the Guerrilla or Bushwhacking war which is now being carried on . . . in Jasper and Newton Counties, Mo. It is my desire . . . to follow . . . all the rules applicable to Civilized warfare. I therefore propose that you . . . come to some point and attack me, or give me notice where I can find your force and I will fight you on your own grounds. But if you persist in the system of Guerrilla warfare heretofore followed by you and refuse to fight openly like soldiers fighting for a cause I shall feel bound to treat you as thieves and robbers who lurk in secret places fighting only defenceless people and wholly unworthy [of] the fate due to chivalrous soldiers engaged in honourable warfare, and shall take any means within my power to rid the country of your murderous gang.[25]

In that same period, Major Edward Eno, of the Eighth Missouri State Militia Cavalry (Union) was on a scout with 180 men in southwestern Missouri, specifically seeking out Livingston's Confederate Battalion. They engaged Livingston on May 14, near Sherwood inconclusively, killing one. They captured two more in a skirmish the next day. Livingston broke his command down to small teams designed to disappear into the countryside, and reform elsewhere. Eno's blue-jacketed troops chased down and killed some of the rebels. On the eighteenth, Eno's troops returned to their base, having lost four killed and two wounded. People present at the burial of Livingston's men counted fifteen dead, and fifteen to twenty wounded.[26]

On May 18, a detachment of forty-five men, twenty-five from the First Kansas and twenty from the Second Kansas Battery, under the command of Major Richard Ward of the First Kansas, were on a foraging mission near Sherwood, Missouri. They were approximately fifteen miles from Baxter Springs. The men, other than a few pickets, had stacked their muskets, and were loading corn into their wagons. Livingston and his First Missouri Cavalry Battalion took them by surprise in a brutal attack.[27] Most of them were far enough away from their weapons that they never had a chance to respond. For the Confederates, it was a turkey shoot—bodies everywhere. Most of the white men from the Second Kansas, and about half of the First

Kansas managed to flee into the nearby forest. Their losses were sixteen men killed, and five captured.[28] Fourteen of the men killed were black soldiers; two were white. Of the five men captured, three were white men from the Second Kansas Battery, and two were black men from the First Kansas. One author theorized that fewer white artillerymen were killed because they were mounted, and the blacks, who were infantry, could not escape.[29] That may be true, but the artillerymen had dismounted at the time of the attack.

As survivors trickled back to Baxter Springs, Williams became aware of the magnitude of the massacre. He immediately deployed a task force of three hundred men to the scene of the action.[30] The next morning, when they arrived at the farm outside Sherwood, they found a bloody mess of mutilated and mangled bodies strewn around the landscape. Williams was enraged at the sight he encountered. He later reported, "I visited the scene of this engagement the morning after its occurrence and for the first time beheld the horrible evidences of the demoniac spirit of these rebel fiends in their treatment of our dead and wounded." He described the carnage he encountered: "Men were found with their brains beaten out with clubs, and the bloody weapons left by their sides, and their bodies most horribly mutilated."[31]

Williams ordered the mutilated bodies picked up and placed in the farmhouse. He concluded that given the mutilated condition of the bodies and the warm weather, it would be "best to simply cremate the gory remains."[32] On their way to the scene, his men had stopped a man named John Bishop walking down a nearby road. Upon inspection, they recognized him as a Confederate soldier paroled after capture by Union forces. Unfortunately for Bishop, he was wearing items belonging to one of Williams' men killed the previous day. Williams had Bishop shot, and his body thrown in with those of the brutalized Union soldiers. The house became a ceremonial funeral pyre for the slaughtered men.[33]

Williams recognized that many of the Confederates in Livingston's Battalion were from Jasper County, and were receiving aid from the local citizenry. He ordered the destruction of the town of Sherwood and utter devastation of the countryside within a five-mile radius of there. Sherwood never recovered, and ultimately ceased to exist.[34]

On May 20, Livingston sent a letter through an intermediary to Williams. The text of that letter clearly framed the Confederate government's policy concerning black prisoners:

Camp Jackson May 20th 1863
Col Williams

honored sir I have five of your Solgers prisoners three Whight and two
Black men The whight men I propose Exchanging with you if you have
any of My men or other confederate Solgers to exchange for Them as for
the Negros I cannot Reccognise them as Solgers and In consiquence I
will hav to hold them as contrabands of war if my proposels Sootes your
you will Return ammeadately my men or other confederate Solgers and
I will send your your men x arrested a citizen of this Naborhood by the
name of Bishop If that is your mode of warefair to A rest civil citizens
who air living at home and trying to Rase a crop for their familys Let
me know and I will try to play to your hand Mr Bishop was once arested
taking to Fort Scott Examoned Released and past home a civil citizen
Sum of your men stated that he was burnt up in Mrs Radors House
but I am sadisfied that you are to high toned a jentelman to stoope or
condescend to such Brutal deeads of Barbarity.

I remain yours truly
T. R. Livingston, Maj Comdg Confederate forces.[35]

Thus began a war of words and the exchange of a number of letters
between the two men, culminating ten days after the incident. It was a direct
result of a policy enacted by the Confederate Congress that black men in
uniform captured by Confederate forces were not soldiers. Military captors were to turn black prisoners over to civil authorities and, if found to be
escaped slaves, returned to their owners. If ownership were not established,
Confederate authorities would sell the captives. Williams' barely contained
fury was evident in his response to Livingston:

Head Quarters 1st K.C.V. Camp Hooker Ks. May 21st 1863—
Maj T. R Livingston Commanding Confederate forces

Sir Yours of the 20th inst is at hand, you have in your custody as I believe
Privates, Pipkins & Whitstine of the 2nd Kansas Battery for which I will
exchange two confederate Soldiers, now prisoners in my camp, in regard
to the other white man now a prisoner with you, I do not know of any
man belonging to my command not otherwise accounted for. And you

can arrange for his exchange at Fort Scott. In regard to the colored men, prisoners, belonging to my Regiment, I have this to say, that it rests with you to treat them as prisoners of war or not but be assured that I shall keep a like number of your men as prisoners until these colored men are accounted for, and you can safely trust that I shall visit a retributive justice upon them for any injury done them at the hands of the confederate forces, and if twenty days are allowed to pass without hearing of their exchange I shall conclude that they have been murdered by your Soldiers or shared a worse fate by being sent in chains to the slave pens of the South, and they will be presumed to be dead.[36]

The exchange of white prisoners took place as requested. Williams then discovered that Livingston's men killed one of the two black prisoners in Livingston's custody. Williams made it very clear that he considered the murder of the prisoner to be intolerable. He demanded that Livingston return the body of the black prisoner. He included an ultimatum that Livingston comply within forty-eight hours, or he was going to hang a rebel prisoner. He also headed off an assertion that the death of the black prisoner was beyond Livingston's ability to control by pointedly remarking, "If you are fit to command, you can control your men, and I shall act from the belief that the murder was committed by your consent and will receive no excuse therefore."[37]

Livingston wrote a rambling note back to Williams, claiming that the man who killed the prisoner was not a member of his command, but a visitor who had become enraged at the sight of a black Union soldier. Much of his letter was limited to imprecations to Williams that what he was doing was a terrible thing, and he would forward the threatening letters through channels in protest.[38]

Williams determined that he would prove the value of his word. He had a Confederate prisoner executed to back up his promise. He commented, "Suffice it to say that this ended the barbarous practice of killing prisoners as far as Livingston was concerned."[39]

The exchange of written potshots went on into early June. Beyond that point, neither Williams nor Livingston accrued any further gains. They both had missions to fulfill, so they went about their business.

Williams' decision to savage everything within a five-mile radius of the massacre site had a significant impact. His soldiers destroyed twelve farmhouses. The destruction precipitated actions in other parts of the county that in turn resulted in devastation of the entire county.[40]

James Williams and the First Kansas Colored Volunteer Infantry would soon move on to be victorious in larger scale engagements in Indian Territory and Arkansas. However, on two future dates, Rebels would slaughter black soldiers of the First Kansas without quarter, solely because of their race and the policies created by the Confederate government.

Chapter Six

Into Indian Territory:
First Battle of Cabin Creek

The Civil War was savage in the Trans-Mississippi region of the United States, particularly in Indian Territory (now Oklahoma). Battles were smaller in total numbers, but they were no less brutal than those in the east; they were, perhaps, even more so. Old animosities pitted neighbor against neighbor. Opposing forces knew each other well and fought over and over again. Guerrilla forces terrorized, murdered, and burned almost as they pleased without regard to the ideologies of their victims. Along the Kansas-Missouri border, the fighting continued from 1855 to 1865, costing thousands of soldiers and civilians their careers, homes, and lives.

Conflicts within Indian nations stemmed from President Andrew Jackson's forced relocation of the Indians from southeastern states to Indian Territory. Violent factions emerged between those who supported the relocation and those who did not. Confederate and Union governments sought Indian loyalty, creating schisms within families and friendships. Political systems of the Indian nations fell apart. The result was a civil war within the Civil War. Tribes fought each other, as did factions within each tribe, particularly the Creeks and Cherokees. Families were wiped out, towns burned, farm fields lay fallow, and the residue of combat littered the landscape.

Indian Territory was strategically valuable to Union and Confederates alike. It was a source of cattle for beef and leather, grain, salt, lead, and Indian labor. It could serve both sides of the conflict as a barrier between Kansas and Texas, while protecting the western border of Arkansas from Union attack. Control of Indian Territory would enhance Confederate access to the western territories.[1]

The Confederacy ultimately established formal ties with most of the Indian tribes in the Territory, securing commitments from Indians to fight in the Confederate Army. These Indians had been adherents to the Southern lifestyle, including slave ownership. Confederate Indians brutally drove all who were loyal to the Federal government north toward refuge in Kansas. Hundreds were killed, yet even larger numbers died of starvation or froze to death. Into the mix came Union and Confederate armies with whites and Indians on both sides. On the Union side, the black men of James Williams' First Kansas Colored Volunteer Infantry joined the fray.[2]

By early 1863, the Confederacy had control of essentially all of Indian Territory. A Federal incursion in 1862 had collapsed under the inebriated and incompetent leadership of Colonel William Weer, arrested by his subordinates, who then pulled back north. Confederate troops, including regiments from Texas, occupied all the forts abandoned by Federals in 1861.

Confederate Indians soon formed regiments. The First Regiment of Cherokee Mounted Rifles, commanded by Colonel John Drew, consisted of Cherokees—or "Pin Indians"—loyal to John Ross, titular head of the Cherokee Nation. Colonel Stand Watie, an outstanding Confederate leader with combat experience, commanded the rival Second Regiment of Cherokee Mounted Rifles.[3] Watie headed a faction of mixed blood Cherokees at odds with John Ross' Pin Indians, stemming from the Indian Removal when Ross' group killed Watie's half-brother, uncle, and cousin. Watie would ultimately emerge as the preeminent Indian military officer in the South. In spite of internecine conflicts, these and several other Confederate Indian units would figure prominently in James Williams' future.[4]

The flood of Indian refugees with Union sympathies north to Kansas prompted the creation of three Indian regiments in blue uniforms. These Yankee regiments became the nucleus of an Indian Brigade commanded by Colonel William A. Phillips, a competent commander at the head of the Third Indian Regiment. His brigade consisted of the First, Second, and Third Indian Regiments, the Sixth Kansas Cavalry (one battalion), and Captain Hopkins' Battery of Artillery.[5] Many of the Indians' former black slaves, now free, enjoyed a level of equality with their former masters not enjoyed between blacks and their former white masters.[6] Some of those former slaves joined Williams' regiment.

In the spring of 1863, General Blunt, headquartered at Baxter Springs, Kansas, just across the border from Indian Territory, determined it was time to restore the Union presence there. Accordingly, he directed Colonel Phillips with his brigade of Indians to move on Fort Gibson, in eastern Indian Territory. Fort Gibson, just east of present-day Muskogee, was located on the banks of the Grand River near its confluence with the Arkansas River, a strategic location.

Fort Gibson's lifeline to the north was the Military, or Texas, Road, which connected to Baxter Springs, Fort Scott and Fort Leavenworth. The road extended south from Fort Gibson through Confederate territory to the Texas border.[7] Phillips, well aware of the presence of multiple brigade-sized Confederate commands in the area, cautiously worked his way in that direction, with advance cavalry units leading the way. His lead units took Fort Gibson from a small Confederate garrison in short order, and Phillips moved in on April 13.[8]

Life at Fort Gibson proved to be a source of nerves for Colonel Phillips. Confederate Brigadier General Douglas Cooper, with his Indian-Texan Brigade, set up camp across the Arkansas River within sight of Fort Gibson, monitoring every move made by the Yankee Indian Brigade. Phillips was also very much aware of the proximity of Confederate Brigadier General William L. Cabell and his Arkansas cavalry brigade. Phillips was dependent upon periodic resupply of his brigade by wagon trains from Fort Scott, 160 miles distant, along a vulnerable lifeline.[9]

Phillips needed supplies and reinforcements. His troops had been on half rations since the beginning of the year.[10] It was obvious that the Confederates were marshaling more and more troops in his area, with less than congenial intentions.[11]

General Blunt dispatched a wagon train of two hundred wagons from Fort Scott loaded with supplies, foodstuffs, ammunition, and equipment. Blunt provided a military escort with the mission of protecting the train, and reinforcing the Federals at Fort Gibson. Included were six companies from the Second Colorado Infantry, one company from the Third Wisconsin Cavalry, one company from the Ninth Kansas Cavalry, a section of the Second

Figure 10   Major General James M. Blunt, USA

General Blunt was Commander, Department of Kansas; Army of the Frontier; and was Union Commander at the Battle of Honey Springs. Before getting involved in the Kansas Free-State movement, he was a merchant sailor and physician. LIBRARY OF CONGRESS PHOTOGRAPH.

Kansas Artillery, and a twelve-pounder mountain howitzer. The commander of troops was Lieutenant Colonel Theodore Dodd, with his battalion of the Second Colorado Infantry. The column left Fort Scott on about June 20 heading down the Military Road. After an uneventful few days, they arrived at Baxter Springs, in southeast Kansas. They picked up six hundred more cavalrymen from Kansas under the command of Major John Foreman of the Third Indian Home Guards, and continued their journey south on June 26. The column proceeded only fifteen miles farther south, before being forced to pause two days because of high water on the Neosho River (another name for the Lower Grand River).

While the wagon train waited, Colonel James Williams received word of an imminent attack on the column and moved his regiment to overtake it. Lieutenant Colonel Dodd was pleased to receive additional help and displayed little or no reservations about black troops being on the same expedition.[12]

Williams' primary mission, as directed by General Blunt, was to reinforce Phillips at Fort Gibson.[13] A supplement to Williams' orders contained instructions with somewhat convoluted verbiage indicating that if he chose to accompany the column, he would only be along for the ride—Lieutenant Colonel Dodd would remain in command of the escort. The instructions read:

> If by any means you have failed to move your command and reinforce Col. Phillips as directed per Special Orders from Hd. Qtrs. Of Ks., before the command of Lieut. Col. Dodd, 2nd Colorado reaches you; your forces will not be united for the purpose of escorting the train and you assume command as the ranking officer, but comply with previous orders issued you, reporting in person to Col. Philips with your command.[14]

The intent of the message appears to be compliance with Federal policy that segregated the chain of command of black troops from white troops, as well as the troops themselves. Williams' actions with respect to these instructions would be significant in a few days.

Transit of the wagon train to Fort Gibson was crucial. Failure would mean a threat to the viability of the Union presence in Indian Territory. Confederate forces would be substantially stronger at the expense of the Federals if the wagon train's cargo were to fall into their hands. Thus, there was little doubt that the massed Confederate forces would be attacking the wagon train. Major

Livingston monitored its progress and reported its status to the Confederate command as it passed through Baxter Springs. Livingston's message arrived at Confederate Brigadier General William Steele's headquarters on June 29. In response, Steele immediately sent a message to General William Cabell, directing him to move his brigade at once to reinforce Cooper's brigade. On the same date, General Steele directed Cooper to ride quickly to intercept the wagon train with every soldier he could find.[15] Four salient observations emerge from the messages:

- General Steele was not sure if the large escort was going to remain with the wagon train, or most of it was going to move out to attack Cooper's camp in his rear. The escort stayed with the wagon train.
- General Steele did not believe the escort was as large as reported. The reports he received indicated a force of 2,000 men. The actual strength was 1,600, probably still more than he expected.
- General Steele believed that General Blunt would accompany the wagon train. He did not.
- General Steele believed that the wagon train would not leave Baxter Springs until June 29. It left on the twenty-sixth. Although it paused at a ford fifteen miles south of Baxter Springs, it still had a slim edge on Steele's estimated timeline.

These observations demonstrate that the Confederates had to scramble to act, and they may have had to split their forces to handle eventualities. Cooper had Colonel Watie in command of a task force blocking the Military Road, with General Cabell's brigade coming to reinforce him. Watie's command consisted of his Second Cherokee Mounted Rifles, the First Creek Cavalry Regiment, and six hundred men from the Twenty-Ninth Texas Cavalry and Fifth Texas Partisan Rangers. His total force was between sixteen and eighteen hundred men.[16] If Cabell's brigade could get there in time, their combined commands would easily carry the day.

The wagon train lumbered along slowly, its two hundred wagons and sixteen hundred men stretched out across nearly two miles of the Military Road, Williams' First Kansas in the midst. On June 30, Foreman's scouts discovered a fresh trail and tracked down thirty Confederates, who proved to be advance pickets for Stand Watie's command. Foreman's Indians attacked, killing four and capturing three. They knew a larger confrontation was imminent.[17]

Figure 11   **Brigadier General Stand Watie, CSA**

General Stand Watie, a Cherokee Indian, proved an able combat commander for the Confederate Army. He commanded the Cherokee Mounted Rifles and, later, the First Indian Brigade as a brigadier general. Watie commanded Confederate troops in the First Battle of Cabin Creek. His troops were a large component of the Confederate line at the Battle of Honey Springs. He commanded his brigade in the Second Battle of Cabin Creek. Watie was the highest-ranking Indian officer in a field command on either side during the Civil War. He was also the last Confederate general in a field command to surrender at war's end. RESEARCH DIVISION OF THE OKLAHOMA HISTORICAL SOCIETY.

Figure 12   Brigadier General William Cabell, CSA

General Cabell, a West Point graduate, commanded an Arkansas cavalry brigade. High water on the Grand River delayed his mission to reinforce Watie's troops at the First Battle of Cabin Creek in Indian Territory. Similarly, he was a few hours too late to make a difference at the Battle of Honey Springs. His command played a key role in the later Battle of Poison Spring in Arkansas. LIBRARY OF CONGRESS PHOTOGRAPH.

On the next day, July 1, the column approached the Cabin Creek crossing in northeast Indian Territory. As they slowly worked their way down a hill to the creek, they drew fire from thick brush on the north side of the creek. A skirmish ensued, in which Foreman's troops killed three Confederates and captured three more.[18] Colonel Dodd ordered the deployment of Foreman's troops in a skirmish line left and right of the road at the fording point. He had the wagons moved into defensive positions back up the hill as they arrived, with security from one company from the First Kansas, one from the Sixth Kansas, and the companies from the Second Colorado. Unlimbering their mountain howitzer, they opened fire on the enemy positions, causing the enemy riflemen to stop shooting and pull back. This led to about three to four hundred Confederate skirmishers trapped between Foreman and the stream. Some attempted escape by running downstream on the bank; others headed upstream. Others sought to swim themselves, or their horses across, the stream. Many of them drowned. Foreman and his troops pushed forward to the creek, attempted to wade across it, and found the water to be too deep and fast from recent rains upstream. Testing the enemy's lines on the opposite bank, they determined that the Confederate positions extended for a mile in either direction from the ford. They fell back to regroup and allow the water to subside.[19]

Cabin Creek, at the fording point, posed a challenge for troops coming from the north. Thick growth of brush and trees all along both sides afforded close range cover for riflemen. The creek itself was forty to fifty yards across, with steep banks of thirty feet or more on both sides. With deep and fast water, it was more like a small river than a creek. The Military Road at that point (just as it is today) was a narrow path—one set of wagon ruts wide—which curled down to the creek. When wet, as it was, it was very slippery.

That night, Colonel Williams, Lieutenant Colonel Dodd, and Major Foreman met to put together a plan. There was no choice in direction; the supplies and men had to get through. They had to act fast and decisively before enemy reinforcements arrived. They concluded that as many men as reasonable (but not too many) be removed from the security of the wagon train, and agreed that unity of command was critical. Colonel Williams would command the action the next day. The assault element would include the First Kansas Colored, three companies from the Second Colorado Infantry, Company B of the Third Wisconsin Cavalry, Company C of the Ninth

Kansas Cavalry, Company B of the Fourteenth Kansas Cavalry, all of Major
Foreman's Indian command, and a section from the Second Kansas Battery.
The assault force totaled nine hundred men.[20]

The plan was to place artillery on the left and right flanks and in the center to provide covering fires for the assault. Major Foreman had responsibility
to lead the assault with a company of the Third Indian Home Guards, followed by the First Kansas led by Lieutenant Colonel John Bowles (the executive officer); the Second Colorado Infantry, and a battalion of three cavalry
companies. The remaining companies of the Third Indian Home Guard took
position on the flanks of the assault force and covered the creek.[21]

The following morning, Williams determined that the water level had
subsided enough to attempt the crossing. At 8:00 a.m. Yankee bugles shattered the quiet morning, and the Federal column stormed into the waters of
Cabin Creek. Simultaneously, Williams' artillery erupted, blasting shot and
shrapnel along the rebel lines to either side of the charging bluecoats. In spite
of the fierceness of the attack, the Confederate troops, shielded behind fallen
trees and logs, held their positions. Just as Major Foreman's cavalry entered
the creek, large numbers of Confederates charged out of the woods, deliver-
ing a volley of small arms fire into the Federal column, felling several men.
With the movement of Confederates into the open, the Union artillerymen
switched to canister and spherical case shot designed to savage enemy formations. The Confederates quickly withdrew back into their protective cover,
and the bluecoats resumed their advance. The next volley of fire from the
Confederates caught the Federals mid-stream, bringing down several more of
them, including Major Foreman.[22]

Foreman had two wounds; his horse had five. His troops, confused, fal-
tered. Williams had the leading companies file to the right to stabilize, and
then resume fire with the artillery. In short order, he placed a company of horse
soldiers from the Ninth Kansas Cavalry in the lead, followed again by the three
Indian companies, with volleys of suppressing fire from the black infantry.[23]

The lead company of the Ninth Kansas Cavalry, with sabers high, charged
into the water, forcing themselves through the flank-deep current. They made
it across the creek to the south bank, and secured the ford. The rest of the
Union command charged across with the Kansans followed by the Indian
cavalry, elements of the Sixth Kansas Cavalry, and the First Kansas Colored

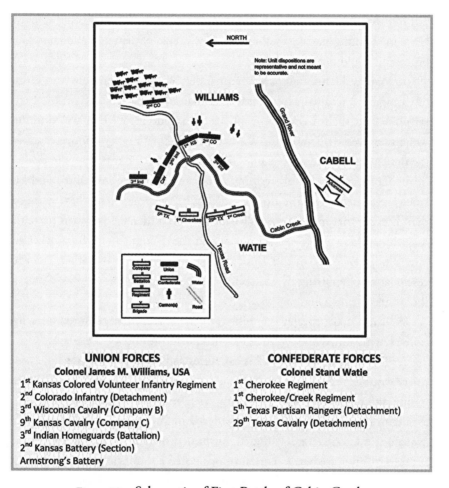

NORTH

Note: Unit dispositions are
representative and not meant
to be accurate.

WILLIAMS

2nd CO

1st KS   2nd CO

2nd Inf

Cav

3rd Inf

3rd Ind

5th TX   1st Cherokee   29th TX   1st Creek

Grand River

CABELL

Arkansas

Cabin Creek

WATIE

Texas Road

Company
Battalion
Regiment
Brigade

Union
Confederate
Cannon(s)

Water
Road

UNION FORCES
Colonel James M. Williams, USA
1st Kansas Colored Volunteer Infantry Regiment
2nd Colorado Infantry (Detachment)
3rd Wisconsin Cavalry (Company B)
9th Kansas Cavalry (Company C)
3rd Indian Homeguards (Battalion)
2nd Kansas Battery (Section)
Armstrong's Battery

CONFEDERATE FORCES
Colonel Stand Watie
1st Cherokee Regiment
1st Cherokee/Creek Regiment
5th Texas Partisan Rangers (Detachment)
29th Texas Cavalry (Detachment)

Figure 13   Schematic of First Battle of Cabin Creek,
July 1–2, 1863 (Not to Scale)

Volunteer Infantry Regiment, with fixed bayonets and Colonel Williams in the lead. As fast as the Federals crossed the stream, they deployed into an offensive line. Again, the bugler sounded the signal, and the line surged forward. One of the men in that formation later recorded, "When the enemy saw our troops approaching them in double quick time with glittering bayonets and flashing sabers, they made a few feeble efforts to stand, but soon broke and could not be rallied."[24]

One of Williams' company commanders, Captain Benjamin Van Horn, of Company I recalled exuberantly, "We run our howitzers up on the highest point and shelled the brush on the other side for all that was out, and while they were still throwing shells we made for the creek and crossed on the double-quick, the water came to about the top of our pants." He exulted in the Confederate retreat, writing, "They made some show of a stand but when we came out on the double-quick with bayonets fixed they broke for their horses, what mounted men we had followed them and in their haste the majority ran down between the bayou and the river, many of them never got out."[25] G.S. Killgore, of the Third Wisconsin Cavalry, raved about the successful attack, reporting that as commander, Williams "was as brave a man as the western army had.[26]

All the Yankee cavalry combined for the chase. They returned after five miles, having killed and wounded an unknown number of the enemy.

Williams determined that his casualties had been light—three killed and thirty wounded. Major Foreman would recover; Captain Earle of Company F only suffered a slight wound. Enemy casualties were much more difficult to ascertain. Estimates were at least fifty dead, and nine captured. No data were available on Confederate wounded, or those drowned in the flooded creek.[27] A few days after the battle, Union troops noted a significant number of dead Confederate soldiers and horses as they floated past Fort Gibson, well downstream from the battle site.[28]

General Cabell's Confederate brigade did not make it to the battle scene in time to reinforce Stand Watie's brigade. High waters stymied him as he attempted to ford the Grand River downstream from where Cabin Creek fed into it. The rain-swollen river was even deeper and swifter than had been Cabin Creek when Williams initially attempted to ford it. Cabell and his brigade returned to Arkansas.[29]

Figure 14   Wagon Train Parked, Ready to Move

This photograph shows approximately 230 wagons parked in a field— comparable to the 200–300 that were attacked at Cabin Creek. Judging by this photo, it would have been difficult to defend so many wagons, whether parked or spread out along the road. A column of this many wagons would have been as many as two miles long. LIBRARY OF CONGRESS PHOTOGRAPH.

Pursuing the fleeing Confederate enemy would have been imprudent; the wagons and their precious cargo were much more important. The column reorganized and continued on its way, closing successfully on Fort Gibson by July 5. No supplies were lost, the command was intact, and victory was sweet.

The victory at Cabin Creek did not draw major attention. It took place on the first and second of July 1863 on a remote prairie in the Trans-Mississippi Theater of War. It only involved a few thousand troops. At the same time, one thousand miles east of Cabin Creek, over a hundred thousand men were in the grip of the bloodiest battle in American history in a little town named Gettysburg. Only four hundred miles to the southeast of Cabin Creek, a Union army under General Grant was in the last stages of starving the resistance out of 29,500 Confederates at Vicksburg. Both those battles ended before the wagon train arrived at Fort Gibson. Nevertheless, the arrival of the supplies and reinforcements at Fort Gibson generated the same enthusiasm as was celebrated by the winners of the larger battles in the East.

The Federals' victory had a significant impact upon the course of the Civil War in Indian Territory. Union forces now controlled most of Indian Territory north of the Arkansas River. The victory and success of the column provided the Union troops based at Fort Gibson the resources necessary to carry the war to the Confederates and terminate their control of much of the Indian Territory for the rest of the war.

Williams' victory was notable for other reasons as well. It was the first time non-white troops engaged in battle opposite each other. Whites, blacks, and Indians joined to fight the Indians and whites on the Confederate side. It was the first time in the Civil War that whites and blacks fought alongside each other under the same commander, breaking a structured color barrier. It incidentally meant that Colonel James Williams violated a written direct order by unifying all the troops with the wagon train under his single command.[30] The senior officers present recognized the need for unity of command, and overrode a social structure—a basic principle of war prevailed. Williams became a hero because he won. Had he lost, the story would have been different: his violation of the written order could have resulted in court martial. Nevertheless, the same conditions would be repeated within a few weeks.

Chapter Seven

The Battle of Honey Springs, Indian Territory

Having heard of Williams' victory at Cabin Creek, General Blunt was enthusiastic about his achievement and its potential impact upon the course of the war in Indian Territory. He immediately left Fort Scott on July 6 on a forced march south to Fort Gibson with four hundred men and eight cannons. He was intent upon exploiting the Cabin Creek victory with a campaign to push the Confederate army out of Indian Territory. His options were either to drive the enemy east to Arkansas, or south to Texas. His total resources, with the new reinforcements, would include twelve cannon and four thousand men.[1] Blunt made the 175-mile trip in five days, pushing hard. The garrison at Fort Gibson treated him to a grand reception upon his arrival. Phillips was of the opinion that the mere presence of Blunt and his command would cause Confederates to leave the area. Blunt reported the Union victories at Gettysburg and Vicksburg, speculating that they would prompt the return of troops to his command taken for the campaigns in the east, giving him even more resources.[2]

The same day Blunt closed on Fort Gibson, the empty wagon train—the survivor from the Battle of Cabin Creek—was returning north to Baxter Springs. The main threat en route to Baxter Springs was Confederate Major Livingston and his command of bushwackers—the ones who massacred the

First Kansas soldiers at Sherwood, Missouri. He was known to prey on Union activity along the Military Road, but on that day he was conducting a raid on Stockton, Missouri, some distance away, leaving a safe trail for the wagon train. The Stockton raid would be Livingston's last. Union soldiers killed him that night in Stockton, eliminating a major source of fear to Unionists in southwest Missouri and Federal troops in southeast Kansas.[3]

Meanwhile, General Blunt rounded up resources for an expedition against the Confederates, hard on the heels of Williams' victory at Cabin Creek. He was aware that the Confederates were building up their forces for an attack upon him at Fort Gibson. To the Confederate command, this effort had taken on a high priority. Even before the losses at Gettysburg and Vicksburg, they wanted to push the Yankees out of Indian Territory and force the diversion of federal troops westward. That priority did not change as the calendar slipped into mid-July. Confederate President Jefferson Davis put his stamp clearly on the Trans-Mississippi. He reinforced its importance, asserting, "No effort shall be spared to promote the defense of the Trans-Mississippi Department, and to develop its resources so as to meet the exigencies of the present struggle."[4]

Confederate leaders, reviewing the loss at Cabin Creek, were concerned that Phillips, with his new reinforcements, would press south of Fort Gibson after the Arkansas River became fordable, just as Williams had done.[5] On July 8, Brigadier General William Steele, the senior Confederate commander in the Indian Territory, began organizing an attack on Fort Gibson. He ordered General William Cabell's and General Douglas Cooper's commands to join approximately fifteen to twenty miles south of Fort Gibson and prepare for an attack.[6]

Confederate preparations for their campaign to push the Yankees back out of Indian Territory were ongoing ever since Colonel Phillips had taken Fort Gibson early in the year. They established a secret supply depot at the village of Honey Springs, near the point where the Military Road crossed Elk Creek, about twenty-five miles south of Fort Gibson. They began stocking supplies and munitions at the depot early in 1863.[7] Supplies poured in from the territory's Confederate military installations and Arkansas. Amongst the munitions were many barrels of gunpowder that the Confederate government had procured from Mexico and shipped from San Antonio, Texas. In addition to munitions, large quantities of food, clothing, and tentage arrived. Confederate facilities at the Honey Springs Depot included a Commissary, hospital, powder magazine, some officers' quarters, and warehouses.[8]

Available Confederate forces numbered between 3,500 and 6,000 men, depending upon the source of the estimate. Six thousand was unlikely. A better estimate would be 4,000–4,500 men. Those under General Cooper were:

- First Cherokee Mounted Volunteers
- Second Cherokee Mounted Rifles
- First Choctaw and Cherokee Regiment
- First Creek Mounted Rifles Regiment
- Second Regiment Creek Mounted Volunteers
- Fifth Regiment Texas Partisan Rangers
- Twentieth Texas Cavalry Regiment–dismounted
- Twenty-Ninth Texas Cavalry Regiment
- Gillette's Squadron of Texas Cavalry
- Scanland's Squadron of Texas Cavalry
- Lee's Light Battery of Texas Artillery

An additional force of three thousand Confederate cavalry was en route under command of General Cabell. Once they made it to Honey Springs, the size of their command would be more than sufficient for an attack on Fort Gibson.

Blunt was not at all ignorant of the Confederate buildup. His spies and informants had kept him well informed, and he elected to hit the Confederates before General Cabell arrived to team up with General Cooper.[9] Figuring he only had a few days, he moved quickly. He rounded up all the flat boats he could find and built others to get his troops across the Arkansas River, then he organized his troops into two brigades:

- First Brigade–Colonel William R. Judson
    - First Kansas Colored Infantry Regiment
    - Second Indian Home Guards Regiment-dismounted
    - Third Wisconsin Volunteer Cavalry Regiment
    - Second Kansas Battery

- Second Brigade–Colonel William A. Phillips
  - ❖ Second Colorado Volunteer Infantry Regiment
  - ❖ First Indian Home Guards Regiment
  - ❖ Sixth Kansas Volunteer Cavalry Regiment–four companies, two mountain howitzers
  - ❖ Third Kansas Battery–four guns
- Unassigned
  - ❖ Third Indian Home Guards Regiment[10]

James Williams' combat-tested First Kansas Colored was the largest regiment in the command. General Blunt, impressed by their successes, selected them to play a key role in the upcoming confrontation.

General Blunt kicked off his offensive in the middle of the night of July 15–16, 1863. He forded the Arkansas River several miles above Fort Gibson with elements of the Sixth Kansas Cavalry and the Second Kansas Battery. Their plan was to get between the Confederate pickets and their lines, capture them, and prevent them from alerting the Confederate command. Unfortunately, some of the pickets evaded capture and managed to get the word back to a forward outpost north of Elk Creek that Blunt was on the move.[11]

The bulk of Blunt's command, using flat boats, crossed the river close to its junction with the Grand River the following night, finally clearing it around 11:00 p.m. At dawn, on July 17, point men from the column encountered advance pickets of the alerted Confederate forces about five miles north of Elk Creek. Quickly reinforced, Federal cavalrymen pushed forward, and Confederate pickets pulled back to their main lines on the north side of Elk Creek.[12]

Confederate General Cooper arrayed his command for more than a mile along Elk Creek. The right wing comprised the First and Second Cherokee Regiments under Colonel Stand Watie, although Cooper dispatched Watie on a special mission to Arkansas before the engagement began. On the left, Colonel D.N. McIntosh commanded the First and Second Creek Regiments. The center of the Confederate line included the Twentieth Texas Cavalry (dismounted), Twenty-Ninth Texas Cavalry, Fifth Texas Partisan Rangers, and Lee's Light Battery, all under command of Colonel Thomas Bass. The Confederate reserve, commanded by Colonel Tandy Walker, included Scanland's Squadron, L.E. Gillett's Squadron, and Colonel Tandy Walker's

First Choctaw and Chickasaw Regiment. Cooper positioned each of the three line elements to cover possible crossing points along Elk Creek, and located the reserve near the Honey Springs Depot.[13]

During the overnight period, it began to rain, and continued to do so until about 8:00 a.m.[14] Aside from making the column of soldiers miserable, and the following morning hot and humid, the rain had a significant impact upon the battle's outcome. It dampened the Confederate's poor quality gunpowder, making their weapons unreliable. Confederate soldiers could not count on their weapons to fire every time they pulled the trigger. They were already at a disadvantage as many of their weapons were shotguns and smoothbore muskets—efficient only at short range.[15] Union troops were equipped with more modern rifled muskets and carbines.[16]

As the main elements of Blunt's column marched close to the enemy, he took a couple of imaginative steps. First, recognizing that they were exhausted after an all-night march, he stopped their advance behind a ridge, and out of sight of the enemy, about a half-mile from enemy lines. He gave his hot and weary soldiers a two-hour break, in which most of them slept where they stopped, and ate a meal from their knapsacks. Meanwhile, the Confederate troops were anxiously awaiting the inevitable attack of the enemy behind the ridge to their front. The delay only heightened the suspense.[17]

By 10:00 a.m., General Blunt determined his troops had sufficient rest, and formed them into two parallel columns on either side of the Texas Road. As the regiments moved into their assigned place, Williams, tall in the saddle, called his own men to attention, and addressed them:

> This is the day we have been patiently waiting for. The enemy at Cabin Creek did not wait to give you an opportunity of showing them what men can do fighting for their natural rights and for their recently acquired freedom and for the freedom of their children and their children's children. . . . We are going to engage the enemy in a few moments and I am going to lead you. We are engaged in a holy war; in the history of the world, soldiers never fought for a holier cause than the cause for which the Union soldiers are fighting, the preservation of the Union and the equal rights and freedom of all men. You know what the soldiers of the Southern armies are fighting for; you know that they are fighting for the continued existence and extension of slavery on this continent,

and if they are successful, to take you and your wives and children back into slavery.

Show the enemy this day that you are not asking for quarter, and that you know how and are eager to fight for your freedom and finally, keep cool and do not fire until you receive the order, and then aim deliberately below the waist belt. The people of the whole country will read the reports of your conduct in this engagement; let it be that of brave, disciplined men.[18]

Colonel Judson's brigade was on the right side of the road, and Colonel Phillip's brigade, including Williams' regiment was on the left side. He arranged the columns with infantry units in companies, cavalry by platoons, and artillery by sections. He then closed up the entire formation into a tight column, with the intent of making it look smaller than it actually was as it came over the rise at the Confederate enemy's front. His preparations complete, Blunt led the entire column down the road to a point about a quarter mile from the Confederate line at Elk Creek, where he suddenly deployed the two columns left and right into a line of battle. Within five minutes, the troops completed their deployment and, with skirmishers in the lead, moved forward on the enemy. The cavalry dismounted and covered the flanks. Fighting began in earnest almost immediately, with the Confederate shooters revealing their positions to the Yankee artillery.[19]

Williams' men were combat veterans, who had proved themselves in battle. General Blunt entrusted Williams and his regiment with an assignment near the center of the Union line, where the heaviest concentration of Confederates was expected. The Second Indian Home Guard Regiment was to their right; the Second Colorado Infantry to their left. The Twentieth and Twenty-Ninth Texas were opposite them. The First Kansas was to work with an artillery battery as it moved into the enemy. They deployed into battle formation, and the battery opened fire. General Blunt then came to Colonel Williams with direction, "I wish you to move your regiment to the front and support this battery; I wish you to keep an eye to those guns of the enemy, and take them at the point of a bayonet, if an opportunity offers." Williams passed this instruction to the men of his regiment, and then ordered, "Fix bayonet." They were already three hundred yards from the enemy exchanging artillery fire with the foe.[20]

His men stepped off smartly, and moved in line to within just forty paces of the enemy. Williams—raised in his saddle—commanded, "Ready, aim, fire!" He accompanied the command with a swing of his saber, pointing it to the enemy. Yankee and Confederate lines simultaneously belched enormous gouts of flame and smoke, as if both were responding to his command. Confederate gunfire quickly felled Williams and his horse. Williams received wounds in the face, chest, and hand. He survived; the horse did not.[21]

Firing from opposing sides continued without letup, at near point-blank range. First Kansas soldiers proved their training and experience once again; they did not waver. At one point, for reasons unknown, some Federal Indians from the regiment on the First Kansas' right flank rode through the brush between the enemy and the First Kansas, exposing themselves to cross-fire. Lieutenant Colonel Bowles yelled at them to fall back. The men of the Twenty-Ninth Texas, hearing the order, misinterpreted it as a command for the First Kansas to retreat, took it as an opportunity to charge, and surged ahead. The soldiers of the First Kansas stood their ground, and when the Texans were within twenty-five paces, the First Kansans unleashed a musket volley savaging the Texans. The Texan ranks broke, and they pulled back in disorder. Their color bearer went down in the next volley. Another Texan immediately picked up the flag and the Federals shot him down just as fast. Still another did the same, and met the same fate. After that, the Texans left the flag and scrambled for cover with the First Kansas in pursuit. The commander of the Second Indian Regiment sent a messenger asking to pass in front, so the First Kansas would hold their fire. On their way by, the Indians picked up the Twenty-Ninth Texas colors.[22]

Just as the Indian soldiers scooped up the Confederate colors, Lieutenant Colonel Bowles, having previously been on the right of the First Kansas line, discovered that Williams was shot and removed from the field. Bowles quickly assumed command of the regiment as the clamor over the stolen colors erupted. Bowles refused, appropriately, to allow his men to chase them down. Unfortunately, the First Kansas never recovered the Twenty-Ninth Texas colors, and there is no record today of what happened to them. Blunt ordered his line to advance, and the First Kansas pushed the fleeing Texans across Elk Creek and three miles farther south before calling off the chase and bivouacking for the night. Union regiments up and down the line all surged forward together, forcing the Confederates to retreat.[23]

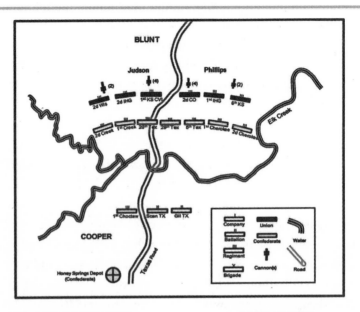

CONFEDERATE FORCES

Brigadier General Douglas H. Cooper, CSA
1st Cherokee Mounted Rifles Regiment
2d Cherokee Mounted Rifles Regiment
1st Chocktaw and Chickasaw Regiment
1st Creek Mounted Rifles Regiment
2d Creek Mounted Rifles Regiment
5th Texas Partisan Ranger Regiment
20th Texas Cavalry Regiment (Dismounted)
29th Texas Cavalry Regiment (Dismounted)
Gillette's Squadron of Texas Cavalry
Scanland's Squadron of Texas Cavalry
Lee's Light Battery of Texas Artillery

UNION FORCES

Major General James G. Blunt, USA
1st Brigade: Colonel William R. Judson
1st Kansas Colored Volunteer Infantry Regiment
2nd Indian Home Guards Regiment
3rd Wisconsin Volunteer Cavalry (Detachment)
2nd Kansas Battery
2nd Brigade: Colonel William A. Phillips
2nd Colorado Infantry (Detachment)
1st Indian Home Guards Regiment
6th Kansas Cavalry (Detachment)
3rd Kansas Battery
Unassigned
3rd Indian Home Guards Regiment

Figure 15 Schematic, Battle of Honey Springs,
Indian Territory July 17, 1863 (Not to Scale)

A few hours later, Confederate General Cabell arrived, again too late to reinforce the Confederate command. His brigade included more than two thousand additional men and four pieces of artillery. They likely would have made a difference. As it was, the Confederate command that faced off with the Yankees had eight regiments of infantry and two squadrons of cavalry, to Blunt's three regiments and three battalions. Blunt, however, had a decided advantage in artillery of eight cannon and four mountain howitzers to the Confederate's one battery of four cannon.[24]

Casualties for the First Kansas were two killed and thirty wounded. Twenty-Ninth Texas casualties were fourteen killed, twenty wounded, and eight missing.[25] Interestingly, their commander, Colonel Charles DeMorse, was wounded seriously early in the battle just as had been Williams. This was the second time the First Kansas had met and humiliated the Twenty-Ninth Texas on the field of battle. The two regiments would meet again, however, giving the Texans still another chance to redeem themselves.

Total Confederate casualties that day were 627: 150 dead, approximately 400 wounded, and 77 captured. Union fatigue parties buried the Confederate and Federal dead side by side on the battlefield.[26] Overall, the Federal casualties numbered a total of 75: 13 killed, 62 wounded. Williams, among the wounded, would return to duty shortly, in spite of a serious wound to his chest. His other wounds to his face and hand had no lasting impact.

In his official report to Major General John M. Schofield, commander of the Department of the Missouri, General Blunt singled out the First Kansas Colored Infantry. Of them, he said, "The First Kansas (colored) particularly distinguished itself; they fought like veterans, and preserved their line unbroken throughout the engagement. Their coolness and bravery I have never seen surpassed." He went on, "they were in the hottest of the fight, and opposed to Texas troops twice their number, whom they completely routed. One Texas regiment (the Twentieth) that fought against them went into the fight with three hundred men and came out with only sixty."[27]

A Confederate soldier, Private McDermott, of Company C, Twentieth Texas Cavalry later wrote of his experience that day. He was not as effusive about the Yankee troops as was General Blunt. He wrote, "We had a fight with the enemy and they whipped us bad. . . . When they came near enough, we let them have it and killed lots of them, though they made no halt, and the Texas boys had to fly." He continued to describe the torrent of fire from

Figure 16   Battle of Honey Springs, Indian Territory, July 17, 1863

Leslie's Illustrated Newspaper *published this somewhat fanciful sketch of the Battle of Honey Springs, drawn by James R. O'Neill on August 29, 1863. William Clark Quantrill's raiders killed O'Neill in their raid on Baxter Springs, Kansas on October 6 that same year.*

the First Kansas soldiers to his front: "The bullets came faster than we ever saw before. . . . I believe they will whip us all the time . . . they are as good as we are, better drilled and better armed."[28]

Another Confederate soldier, Private Wesley Bradley of the Fifth Texas Partisan Rangers seemed to sum up their point of view after the battle: "Since I last wrote to you, we have had another battle with the feds which resulted, as usual, with our defeat."[29]

Decades later, long after the close of the Civil War, an elderly, former slave of Indians who lived near the battle site, provided one of the best and certainly most colorful descriptions of what happened at Honey Springs. Her name was Lucinda Davis. She interviewed in 1937 as part of a Works Progress Administration (WPA) project to capture history of former slaves, using the first-person dialects of those still alive who had been slaves. Even though she was a child at the time, her perceptions are truly sharp. Some of her narrative follows:

> I never forgit de day dat battle of the Civil War happen at Honey Springs! . . . I was swinging de baby, and all at once, I seen somebody riding dis way 'cross dat prairie – jest coming a-kiting and a-laying flat out on his hoss. When he see de house he begin to give de war whoop – he holler to git out de way 'cause dey gwine to be a big fight, and old master start rappin' wid his cane and yellin' to git some grub and blankets in de wagon right now! We jest leave everything settin right whar it is. Den jest as we starting to leave here come something cross dat prairie sho-nuff! We know dey is Indians by de way dey is riding, and de way dey is strung out. Dey had a flag, and it was red and had a big criss-cross on it – den long come more soldiers dan I ever see b'foe. Dey all white men, and dey have on dat brown clothes, dyed wid walnut and butternut, and Old Master say dey Confederate soldiers. Den we hear de fighting up to de north long 'bout whar de river is. De head men start hollaring and de soldiers start faster up de road.
>
> We get in a big cave and spend de whole day and dat night listening to de battle going on. Dat place 'bout half-mile from the wagon depot at Honey Spring. We can hear de guns going on all day and along in de evening here come de South side making for a get-away. Dey com ridin and running by whar we is, and it don't make no difference how much

Figure 17   Colonel Charles DeMorse, CSA

Charles DeMorse, Colonel of the Twenty-Ninth Texas Cavalry at the Battle of Honey Springs was a casualty of a gunshot wound at the same time as James Williams. They faced each other again at the Battle of Poison Spring in Arkansas, when DeMorse was commanding Gano's Texas Brigade. DeMorse was a newspaper publisher and veteran of service in the Texas Navy during its revolution from Mexico. COURTESY HISTORICAL RESEARCH CENTER, TEXAS HERITAGE MUSEUM, HILL COLLEGE, HILLSBORO, TEXAS de head man hollars at 'em day can't make dat bunch slow up and stop. After a-while here come de Yankees, right after 'em and dey goes on into Honey Springs and pretty soon we see de blaze whar dey is burning de wagon depot and de houses.[30]

Private McDermott of the Twentieth Texas must have run right by Mrs. Davis. He said he and his compatriots ran fifteen miles, and "got so much scatterdness in the stampede that [they] was three days getting together and not all have come in yet."[31]

The Battle of Honey Springs had a decisive impact upon the Civil War in both Indian Territory and the Trans-Mississippi Theater. It ended any further possibility of Confederate control of the Indian Territory. It provided access to Confederate Arkansas for the Union army. It secured the southern border of Kansas from guerrillas and Confederate troop incursions. James Williams and his First Kansas Colored were central to that success.

The loss dramatically impacted the morale of the Confederate Indians. They had been defeated under Confederate leadership, weakening the alliance between the Indian Nations and the Confederate government. After the Battle of Honey Springs, Union troops occupied much of Indian Territory north of Boggy Depot—lands that were supposed to be under Confederate protection.[32] The Confederate Indians found themselves in straits similar to those of their Union-oriented brethren who had fled north to Kansas. They abandoned their farms and homesteads, clustering in refugee camps, suffering from hunger and lack of basic necessities. The Confederate government, to which the Indians had looked for protection, was no longer dominant.[33]

During the post-battle period, the First Kansas was not idle. There were constant foraging missions, drills, and guard duties to perform.[34] Williams, out of the hospital and recuperating from his wounds, busied himself with the daily details of life in the regiment. He established a daily routine that began early. After the troops were up, there would be a formation and roll call, after which each company would drill until 6:30 a.m. After the events of the day, there would be a dress parade and drill from 6:00 p.m. until twilight.[35]

Blunt was intent upon exploiting the victories at Cabin Creek and Honey Springs. He received reinforcements in the form of a brigade commanded by Colonel W.F. Cloud from southwest Missouri. Cloud's brigade included fifteen hundred men from the Second Kansas Cavalry, Sixth Missouri Cavalry, and artillery including Rabb's Second Indiana Battery (two sections), and two mountain howitzers.[36]

A month after the Honey Springs battle, Blunt again crossed the Arkansas River on August 22, 1863 with forty-five hundred troops, including the First Kansas. His target was the consolidated Confederate commands of Generals Cabell, Cooper, and Stand Watie, with nine thousand troops. Upon arrival at the site where the Confederate camp was supposed to be located, Blunt found that the enemy commands had split up, with Cabell headed for Fort Smith, Arkansas; David McIntosh up the Canadian River with his Creeks; and Steele, Cooper, and Stand Watie to the Red River. Blunt elected to chase the latter group. He caught up with the tail of the column at Perryville, Indian Territory, on August 25.

A brief skirmish ensued with light casualties. Blunt stopped the pursuit to allow his weak, tired horses rest; meanwhile, the Confederates had fresh stock. Steele and his command abandoned Perryville, and continued south down the Military Road. Blunt's troops discovered Perryville was a supply depot for the Confederate army. After destroying the supplies and equipment his column could not carry, Blunt split his own command, giving Judson's brigade the mission of dealing with the Creek Indians under McIntosh, and taking Cloud and his brigade to Fort Smith, Arkansas to deal with General Cabell.[37]

General Blunt, with Cloud's brigade made the hundred-mile march to Fort Smith in four days. Confederate General Cabell evacuated Fort Smith, and Blunt's Yankees took it without a shot fired. He sent Colonel Cloud to chase Cabell to the south. Cloud fought a short, nasty engagement at Devil's Backbone with Cabell, did some damage, and drove Cabell farther away. Cloud moved on to take command of Fort Smith.[38] In two months, Blunt's command had cleared the way down the Military Road to Boggy Depot and over to Fort Smith. He destroyed the Confederate presence in Indian Territory and established a Federal presence in western Arkansas. Blunt then returned to Fort Scott on September 23 to handle the details of moving his district headquarters to Fort Smith. He received a grand welcome in spite of the heightened concerns in Kansas following Quantrill's August 21 raid on Lawrence, the imposition of General Order 11 (which mandated the depopulation of four border counties of Missouri), and an increase in Guerrilla activity.[39]

Williams apparently made a dramatic impression as commander of the First Kansas. On August 10, a letter to Senator Lane noted that two colored regiments (First and Second Kansas Colored Volunteers) had mustered in Kansas, and a third was in the planning stage. The letter recommended placing these regiments under the command of a single brigade. It also recommended promotion of Colonel James Williams to brigadier general and assignment to command the brigade. The letter bore signatures of 143 officers from all regiments with whom the First Kansas Colored had served in combat. The letter went to the general-in-chief, who took no action at that time.[40]

Williams and his regiment marched into Fort Smith early in September.[41] They transitioned into garrison and occupation duties. The tasks of constructing fortifications and foraging consumed their time. After a month, they relocated to Bauldinsville (about fifty miles away) and spent a couple weeks there gathering wheat and milling it into flour. They moved on to Roseville, on the Arkansas River (about forty miles downstream from Fort Smith), and wintered there until March 1864. Soldiers in the regiment were put to work gathering cotton. This foray into agriculture yielded a lucrative cash crop needed by northern factories and provided money for the continuation of the Federal war effort.[42]

While the First Kansas was engaged in these pursuits, Williams' chain of command underwent a change. General Blunt returned to Kansas in October, barely surviving an attack by the infamous Confederate guerilla William Quantrill, near Baxter Springs. This, on the heels of Quantrill's disastrous attack on the city of Lawrence, thrust Kansas into turmoil. Blunt was relieved of his command. Williams and his regiment, busy in Arkansas, were placed under command of Brigadier General John McNeil.[43]

As winter melted into spring in 1864, the Union Army monolith throughout the North and South prepared to flex its mighty muscles. President Lincoln named General Ulysses S. Grant as General-in-Chief of all the United States Armies. At the same time, he promoted Grant to lieutenant general. Grant introduced the concept of coordinated actions of his armies in all theaters of war, which balanced pressure upon the Confederates everywhere. This denied the Confederacy the ability to move resources around to meet isolated demands. Grant's two most powerful field commanders, Generals Sherman and Meade, would initiate major offensives against the Confederates east of the Mississippi. West of the Mississippi, plans for another major offensive were expected to change the shape of the war in that theater. James Williams would be deeply involved.[44]

Chapter Eight

The Red River Campaign and the Camden Expedition

The Red River Campaign was a Union effort to take the war into Texas. Its objectives were to stall Emperor Maximilian of Mexico in his threats to the borderlands and potential alliance with the Confederacy; take control of cotton production resources in the Southwest; and crush the Confederate determination west of the Mississippi. The stage for this campaign was set with the Union victories at Vicksburg and Port Hudson in July 1863. The Union had successfully cleaved the Confederacy. It was time to exploit the gains.[1]

The overall strategy was a multi-axis attack on Confederates in the Trans-Mississippi southwest. Army and Navy would work together under Major General Nathaniel Banks and Rear Admiral David Porter. Banks would move west from New Orleans overland and link up with Admiral Porter, and his flotilla of gunboats moving up the Red River. They would then push north up the Red River with Shreveport as their target. Simultaneously, Union Major General Frederick Steele's VII Corps (with thirty-eight regiments in three divisions, with approximately twelve thousand men) was to strike southwest from Little Rock to Shreveport and link with Banks—setting the stage for an invasion of Texas.[2] Williams' First Kansas Colored Infantry was part of Steele's command.

In concept, the plan had merit. An overwhelming force of Union troops would converge upon Confederates near Shreveport, cut off their avenues of escape, crush them, and secure access to Texas. The naval component had enormous firepower; however, the seeds of failure also resided in the concept of execution. There was no unity of command; no one was in charge. Admiral Porter proved to be a fine commander; General Banks, on the other hand, did not. Banks was one of the most senior political generals, having held a number of commands, but his overall performance, though enthusiastic, proved to be mediocre. His background as a politician left him poorly prepared to serve as a general officer in the army.[3]

Major General Frederick Steele was the commander of VII Corps and the Department of Arkansas. A West Point Graduate (class of 1843) he was a career infantry officer. At West Point he was known as a prankster and advocate of anything humorous, but he became increasingly sober with age. He distinguished himself at the Battle of Chapultepec in the Mexican War with his leadership in the assault on the Mexican military academy. In the Civil War, he established a reputation as a courageous and competent fighting commander who stayed with his troops. He achieved notable success as a battalion commander at Wilson's Creek and as a division commander at Vicksburg.[4] Upon taking command of the Department of Arkansas, he led a campaign to wrest control of Little Rock from the Confederates. He succeeded in dislodging General Sterling Price—senior Confederate commander in Arkansas—from his base headquarters at Washington, Arkansas (the state capital), forcing him to retreat to the southwestern part of the state.

General Steele's superior combat record proved his competence as a campaigner and his willingness to join the fray, but he was tentative about this project. His greatest concern was General Banks who, in spite of commanding the largest number of troops, was a terribly weak leader. Banks had an extensive resume as a politician at state and federal levels, but his military training consisted solely of figuring out how to get an appointment as a general.

Steele was reasonably concerned that Banks lacked the timing and communication skills necessary for a successful mission, especially since Steel was at least four hundred miles from the advancing gunboats, steamboats, and their infantry. All of those four hundred miles were in Confederate territory, which the rebels would not yield willingly. Banks had to arrive with his troops at Alexandria, Louisiana at the right time to coordinate with Admiral Porter, and then make the transit farther up the Red River through Confederate territory to Shreveport. Communication between Banks, Porter, and Steele would be nearly impossible.

The southern axis of Yankee advance was already on the way upstream by early March 1864. Three divisions of infantry and a separate brigade of marines accompanied Admiral Porter's fleet of a score of brown water gunboats, monitors, and myriad others. Banks' overland element of the converging force was underway to the linkup point at Alexandria. It included 32,500 men and 90 cannon.[5]

General Steele, in command of VII Corps and the District of Arkansas, marched out of Little Rock on March 23, 1864, en route to Shreveport with sixty-eight hundred men in two divisions. The day before, General John Thayer, commanding the Frontier Division(also part of VII Corps), left Fort Smith with thirty-six hundred men headed south to join Steele at Arkadelphia.[6] The same day, a column consisting of Colonel James Williams' First Kansas and Lieutenant Colonel William Campbell's Sixth Kansas Cavalry left Roseville, marching through the Ouachita Mountains to link up with Thayer and Steele. These units were part of Thayer's Division. Williams' column at that time numbered about 900 men, 11 cannon, and 150 wagons.[7]

As Steele's command was preparing for the march on Shreveport, the Confederate commander of the Trans-Mississippi, General Edmund Kirby Smith, on March 16 appointed Major General Sterling Price commander of Confederate forces in Arkansas. He ordered Price not to allow Steele to get to Shreveport.[8]

Sterling Price was a politician, but had seen considerable amounts of combat. A man of distinguished looks with a face surrounded by curly white hair, his men called him "Old Pap." Born in Virginia, he settled into the life of a planter and a career in politics in that part of Missouri known as "Little Dixie". He served as a state representative and in the United States House of Representatives in the 1840s. He raised a regiment of cavalry in the Mexican War and served creditably in New Mexico, earning a brigadier general's brevet. In spite of a generally good record, he was known to be a poor disciplinarian. He also had a bad habit of arguing with his senior officers. Such traits could present problems to command in the heat of combat. After that war, he returned to Missouri, and lived comfortably on his plantation while going deep into debt. He won the governorship in 1853 and presided over the border ruffian days, until 1857, as a competent, but undistinguished governor.[9]

General Steele's doubts about the viability of the Red River Campaign plan loomed ever larger with serious concerns about the desolation and poverty of the route of advance, and its inability to provide forage and commissary supplies for his troops. Confederate foraging had wiped southwest Arkansas clear. His route was over muddy roads, through swamps, and generally difficult territory. Half of his cavalry was travelling on foot. The horses he did have were in poor condition.[10]

On March 28, Williams and Campbell tied their regiments into the rest of their division with General Thayer, and continued their march.[11] Operational plans called for Thayer's division to converge with the main body of VII Corps under Steele at Arkadelphia the next day. Muddy roads and shortages of food and forage delayed Thayer. Steele waited impatiently three days at Arkadelphia, consuming critical rations and forage, and then continued toward the Confederate capital of Arkansas at Washington.[12]

Steele's intent was to threaten Arkadelphia and Washington, to draw Confederate troops out of Camden, which he planned to use as a riverine supply base by way of the Ouachita River to Alexandria.[13] Confederate General Price obliged, sending out Brigadier General Joseph O. Shelby, one of the top cavalrymen in the Confederate army, on hit and run attacks on the rear of Steele's column. He also sent Brigadier General John Marmaduke to inflict similar damage to the head of the column, and Colonel Colton Greene to hammer the column's left flank. Price did not feel he had enough troops at that time for a full-fledged battle with Steele's corps. On April 3, Shelby attacked a brigade of Steele's command, positioned several miles in the rear. A freak hailstorm and a swarm of angry bees ended the battle. The next day, at Elkins' Ferry, there was a brief, but violent engagement. The Confederates withdrew to Prairie D' Ane. There, they received reinforcements from two additional brigades of General Price's garrison army, based in Camden, and two brigades of Indians under Colonel Tandy Walker. Steele and his Yankees waited for General Thayer's division to catch up.[14]

On April 9, Thayer's Frontier Division closed upon General Steele's VII Corps column. Steele now had his three Yankee divisions altogether. On April 9–10, at Prairie D' Ane, the enemies confronted each other with artillery and isolated ground attacks. Williams' First Kansas was there, but only peripherally involved. In spite of having a sizeable command, Price was not confident his Confederates could win. Steele's Yankees were exhausted—his column

Figure 18   Major General Frederick Steele, USA

General Steele commanded VII Corps and US troops in Arkansas during the Red River Campaign and the Camden Expedition. A West Point graduate, he distinguished himself in the Mexican War. He was also a division commander at the siege of Vicksburg. LIBRARY OF CONGRESS PHOTOGRAPH.

Figure 19   Major General Sterling Price, CSA

General Price was overall commander of Confederate troops in Arkansas during the Union's Red River Campaign and the Camden Expedition. He was a brigadier general in the US Army in the Mexican War. Before the Civil War, he served as governor of Missouri. LIBRARY OF CONGRESS IMAGE.

from Fort Smith had been on half-rations for two weeks. Thayer's division, including Williams' regiment, had also been on half-rations, and were nearly out of commissary stores and feed for their animals. The Confederates and Yankees spent the next day staring each other down without contact.[15]

The dawn of the twelfth revealed that Price's Confederates had pulled out overnight, moving down the road toward Washington. Steele—his troops exhausted, hungry, and out of forage—turned his column toward Camden. Camden offered Steele a base from which he could hopefully draw supplies for his people by way of the Ouachita and Red Rivers, and overland from the Union base at Pine Bluff on the Arkansas River. This would enable him to resume the march to his Shreveport rendezvous with Banks. As Steele hoped, Price was forced to abandon Camden in order to defend Washington. The Confederates left Camden with well-constructed defenses Steele could use. He could receive supplies by riverboat on the Ouachita River at Camden, which provided an attractive port with a twenty-four foot deep channel.[16] His corps closed on the town on April 15.[17]

Confederate General Marmaduke was elated with the unfolding events. Knowing that Steele was short of rations, Marmaduke stated that the purpose of the three-day-long dance at Prairie D'Ane was to cause Steele "to waste his time and keep his army starving in a barren country for three days."[18]

Chapter Nine

The Battle of Poison Spring, Arkansas

Steele soon discovered that the ideal base at Camden was as much a trap as a resource. As his corps flowed into Camden, he received word that the Confederate army in Louisiana defeated General Banks' large Union command, forcing Banks to withdraw back down the Red River. Steele had to hold tight in Camden to determine what would be the future course of the overall campaign to Shreveport.[1]

There was nothing available in Camden to sustain Steele's corps. The departing Confederate soldiers had left behind a welcoming gift of water wells contaminated with the corpses of dead animals.[2] The region around Camden for many miles was devoid of forage and rations. Confederate soldiers based in Camden before the Yankee incursion had picked the countryside bare.[3] The wagon train of supplies he so urgently ordered from Little Rock a week earlier was not coming to Camden. To his dismay, an untimely riverboat collision would delay the shipment indefinitely.[4]

Steele was in a bind. He had taken his corps off its route to Shreveport to re-provision at Camden, and now found himself in a siege posture, with no forage. He needed to feed roughly twelve thousand troops, and a like number of horses and mules, as well as the hungry, restive citizens of Camden, and had no way to obtain food.[5] Meanwhile, Confederate General Price's nearby command was growing larger by the day. To make matters worse, Steele learned that Confederates were burning any remaining large stocks of corn in the immediate area. His only glimmer of hope was a report of a remaining stash of five thousand bushels of corn about fifteen miles west toward Washington. It would give him a few more days of cushion. He either had to act, or face the prospect of his corps decimated by starvation. On April 16, he directed the organization of a foraging expedition to that site.[6] The mission was fraught with risk, but he was desperate.

That night, General Thayer visited his Second Brigade headquarters. Colonel Adams, the brigade commander, was not available, so Thayer met with the brigade's assistant adjutant and, together, they went to see Colonel Williams. They roused Williams from his bunk, and Thayer told Williams he was to command the foraging expedition. Thayer explained that General Steele had instructed him to select a good officer. Thayer believed Williams was best suited for the task, with no disrespect meant to Colonel Adams. Thayer ordered Williams to be ready to march at 5:00 a.m. the following morning with his own regiment, four squadrons of cavalry, and one section of Rabb's Indiana battery.[7] He was to take his foraging party back to the White Oak Creek area where the division headquarters had been the night of the fifteenth. There was said to be plenty of forage in the area.

Thayer committed to sending out additional troops later in the day to reinforce Williams, if needed.[8] This was some consolation as General Steele's quartermaster originally specified several hundred more men when he determined the organizational strength of the wagon train escort. Steele's adjutant overrode the request, ordering the reduced troop strength.[9]

The next morning, April 17, Williams and his foraging party marched out of Camden. His command at that time consisted of five hundred men from the First Kansas Colored Volunteer Infantry under the command of Major Richard A. Ward, the regiment's executive officer; fifty men from the Sixth Kansas Cavalry; seventy-five men from the Second Kansas Cavalry; seventy men from the Fourteenth Kansas Cavalry, and one section of the Second Indiana Battery. His total strength was 695 men, 2 cannon, and 198 wagons.[10]

Williams took the forage train about eighteen miles northwest from Camden toward Oak Creek, and established a command post. Major Ward deployed the wagons with security troops out in all directions to a radius of six miles. There was reason for caution because of the presence of Confederate patrols. The wagons returned to camp that night around midnight without incident. Soldiers successfully filled over 140 of the wagons with corn. The stockpiles Williams' men located were expected to have had five thousand bales of hay, but rebels had burned half of them before the forage parties managed to get there.[11]

Confederate troops monitored Williams' progress every step of the way. Colonel Colton Greene, commanding a brigade in General Marmaduke's division, tracked Williams from the time the Federal troops set forth out the Washington road. Armed with accurate information, Marmaduke rounded up his division and rode out to cut Williams off that night. A couple miles along the way, he discovered the promised relief force General Thayer had dispatched from Camden to back up Williams. Marmaduke decided his brigades did not have enough force to overwhelm Williams and his reinforcements, so he backed off for the moment. He contacted General Price for reinforcements. Price quickly directed General Samuel B. Maxey and his division to reinforce Marmaduke.

The following morning, April 18, at sunrise, the wagon train formed up and began its trek back toward Camden with its armed escort. Williams had his men continue limited foraging along the way, sending out occasional parties in various directions, but realized little in the way of positive results. Nevertheless, the volume of corn they had gathered would be welcome in Camden.[12]

The promised reinforcements rendezvoused with Williams' column at a crossroad four miles closer to Camden. Although the reinforcements left Camden on time the previous day, they were delayed by frequent encounters with roving Confederate patrols. The additional escort included 465 men from the Eighteenth Iowa Infantry, Sixth Kansas Cavalry, Second Kansas Cavalry, Fourteenth Kansas Cavalry, and 2 mountain howitzers from the Sixth Kansas Cavalry. Captain William Duncan commanded the relief force. Their arrival brought Williams' command to 1,160 men: 875 infantrymen, 285 cavalrymen, and 4 cannon.[13]

In spite of the numbers, Williams was concerned about the fighting ability of his men. He later reported that the energy expended on the foraging mission, following twenty-four days of uninterrupted campaigning on half rations seriously diminished the combat effectiveness of his command. At least one hundred soldiers of the First Kansas Colored were unfit for duty, placing added burden on the others. He faced an incremental problem as many of the cavalry troopers strayed all across the countryside in spite of orders to remain close in.[14] Lieutenant Barrett Mitchell of the Second Kansas Cavalry later corroborated the problem with the cavalrymen, noting: "During the engagement my detachment was necessarily so scattered that I cannot say what they did or did not."[15]

About a mile east of the crossroads, troops forming the Federal vanguard encountered a Confederate patrol and drew sporadic fire. The exchange of fire generated a dramatic step up in alertness of the escort. There was little doubt that the country was crawling with Confederates. The Yankee wagons continued to roll, and the Rebels pulled back as the column advanced for another mile. Suddenly, at a site known as Poison Spring, a strong line of enemy skirmishers appeared on a hillcrest, deployed astride the road. The skirmish line's strength was a signal that there was a greater enemy presence hidden from view. The blue-coated point men leapt from their horses, taking defensive positions. Their officers immediately dispatched messengers to Colonel Williams, alerting him to the Confederate presence. When messengers galloped up to warn Williams of the contact, he halted the train, and ordered the wagons closed up. The wagons were parked up to three abreast, whenever terrain permitted.[16]

Williams had the First Kansas double time, from the rear to the front, to join the vanguard. The First Kansas extended across the front and angled down the right flank of the now stalled wagons. The train was vulnerable, stretched over one and a half miles with pine forest and thick undergrowth extending back from both sides of the road. Occasional small open fields along the road penetrated the forest. The terrain was irregular, with the road following the route of least resistance between hills. It was a much different scenario than Cabin Creek, where the enemy concentrated at the head of the column. This time, enemy skirmishers were on the flanks as well as at the front, signaling an enemy deployed in multiple directions.[17]

Williams immediately called for the Second Indiana Battery, which quickly rumbled forward. The artillerists jumped to their tasks and unlimbered their guns. At Williams' command, they opened fire into and beyond the skirmish lines. His purpose was to elicit a response revealing enemy forces, their positions, and if they had any artillery with which to respond. He also intended for the artillery fire to signal his forage teams to return to the column. The Confederates did not take the bait, but heightened their firing. The rattle of musketry punctuated by crashing artillery increased in intensity.[18]

Williams then sent for the detachments of the Second and Sixth Kansas Cavalry, which were farther back down the column. They galloped forward, and immediately deployed along the right flank of the column past the First Kansas. The Fourteenth Kansas Cavalry spread down the left flank. A messenger rode hard to the rear of the column with orders for Captain Duncan. He was instructed to deploy the Eighteenth Iowa, along with its accompanying cavalry and artillery to cover the rear of the column.[19]

At that point, Williams had little idea of the magnitude of the units he faced. The use of skirmish lines indicated only that the enemy had enough strength to deploy in battle formation, rather than hit and run. General Marmaduke, in command of a Confederate division, was now perched on a hill looking down at his Yankee prey. He had been dogging Steele's command throughout the expedition. Marmaduke's division was part of General Price's command, with the mission of harassing Steele's march to Shreveport; so far, they had been successful. Continuous skirmishing had forced Steele to use up valuable resources in men, time, forage and rations. Steele had turned away from his objective to consolidate his forces in Camden. Now, with large numbers of Confederate troops in the vicinity, Williams' foraging party provided Marmaduke with the opportunity to kill or capture a large number of Steele's soldiers, destroy the wagon train, and continue to deny Steele forage for his starving command.

Marmaduke's Confederate scouts provided him all the intelligence he needed to plan an attack on the train. He later reported that Williams' command was twenty-five hundred strong, a dramatic exaggeration of the actual eleven hundred men in William's command (such exaggerations were common in the Civil War and contributed to the scale of the reported action). Marmaduke's scouts determined that the column had 225 wagons.[20]

Marmaduke's initial inclination was to attack Williams the night of the seventeenth, but he determined he did not have enough troops. He called for two brigades from General Fagan's division to reinforce his own and devised a plan to engage Williams the next morning. General Price approved the plan.[21]

Marmaduke had his division on the move at dawn on the morning of April 18. While Williams' column worked its way back toward Camden, Marmaduke positioned his command at Poison Spring. He posted skirmishers on higher ground where they would force the column to stop and regroup. Behind the skirmishers, in front of the column, he deployed two brigades of gray-and-butternut-clad Confederate soldiers across the road under Brigadier General William "Old Tige" Cabell and Colonel William A. Crawford. These were the brigades he borrowed from General Fagan. He placed another brigade under Colonel Greene in reserve, and two more cavalry battalions to Crawford's right. At that point, General Sam Maxey arrived with his division. Maxey was senior to Marmaduke, but deferred overall command to Marmaduke because the plan of operation was Marmaduke's idea. Marmaduke asked Maxey to deploy his division in the trees south of the road, along Williams' approaching right flank.[22]

General Maxey was an impressive man with pronounced cheekbones and brow framing his intense eyes and a thick, curly beard over his jutting chin. He graduated from West Point in 1846, along with George McClellan, George Pickett, Thomas J. (Stonewall) Jackson, and a number of other future generals. He served in the Mexican War and was brevetted twice to captain for gallantry in action. He resigned his commission in 1849 to study law, and eventually settled in Paris, Texas, to practice with his father. He served in the Texas Senate in 1861, but resigned to accept a Confederate commission and command the Ninth Texas Cavalry. After serving in a number of campaigns east of the Mississippi, he took over his brigade in the Trans-Mississippi. He knew what he was doing.[23]

Maxey's division had two brigades, one commanded by Colonel DeMorse and the other by Colonel Tandy Walker. DeMorse had led the Twenty-Ninth Texas Cavalry when Williams' First Kansas Colored Infantry humiliated them at Cabin Creek and Honey Springs. Now, recovered from his wounds, he had a brigade with three Texas cavalry regiments, including the Twenty-Ninth, two separate cavalry units, and an artillery battery. He had recently taken over as interim commander of the Fifth Texas Cavalry Brigade while Brigadier General Richard Gano recovered from gunshot wounds.

Charles DeMorse, originally from Massachusetts, had gone to Texas in 1836 with a New York volunteer battalion intent on serving in the Texas war for independence. After they were captured by a British ship and later released, he served as a marine first lieutenant aboard the Texas ship *Independence*, learning military skills under the tutelage of Albert Sydney Johnston. He remained in Texas as a newspaper publisher, and with the onset of the Civil War, raised and commanded the Twenty-Ninth Texas Cavalry Regiment.[24] As previously noted, the First Kansas Colored defeated this regiment twice and left him with an arm wound that troubled him for the rest of his life. He could not wait to return the favor.

Figure 20   **Brigadier General John S. Marmaduke, CSA**

General Marmaduke commanded one of the Confederate Divisions at the Battle of Poison Spring, and was the overall commander of Confederate forces in that action. A West Point graduate, Marmaduke came from a political family. His father and uncle were both governors of Missouri, and a great-grandfather was governor of Kentucky. In 1863, Marmaduke shot and killed his commanding officer, Major General Lucius Walker, in a duel. After the Civil War, Marmaduke served as governor of Missouri. LIBRARY OF CONGRESS PHOTOGRAPH.

Figure 21   **Brigadier General Sam Bell Maxey, CSA**

General Maxey commanded a division at the Battle of Poison Spring. Although he was senior, he yielded command to General Marmaduke (another division commander), who had formulated the attack plan. He was commander of Confederate forces in Indian Territory from 1863–1865. A West Point graduate, he distinguished himself in the Mexican War. After the war, he represented Texas as a two-term US Senator. Library of Congress photograph.

Colonel Tandy Walker commanded a brigade consisting of two unruly regiments of Choctaw Indians. They were enthusiastic about being in on the killing. Maxey jockeyed his brigades into position in the pine forest, spreading them along the wagon train's south side. He pulled one regiment from DeMorse's brigade and sent it along the road to Camden as a blocking force for any Federal reinforcements.[25]

The Confederate troops arrayed themselves in an L-shaped formation, blocking Williams' column, and mirroring Williams' deployed line of troops to the front and right flank of the train. Marmaduke compressed his division into the short leg of the "L." The division blocked the road with two brigades of six regiments. He took his other brigade, under Colonel Greene, out of reserve and deployed it into position on the angle of the "L" with five more regiments. Maxey's division spread out on the long side of the "L" with two brigades of six regiments. These two divisions, with their seventeen regiments, four separate battalions, and four batteries of artillery, although not at full strength, badly outnumbered Williams. He would have to tangle with a small corps.

Williams' soldiers spotted the Confederates moving into position in the underbrush of the pinewoods on their right flank and quickly reported it. Directing his attention to the movement, Williams immediately ordered two of his Kansas cavalry units to punch into the Confederate lines, breach them (if possible), and assess the enemy's strength. Just at that moment, a Confederate soldier, oblivious to what was taking place and who the actors were, rode into the Union line asking for directions to Colonel DeMorse. The soldier was immediately taken into custody and interrogated. The interrogation gave Williams a picture of DeMorse's command on his flank. He also gleaned from the man that General Price was the overall commander of the operation.[26]

By then, Williams' cavalry had reached four hundred yards beyond the road near the Confederate line. They encountered heavy fire and lost several men. The cavalrymen pulled back to their original position, aware they faced an enemy of formidable size. Williams sent a messenger to Captain Duncan at the Eighteenth Iowa at the rear of the column, directing him to send some reinforcements up the line. Duncan's short reply was that he was under intense fire from enemy infantry and artillery and could spare no one.[27]

Then, all hell broke loose. The Confederate artillery opened up on Williams with crossfire from the head and right flank of the stalled column. At the same time, Maxey's division emerged from the wood line and opened fire, giving Williams a clear picture of the enemy he faced. In spite of the sudden revelation that his chances of carrying the day were almost nil, Williams resolved to extract a cost from the enemy. He exhibited calm poise as the enemy shelling continued incessantly for a half hour. Ed Bearss, the preeminent Civil War historian, described him:

> Colonel Williams coolly sat his horse a few paces in rear of Ward's battle line with his field glass in his hands, looking through it and watching every movement of the foe so far as they could be seen through opening in the pines, while fragments from bursting shells whizzed about. All the while, Williams kept urging the soldiers to 'keep their eyes to the front.'[28]

The barrage suddenly ended, and a gray-clad mass of men charged the Union line. The din of the artillery, rattle of small arms fire, and yelling of the troops consumed the field of battle. When the men in gray came within a hundred yards of Williams' lines, he yelled at his troops to fire. They blasted the Confederate lines with buck and ball, and after a quarter hour of intense combat, the Confederates withdrew.[29]

Two more regiments joined the attacking Confederates, and again they rushed the Union line. A blood-curdling yell exploded from the throats of over a thousand gray-clad rebels as they charged Williams' line. Mingled with the tumultuous clamor of the battle all around him, the famous rebel yell gave the battlefield a semblance of the gates of hell. Williams was used to being the attacker, not the defender, but still he calmly fended off the Confederate attack. Much of the noise came from the Twenty-Ninth Texas. Noise, smoke, and dust permeated the battle scene. Colonel DeMorse said, "My men went in with spirit, shouting and fighting undauntedly; but in a little time it became evident that we were outnumbered and that the fire upon us was heavier than we could bear, and under it a portion of my center and left fell back into the hollow."[30] Once again, the Confederates were repulsed.

For an instant, the view was sufficient for the closest elements of the combat lines to see their enemy. The blue and gray forces were close enough to recognize each other. The Confederates of the Twenty-Ninth Texas, inflamed by the realization they were in their third battle with the black men from

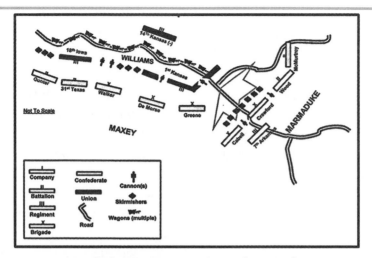

Confederate Command at Poison Spring
Brigadier General John S. Marmaduke*

Marmaduke's Cavalry Division	Maxey's Cavalry Division	Fagan's Division (Cabell)
Greene's Cavalry Brigade	**Gano's Brigade (DeMorse)**	**Crawford's Brigade**
3rd Missouri Cavalry Regiment	29th Texas Cavalry Regiment	Crawford's Cavalry Regiment
4th Missouri Cavalry Regiment	30th Texas Cavalry Regiment	Arkansas Cavalry Regiment
7th Missouri Cavalry Regiment	31st Texas Cavalry Regiment	Wright's Cavalry Regiment
8th Missouri Cavalry Regiment	Welch's Texas Cav Company	Poe's Arkansas Cav Battalion
10th Missouri Cavalry Regiment	Krumbhaar's Texas Cav Battery	Arkansas Cavalry Battalion
Missouri Artillery Battery		
Shelby's Cavalry Brigade	**Walker's Brigade**	**Cabell's Brigade**
1st Battalion, Missouri Cavalry	1st Choctaw Regiment	1st Arkansas Cavalry Regiment
5th Missouri Cavalry Regiment	2nd Choctaw Regiment	2nd Arkansas Cavalry Regiment
11th Missouri Cavalry Regiment		4th Arkansas Cavalry Regiment
12th Missouri Cavalry Regiment		7th Arkansas Cavalry Regiment
Hunter's Missouri Cavalry Regt		

*General Maxey was senior, but ceded command to General Marmaduke, who conceived the attack plan.

Union Command at Poison Spring
Colonel James M. Williams

Forage Column Escort
1st Kansas Colored Volunteer Infantry Regiment
18th Iowa Infantry (Detachment)
2nd Kansas Cavalry (Detachment)
6th Kansas Cavalry (Detachment)
14th Kansas Cavalry (Detachment)
2nd Indiana Light Artillery Battery (1 Section – 2 Guns)
2nd Mountain Howitzers, 2nd Kansas Cavalry (2 Guns)

Figure 22   Schematic, Battle of Poison Spring, Arkansas, April 18, 1864
(Not to Scale)

the First Kansas, yelled, "You First Nigger, now buck to the Twenty-Ninth Texas!"[31] The First Kansas had previously twice defeated the Texans, at Cabin Creek and Honey Springs. Furious Texans attacked again and fought like berserkers to avoid another humiliating defeat. That piece of the overall line of battle became personal. The epithet hurled across the line of battle nevertheless carried a touch of respect. The report submitted by Colonel DeMorse, their commander in the past, and now commanding their brigade, held no animosity for the black Federals, noting the aggressive and disciplined defense he confronted.[32] An officer in DeMorse's brigade commented that the First Kansas' "fire was extraordinarily heavy, and we began to believe the force against which we were contending was decidedly heavier than reported."[33] DeMorse estimated that the troops his brigade attacked outnumbered him by a margin of four to one.[34] His brigade confronted the First Kansas by itself; not the other Federal units spread along the Union line. One Confederate soldier, a sixteen-year-old sergeant, recalled the scene of the fierce combat many decades later: "the ground . . . looked like a cyclone had struck it, the trees and bushes having been mowed down and leveled to the ground, leaving the trunks and stubs splintered like the ends of toothbrushes.[35]

Williams made up his mind to continue the fight, believing that General Thayer in Camden would hear the fearful noise of the cannonade and rush reinforcements. The battle and cannon fire went on, however, for four hours, with no response from Camden.[36] General Steele was aware of the cannon fire, but chose not to send reinforcements. When the survivors returned to Camden, an officer in Steele's command (possibly Williams) stormed up to Steele's headquarters and shouted, "Great God! Why didn't you send us reinforcements?" There is no record of Steele's answer.[37]

The sounds of musket fire, artillery duels, rebel yells, and Choctaw war whoops were overwhelming and incessant. The First Kansas was taking the brunt of the attacks, and their casualties were mounting. Williams, who was constantly surveying his defensive positions, concluded that half his infantry were dead or wounded. Three of his companies had no officers. The weight of the Confederate attack was crushing, and the Federals were running short of ammunition. Assessing the situation, Williams told Major Ward to hold on until the Eighteenth Iowa moved in to cover a withdrawal. Few of his artillerists remained alive and standing, so Williams told them to move to the rear and prepare for withdrawal. Just then, Williams' horse went down, felled by enemy fire. Undaunted, he quickly found another, rode to the rear, and gathered what was left of his men to form a line of battle. Once again, the Confederates swarmed into his last line. Major Ward, forced to withdraw to the rear (on the north of the road), managed to conduct the action in an orderly fashion.[38]

At this point, color proved to handicap some of the remaining line of Federals at the head of the column. They held their fire while nearly one hundred soldiers in blue Union uniforms crossed to their front; some mounted and others on foot. Behind them was a similar force of four hundred or more. There were too many of the foot soldiers to be men from their own command. Only then did the men of Companies C and I of the First Kansas realize those troops were Confederates from a brigade reinforcing General Cabell's attack. Like many rebel units, they outfitted themselves with captured blue Yankee uniforms when there were not enough gray or butternut Confederate uniforms available. Several hundred Confederate soldiers had moved to the First Kansas' left flank. Belatedly, the blacks opened fire.[39]

DeMorse noted that his brigade (including the Twenty-Ninth Texas), Greene's Brigade, and Walker's brigade succeeded with the last charge, mostly against the First Kansas. In his report, DeMorse noted, almost with grudging admiration, that Williams' troops conducted a phased and orderly withdrawal. The Federal artillery, supported by the infantrymen of the First Kansas, made successive stands on a series of ridges. [40]

Captain Duncan, commander of the relief force that had earlier joined Williams' column, received orders similar to those given to Major Ward to protect a withdrawal. His troops covered the rear elements of the column. He fell back across an open field and took up a defensive stance in a tree line. He held the position for about twenty minutes, under heavy fire from his front and both flanks the whole time. He slowly withdrew, reforming his line seven times in a ninety-minute period, checking the enemy advance, and conducting an orderly retreat.[41]

Williams, Ward, and his remaining officers rallied the retreating troops to the rear of the Eighteenth Iowa, and re-established a line of battle. As the enemy charged the Eighteenth, the other Federals stepped forward into line with the Eighteenth and, once again, checked the Confederate advance. That was the last time. Williams ordered the remaining artillery spiked and abandoned, as it could not traverse the terrain through which the action was moving. He gathered his men, took them into the brush, through a swamp, and back toward Camden. Confederates pursued them for about two miles, stopping four or five times to fire volleys at them. General Maxey ultimately recalled the pursuing cavalry to secure the captured wagon train.[42]

Williams led the tattered remains of his troops in a roundabout way through the forests, to avoid Confederate forces. They filed into the Federal lines at Camden until around eleven that night, exhausted, wounded, and hungry.[43] Major General Sterling Price, commander of Confederate forces in Arkansas, reported that his troops had killed Colonel James Williams in the engagement.[44] This report was, as Samuel Clemens would say, "greatly exaggerated.[45]

The contest had been a valiant stand by Williams' men, but a bloodbath. They fended off three enemy attacks against overwhelming odds before their lines collapsed, then conducted a fighting withdrawal. Williams' casualties were horrendous. Of the 1,170 men in the column, there were 301 casualties. The First Kansas suffered 182 of the casualties, 117 killed.[46] Many of the wounded died later, adding to the grisly count. Confederate casualties were light, 111 total, only 16 of which were killed.[47] The Federal soldiers in that engagement fought with honor. The grisly remains of those who died on the field of battle would soon reveal less honorable conduct among some of the Confederate foe.

Chapter Ten

Confederate Atrocities and Steele's Retreat

Confederate soldiers killed many of the First Kansas men who lay wounded on the battlefield at Poison Spring. The wounded Yankees' comrades met the same fate in the previous racial massacre at Sherwood, Missouri. Williams, infuriated by reports from survivors, yet unable to do anything about it, wrote in this report, "Many wounded men belonging to the First Kansas Colored Volunteers fell into the hands of the enemy, and I have the most positive assurances from eye-witnesses that they were murdered on the spot."[1] Major Ward backed up Williams in his own report: "we were obliged to bring our wounded away as best we could, as the rebels were seen shooting those that fell into their hands."[2] An Arkansas Confederate soldier, probably in Cabell's Brigade, wrote home: "If the negro was wounded our men would shoot him dead as they were passed and what negroes that were captured have . . . since been shot."[3] The Choctaw Confederates went upon a gory rampage across the battlefield, scalping the casualties (whether live, dead, black, or white), and mutilating their bodies.[4] To avoid the gruesome fate of their comrades, a few of the wounded lay on the battlefield feigning death until dark, then quietly crawled away. All who remained were murdered. General Cabell recorded that his men killed eighty stragglers.[5]

Multiple reports by Confederate soldiers supported allegations that Union casualties on the battlefield were executed—some were even systematically run over by wagons captured from the Federal column.[6] An Arkansas newspaper later reported that Confederate Indians had buried white Union officers face down in disrespect, then buried one black soldier upright to his waist as a headstone, and another upside down to serve as footstone for each of the white Union officers.[7]

The bias and contempt the white Confederates held for black Union soldiers were widespread. Many years later, for example, an elderly pensioner (who had been a young Confederate soldier in that battle) recollected his impression that the black soldiers must have been placed on the Yankee front line to serve as breastworks. To consider the black men as soldiers, or humans even, was beyond many people's comprehension—such was the bias of the time.[8]

Three days after the battle, a detachment from the Eighteenth Iowa returned to the Poison Spring battlefield to bury their dead. They had fought valiantly, and took heavy casualties. While there, they buried six white officers and eighty black soldiers from the First Kansas in addition to their own. The commander of the Iowans, Major J.K. Morey, wrote, "The white dead were scalped and all were stripped of clothing, which was worn by the rebels. To add insult to the dead officers of the colored regiment; they were laid on their faces, and a circle of dead soldiers made around them."[9] The murders of these black and white Union men, coupled with other atrocities, leave little doubt that what had been a fierce, but one-sided battle had ended as a massacre.

Many accused DeMorse's Confederates of acting out in vengeance against the black soldiers. Instead of taking prisoners, they exacted retribution for their humiliating defeats in previous engagements with Williams' black soldiers. Interestingly, the First Kansas Colored Volunteers never committed any such atrocities on Confederate troops in those contests. At Honey Springs, not one of DeMorse's men, whether captured or wounded, met death at the hands of the Kansas soldiers.[10]

Anne Bailey, in her article, "Was There a Massacre at Poison Spring?" noted that the mix of Confederate soldiers at Poison Spring could have contributed mightily to the zeal with which they set about obliterating the First Kansas Colored Infantry. The brigade under Colonel Charles DeMorse included the Twenty-Ninth, Thirtieth, and Thirty-First Texas Cavalry regiments. All were noted for their lack of discipline, and the Twenty-Ninth and Thirtieth had been humiliated in previous engagements with the First Kansas.

Further, General Marmaduke's command was made up of Missouri troops, who nursed intense hatred for Kansans following five years of antebellum conflicts between Kansas and Missouri over Kansas' future as a slave or free state.[11] General Cabell's Arkansans were generally irate at the black soldiers, and Cabell had been embarrassed by his failure to get his reinforcements to the Confederates at both Cabin Creek and Honey Springs in time to meet the enemy. Had he not failed, Confederate defeat might have been turned into victory.

Bailey also noted that by the time the engagement at Poison Spring took place, Confederate fortunes were diminishing, and the future was looking bleak. Consequently, morale among Confederates west of the Mississippi plummeted, leading to increased frustration. The fall of Vicksburg to Federal forces in July 1863 cut off the Trans-Mississippi region of the Confederacy from the larger campaigns in the East. The war was dragging on toward an unsuccessful and unpopular conclusion, and the landscape was destitute. Further, the Eastern part of the country seemed not to care or even be interested in what happened west of the Mississippi. Frustration characterized the life of rebel soldiers.[12]

The Confederates did not take black prisoners, nor did they treat the white officers who commanded the black soldiers as ordinary prisoners of war. Aside from the hatred of their former slaves serving as soldiers in an enemy army, white officers serving with the black former slaves were targeted by special policies from the Confederate government concerning white officers in black Union regiments. It began with a Confederate War Department general order in August 1862 stipulating that Union officers who organized or trained slaves not be extended prisoner of war status, but rather be confined as felons for execution. The following December, President Jefferson Davis issued a presidential order that field commanders were required to turn over captured slaves (read black Union soldiers) to the executive departments of the various Confederate states for appropriate disposition—meaning returned to their former owners, sold, or executed. Union officers captured with them would be dealt with, by the respective states, as felons inciting a servile insurrection, and subject to execution.[13]

A resolution by the Confederate Congress followed on May 1, 1863. It provided "that commissioned officers commanding, arming, training, organizing, or preparing Negroes for military service should 'if captured be put to death or be otherwise punished at the discretion of a military court.' Black soldiers were to 'be delivered to the authorities of the State or States in which they shall be captured to be dealt with according to the present or future law of such State or States.'" Simply stated, the policy dictated that black captives were to be sold into slavery and their officers were to be executed. Thus James Williams, all his white officers, and all his black soldiers were equally at risk—a commonality that generated mutual respect.[14]

With the new policy in place, Confederates found themselves faced with the problem of sorting out their black prisoners who were considered property in the South, and soldiers in the North. As prisoners, they consumed extensive resources, but the easy solution—executing them—would only bring about Yankee retaliation. In some quarters, the conclusion was to take no prisoners. At one point, an assistant adjutant to Confederate General Edmund Kirby Smith, commander of the Trans-Mississippi Department, sent a message to a subordinate command stating that they were to grant "no quarter" to enemy black troops. He followed with a personal letter noting that the new method was a means of avoiding the issue.[15]

Federal authorities responded in April 1863 with War Department General Order 100, stating that Negro troops and their white officers were soldiers and, if captured, their captors were to afford them the privileges of any other prisoners of war. The Union granted full status as freedmen to any slave passing through Union lines as a fugitive from the Confederacy. Interestingly, the order fell back on international law, which had no racial distinctions with regard to the conduct of war. The Federal order concluded that enslavement of prisoners of war would be met with severe retaliation. Since enslavement by the Federal side would be illegal retaliation, the action by the Union would be prisoner execution instead.[16] President Lincoln followed with General Order 252, July 31, 1863 mandating,

> For every soldier of the United States killed in violation of the laws of war a rebel soldier shall be executed, and for every one enslaved by the enemy or sold into slavery a rebel soldier shall be placed at hard labor . . . until the other shall be released and receive the treatment due a prisoner of war.[17]

The massacre at Poison Spring was only a small event on the larger canvas of the Civil War. Only a week earlier, a similar incident occurred at Fort Pillow, Tennessee. In that action, only a week earlier than Poison Spring, Confederate General Nathan Bedford Forrest led his cavalry to a crushing victory over the Federal garrison at Fort Pillow, killing two hundred black and eighty-five white soldiers, many as they attempted to surrender.[18] Similar slaughters of black Federal troops occurred later at Petersburg, Virginia (Battle of the Crater) in July 1864, and Saltville, Virginia, in October of that same year.[19]

Over time, the issue moderated, and Confederates began to treat black Federal soldiers as prisoners of war, but not in time for the soldiers who died at Poison Spring.[20]

The day after the carnage at Poison Spring, the quartermaster of Steele's command (who had sent Williams' troops went into enemy territory for forage) noted that the Confederates had captured the twenty-five hundred bushels of corn. He ignored the human expense. He suggested that since only a half-day's ration of forage now remained for the animals of the command, perhaps Steele should order the animals placed out to pasture. With a guard of substantial numbers of soldiers, it would be possible to return the animals to Camden in the event of a Confederate attack. General Steele's response went unrecorded; his situation was desperate.[21]

A day later, a supply train of 150 wagons arrived safely at Camden from Pine Bluff. It had enough rations for Steele to feed his men half rations for ten days. Recognizing that this stockpile of rations was miniscule for his needs, Steele turned the train around in two days and sent it back to Pine Bluff with 211 wagons, intent on garnering further resupply. Lieutenant Colonel Francis Drake of the Thirty-Sixth Iowa Infantry commanded the escort, consisting mostly of the Second Brigade of Brigadier General Frederick Solomon's division, augmented by some detachments. It included sixteen hundred soldiers and an advance guard of cavalry. As it passed through the country northeast of Camden, it found itself attached by fifty to seventy-five more wagons, an aggregation of sutlers, refugees, camp followers, and three hundred blacks (mostly contrabands). These people were seeking the security of the train to get them out of the way of the coming collision of Confederate General Price and Yankee General Steele.[22]

On April 25, Confederate General Fagan and nearly four thousand troops pounced on Drake's wagon train near Marks' Mills, immediately attacking it with twenty-five hundred of his gray-and-butternut-clad soldiers. Drake put up a fierce fight for five hours, but was eventually overwhelmed; the Confederates captured his wagon train and either killed or captured all his troops and civilians. Union military casualties (killed, wounded, or captured) numbered no fewer than thirteen hundred. Confederates slaughtered more than half of the black civilians. Estimates were that Confederate casualties were five hundred. Many important documents fell into enemy hands, giving the Confederates detailed information about Steele's command. The treatment of blacks by Confederate troops at Marks' Mills was consistent with their actions at Poison Spring. This blow to Steele's corps was a significantly greater loss than that at Poison Spring.[23]

While all this was happening, Confederate General Price was diverting Steele's attention with a push on Steele's pickets and an artillery barrage at Camden. The diversion was brief, but it reminded Steele of the magnitude of hazards to his mission to Shreveport. He had no forage at all, only a few days' rations, and a large enemy army between himself and his objective. He had lost control.[24]

Fortuitously, General Steele received further details of General Banks' defeat at Pleasant Hill on the night of the ninth, his evacuation of Natchitoches, Mansfield, and Sabine Cross Roads on April 21 and his subsequent withdrawal to Alexandria, all in Louisiana. Banks termed it a temporary withdrawal. In reality, the Red River Campaign was a disaster. Steele no longer had a mission to Louisiana. His dilemma as to a course of action with respect to continuing the campaign to Shreveport had diminished substantially. He was in dire need of supplies from downriver. Foraging was unsuccessful. His wagon train and riverboat supply routes were in shambles. His most recent intelligence indicated the Confederate General Kirby Smith, commanding the Trans-Mississippi, released eight thousand additional troops and artillery from Louisiana to reinforce Price's offensive odds against Steele. Steele had to either make a stand at Camden or take his corps elsewhere.[25]

That night, Steele called together his senior commanders to discuss the options available. There were few. It was too late to cut their losses. Their supply lines were too long, and too tenuous. General Price's already large force was getting much larger, as Confederate General Kirby Smith turned his attention from Shreveport to Camden. They agreed it was time to evacuate Camden. They would pull back to Little Rock, retaining control of Arkansas north of the Arkansas River. On the twenty-sixth, the day after Marks' Mills, they sent wagons toward Little Rock loaded with the accumulated materiel that had defined the base at Camden. That night, their remaining ten–eleven thousand troops, including Williams and his regiment, quietly pulled out of town.[26]

Steele's retreat to Little Rock crossed the Ouachita River, which was not an easy task. Price's Confederates hounded his column every step of the way. Their objective was to overtake Steele before he could cross the Saline River en route to Little Rock. Steele got there first, but still had two miles of wagons and troops not yet across the Saline bottoms and river when the Confederates arrived. A bloody battle ensued at Jenkins' Ferry, involving nearly fifteen thousand men. They fought in flooded, muddy fields by the river. The men of VII Corps successfully repulsed every Rebel attack, pushing them back far enough for the Yankees to get across the river and continue on to Little Rock.[27]

The Second Kansas Colored fought with the battle cry, "Remember Poison Spring!" as they charged and took a Confederate battery at the points of their bayonets.[28] The Second Kansas Colored resolved that to honor Williams' regiment, they would take no prisoners. When they attacked the Confederates, they "easily overran the battery position, impaling every Confederate within reach on their bayonets, including three gunners who raised their hands in surrender. Only the timely and forceful intervention by the Twenty-Ninth Iowa saved the lives of Lieutenant John O. Lockhart, the commander, and his five remaining men."[29] This retaliation clearly showed the frustration, anger, and fear with which soldiers in the colored regiments had to live.

Williams' First Kansas was among the regiments across the river early; they had a limited role in the fighting. They were just beginning to refit after their devastating losses at Poison Spring. When the battle was over, the First Kansas was right there with everyone else, headed for Little Rock. At that point, all the troops wanted were commissary stores. Many of the soldiers had had little or nothing to eat since leaving Camden. On May 2 the column settled in for another hungry night. Suddenly, a wagon train arrived into the camp, which was met with exuberant shouts throughout the camp. It was a train with wagonloads of provisions from Little Rock. Morale soared. The next day, May 3, 1864, the substantially re-invigorated column, including Williams' battered, but proud First Kansas Colored Volunteer Infantry Regiment marched into Little Rock.[30] Four days later, on May 7, James Williams was assigned command of the Second Brigade, First (Frontier) Division, VII Corps.[31]

Chapter Eleven

A Brigade, Another Massacre, and Second Cabin Creek

Shortly after Williams' assignment as brigade commander, Union forces in Arkansas underwent a reorganization. Regiments shuffled to various brigades and locations as dictated by the military threat. Williams' headquarters moved to Fort Smith, on the border of Indian Territory. He was responsible for all aspects of the lives of 2,735 men and 10 cannon. Most of the soldiers in Williams' new brigade were black Americans. They comprised four regiments that were the core elements of the command. His brigade included:

First Kansas Colored Infantry Regiment
Second Kansas Colored Infantry Regiment
Eleventh US Colored Infantry Regiment
Fifty-Fourth US Colored Infantry Regiment
First Arkansas Battery
Third Kansas Battery[1]

By mid-September, Williams' brigade headquarters, and three regiments relocated west of Fort Smith on the road to Fort Gibson, Indian Territory. Along with their garrison equipage, they included brigade medical staff and hospital supplies. The duration of their detachment was indefinite.[2]

Black troops under Williams' command soon experienced another episode of wanton murder of Union soldiers because of their race. Early

★   133   ★

in September 1864, Confederate Brigadier Generals Richard Gano and Stand Watie, both commanding brigades, hatched a plan for a raid into the Union-controlled part of Indian Territory north of the Arkansas River to attack Federal wagon trains on the Military Road from Fort Scott to Fort Gibson. This was the same route on which Williams had successfully won battles at Cabin Creek and Honey Springs.

While en route to a planned attack on a southbound wagon train at Cabin Creek, the two Confederate brigades undertook an attack on a Federal detachment gathering hay.[3] The goal was to to draw Union forces west and south, away from the route of a major campaign by Confederate General Sterling Price northeast from Arkansas into Missouri toward St. Louis, and then westward. Price's campaign kicked off on August 30, 1864, when he successfully penetrated Union defenses taking his army north through Arkansas and into Missouri.[4]

On September 16, 1864, approximately fifteen miles northwest of Fort Gibson, on a large well-known meadow area at Flat Rock, a Federal detachment was cutting hay for forage. The meadow was a couple of miles from the Grand River, fed by a narrow meandering creek which threaded through small ponds or "lagoons" about a hundred yards apart. The low banks of the lagoons were precipitous or caving, with over-hanging boughs of small willows. In some, there were numerous water lilies, with large palm-like leaves floating on the surface.[5]

The haying party consisted of men from the Second Kansas Cavalry and the First Kansas Colored Infantry. Some of the cavalrymen were mounted, providing security while the others gathered hay. The total strength of the haying party was 125, including 37 from the First Kansas. Captain Edgar A. Barker of the Second Kansas Cavalry was in command of the haying party.[6]

General Gano had twelve hundred men in his brigade of Texans, including the Twenty-Ninth, Thirtieth, and Thirty-First Texas Cavalry regiments. General Watie rode at the head of an eight-hundred-man detachment from his own brigade of Indians, giving them a combined command of two thousand men.[7] Gano's scouts spotted the haying party, and he immediately dispatched one of his regiments to circle around to the rear of the Federals. Gano, Watie, and their staffs rode to the top of a nearby hill where they could see the grand panorama of the coming attack. Gano reported, "From our elevated position we could view their camps, and with spy glasses could see them at work making hay, little dreaming that the rebels were watching them." They then deployed their regiments: Watie's regiments went left, some of Gano's went right, and the rest moved down the center with Gano in the lead.[8]

In spite of their large numbers, the Confederate troops managed to deploy into their attack positions with little awareness on the part of the Yankee soldiers. Captain Barker's scouts saw Confederates headed north and reported to him that two hundred were nearby. He quickly mounted and rode out a couple miles to further assess the situation. To his surprise and chagrin, he discovered what he perceived to be 1,000–1,500 Confederates headed his way. Enemy scouts, in turn, spotted him, opened fire, and gave chase. He fought his way back to the hay camp and rounded up his men as the Confederates closed in on the meadow. Barker placed his men in a ravine to the rear of the haying area in the best and most immediate defensive position available. The rebels, with their blood-curdling yells, swooped down on the badly outnumbered Yankees from five directions. General Gano observed, "The clouds looked somber and the V-shape procession grand as we moved forward in the work of death."[9] For the next half hour, the soldiers from the First Kansas Colored Infantry and Second Kansas Cavalry unloaded volley after volley at the mass of Confederates, repelling several charges.[10]

Barker then concluded their position was hopeless. Perceiving a weak point in General Watie's line, he determined to attempt an escape for those of his cavalrymen who had horses. He abandoned a few dismounted cavalrymen and the black soldiers, leaving them to find their way out. Barker had his troopers mount up, and charged through the Confederate line. Only Barker and fourteen of his men made it through; Confederates killed or captured the rest of his mounted cavalrymen.[11]

General Gano sent one of his officers to the small, besieged Federal force under a flag of truce, accompanied by a Union lieutenant who had been captured in Barker's dash to freedom. Gano's message was clear and concise: surrender, or face the consequences. The black troops (according to Gano) replied by firing at the truce flag. The memory of Poison Spring, only four months earlier, was fresh in their minds; they knew the enemy would murder them instead of treating them as prisoners of war, if captured. Gano eloquently described the next phase of the engagement for the two-thousand-man force: "They fired upon my flag and then commenced the work of death in earnest. The sun witnessed our complete success, and its last lingering rays rested upon a field of blood. Seventy-three Federals, mostly negroes, lay dead upon the field."[12] The Union infantrymen, under command of Lieutenant David M. Sutherland of the First Kansas held off the Confederates for nearly two hours until they ran out of ammunition. Watie's artillery then put an end to the fight, firing canister into the Union position. The surviving defenders scrambled in all directions, many of them fleeing into the brush and a nearby creek. Some took cover under the overhanging banks and the lily pads. As the Confederates filtered into the Union defensive positions, it appeared as though there were no survivors. However, Indian soldiers in Captain George Grayson's company from Watie's brigade began to ferret out survivors hidden in the brush and Flat Rock Creek. The discovered soldiers were dragged into the open and shot, despite their attempts to surrender. Grayson reported, "The men proceeded to hunt them out much as sportsmen do quails."[13] Somehow, four of the black soldiers managed to escape.[14] Records indicate that twenty-eight men from the First Kansas Colored Volunteer Infantry died at Flat Rock. Only five others who were captured actually got to live out the remainder of the conflict as prisoners of war.[15]

Once again, Williams' soldiers had faced the black flag of no quarter from the Confederate government. Once again, they had proved themselves to be worthy soldiers. A couple days later, Williams again took his entire command into the fray.

A day after the engagement at Flat Rock, Generals Gano and Watie turned their attention to their primary target, a supply train of 300 wagons destined for Fort Gibson and Fort Smith. Williams' Second Brigade, other troops at those forts, and Union Indian refugees were the intended recipients of that cargo of rations and forage. The train had 205 government wagons, 4 government ambulances, and 91 sutlers' vehicles. The train was more than four miles long, with an escort totaling 360 cavalry and infantry commanded by Major Henry Hopkins. There were also 600 unarmed recruits accompanying the train.[16]

Reports from higher headquarters alerted Hopkins to Price's major troop movements into Missouri, and northward in Indian Territory by Generals Gano and Watie. He posted a fifty-man rear guard behind the column, and anticipated four hundred reinforcements from Major Foreman of the Third Indian Home Guard.[17]

Figure 23   **Brigadier General Richard M. Gano, CSA**

General Gano commanded Confederate troops at Flat Rock and the Second Battle of Cabin Creek in Indian Territory. He fought in a number of campaigns in the Western and Trans-Mississippi theaters of the Civil War. His brigade was a key element of the Confederate attack on Williams' command at Poison Spring, Arkansas, although he was absent recovering from a wound. Later in life, he became a minister, establishing a number of churches in Texas. He was also a cattleman and businessman in the Dallas area. LIBRARY OF CONGRESS IMAGE.

Colonel Stephen H. Wattles, commanding officer at Fort Gibson, had discovered the actual size of the Gano and Watie task force, and dispatched a messenger who passed the information to Hopkins on the evening of September 17. Wattles rounded up all the troops he could spare, and rushed them north to beef up the wagon train escort.[18]

The wagon train reached Cabin Creek on the morning of September 18. Hopkins' Yankees received reinforcements of 140 men from the Third Indian Home Guard, and 170 more from the Second Indian Regiment. His escort strength improved to 610 men, but he was still waiting for the promised 400 men from Major Foreman and the remainder of the Third Indian Home Guard. Hopkins deployed his column into a standard open-camping configuration about a mile and a half across until he became aware that there was a sizeable enemy force in the area. Anticipating an attack, he had the wagons placed in a quarter circle, which was probably just as indefensible as the open configuration. He expected the enemy strength to be 600–800 men—he was greatly mistaken.[19]

Although Colonel Wattles had managed to get reinforcements on the way to Hopkins (they arrived on the 18th), knowledge of the size of the Confederate forces bearing down on the wagon train compelled him scramble for more. He could spare no more from his own garrison at Fort Gibson. He quickly hit upon the idea of using Williams' brigade. Williams' Second Brigade was camped about forty-five miles east, toward Fort Smith near today's town of Sallisaw. Williams had four regiments of infantry and two batteries of artillery, totaling approximately 2,500 men. Wattles immediately sent for them, and Williams hastily brought his brigade into Fort Gibson on September 18, traversing more than forty miles at "double quick march."[20]

Upon meeting with Colonel Wattles, Williams asked him to round up as many wagons as possible so his troops could fill them with rations, ammunition, and some of his soldiers to facilitate a rapid march to Cabin Creek. The soldiers were able to find only a few wagons, which they quickly loaded with supplies, and the brigade was on its way, once again at the double-quick.[21]

That night, near Cabin Creek, the Confederates, seeing the Union camp-fires from some distance away, formed a line of battle all but surrounding around Major Hopkins' Union camp. Captain G.W. Grayson, a company commander in Watie's Brigade, wrote that the unexpectedly poor conduct of the Federals was not what he expected of combat-ready soldiers. He stated,

"While we were quietly awaiting the light, it appeared quite clear from the boisterous and careless talk of the enemy, which we could plainly hear, that there had been some drinking." The partying soldiers picked up the sounds of the Confederates advancing in the darkness, and challenged them, demanding, "What are you doing here? What do you want?" Grayson's men responded, " 'We are after you and your mule teams and your wagons.' " Eventually, one of the drunken soldiers advanced on the Confederate interlopers, shouting insults as he closed. The unrecognized Confederates ordered him to halt, but he ignored their warning. They repeated the process three times, but he was too drunk to care. After the third challenge, there was a brief pop of gunfire, and things were quiet.[22]

Later that night, the Confederates deployed around the Union lines, advanced to within a short distance, and pushed in close to the Yankee pickets. General Gano, in the lead, entered into a "converse" with a Yankee captain on the picket line. Gano began with "What are your men?"

The Yankee responded: Federals. And you?"

Gano's proud response: "Rebels, by God!"

The Yankee captain retorted: "May God damn you sir! I invite you to come forward."

Gano inquired: "Who is your commander?"

Yankee: "A Fed. Who's yours?"

Gano answered: A mixture. Will you protect a flag of truce?

The Yankee responded, "I will tell you in a short time," indicating he had to ask his commander, Major Hopkins.[23]

Here, the stories from the Federal and Confederate sides diverge. A Union report from Colonel C.R. Jennison, then commanding the First Sub-District of South Kansas, indicates that Major Hopkins did approve the flag of truce. However, when the Confederates were told of Hopkins' decision, they did not respond, and subsequently charged the Union line. The Union soldiers immediately opened fire.[24]

Other accounts of the incident describe the same exchange, but with the Yankee response to Gano's question of Federal support of a truce being, "I will tell you in five minutes." Gano waited five minutes, then ten, then fifteen. There was no response. The absence of an answer by Major Hopkins or his representatives yielded two possible conclusions: the answer to the truce inquiry by Gano was a refusal to respond, or that the Yankees were too drunk to provide an answer.[25] The latter conclusion is supported in the report of Captain Curtis Johnson, of Company D, 14th Kansas Cavalry, who noted that a lieutenant from Company E was captured by the Confederates "in a state of beastly intoxication."[26] The outcome was the same with either Jennison's or Gano's version, but leaves the question of which side's silence prompted the subsequent action.

Around 3:00 a.m. in the morning of the nineteenth, Confederate troops moved even closer to the Yankee line. The bluecoats opened fire, and a withering gout of flame and smoke erupted from the small arms of the Confederates. An explosive barrage from the Confederate cannon accompanied the musket fire. Although there was a bright moon, the muzzle flashes and explosions of artillery shells rent the night with an Armageddon roar. Terrified mules, still hitched to their wagons, ran in all directions, colliding with each other, with trees, and rolling over the 100-foot bluffs into the creek. Hundreds of unarmed Union recruits and civilian teamsters ran toward the road leading back to Baxter Springs. Soldiers in camp, hearing the hoof beats of stampeding animals in the darkness, shot many of them down, believing them to be Confederate cavalry.[27]

With the coming of dawn, the carnage became evident. Dead and dying animals were everywhere, many of them still hitched to overturned wagons. Dead soldiers lay here and there. Some of the Union troops managed to keep their wits about them and stay in a defensive line. Many others had run for their lives. Confederate shells continued their merciless destruction of the Union positions. By 9:00 a.m., it was all over. The Federals surrendered. Given the intensity of the battle and how many troops were involved, casualties were relatively low. Union casualties were around thirty-five, not counting those captured by the Confederates, and the hundreds who had fled for peaceful locales. Confederate casualties were only ten dead and an unknown total wounded.[28]

In spite of leading his men faster than should have been humanly possible, Williams did not make it to Cabin Creek in time to participate in the fighting. They arrived at Pryor Creek, a few miles short of Cabin Creek at 11:00 a.m., just as the captured wagon train and Confederate troops were lined up and headed southwest. Williams' men had marched more than eighty miles in forty-six hours—an astonishing achievement. One of his soldiers from the

First Kansas, Corporal Allen Lynch, recalled the forced, eighty-mile march years later as "the longest walk I ever took."[29]

When they arrived, they were so exhausted they could hardly stand, but they had no time to rest. They were faced with more than two thousand Confederates and the remnants of the captured wagon train loaded with booty. Williams formed his brigade in a line across the prairie, anchored on the left at Pryor Creek. He knew his twenty-five hundred men were good. Many of them had abundant combat experience. All were well trained, well-armed, and willing to fight. Moreover, he had artillery support.[30]

Skirmishing began immediately, and continued for the entire day. At one point, Williams pushed out a double skirmish line, aggressively pumping volleys of fire into Gano's line. He knew his troops would not be able to fight if he failed to spark a contest. He wanted the rebels to respond and come at him; he was ready.

That afternoon, Gano and Watie took the bait and came at Williams. Williams' artillery, which had been silent until then, opened fire with a barrage. Catching the Confederate line by surprise, the Yankee artillery blasted the landscape, forcing the southerners to retreat. Gano's artillerists unlimbered and responded to Williams' ballistic greetings. The enemies spent the rest of the afternoon in an inconsequential, but noisy artillery duel, which ended with few casualties. Major Foreman wrote a message to Colonel Williams the next day (September 20) writing that in tracking the Confederate column he found numerous graves of their soldiers killed by Williams' artillery.[31]

Gano knew he could not fight a pitched battle and still get his prized wagon train far enough south to the comfort of Confederate territory unless he moved quickly. As daylight dimmed into darkness and the shooting died out, he carried out a superb ruse on Williams. He had men silhouetted against the moonlit sky, reinforcing his presence. Campfires dotted the landscape beyond the Confederate lines. Wagons rattled back and forth in the night, ostensibly moving into place for the next day. While all that was happening, Gano and the wagon train pulled out and disappeared off the landscape. Watie and a small element of his command served as a stay-behind rear guard until just before dawn, and then quietly withdrew into the darkness. When Williams and his men prepared for battle at first light, they discovered there was no one to fight. Gano and Watie had made good their escape.[32]

Major Foreman and his relief force did not get to the Cabin Creek battle site until the next day. He put his men to work burying the dead and
gathering up government debris from the battle site. He reported to Colonel
Wattles, "The destruction is complete. Colonel Williams, with his brigade,
came upon them at Pryor's Creek, and after an artillery duel, the enemy
retreated southwest.[33]

The Confederate raid was a huge success. Aside from the damage done
at Flat Rock, their take from the wagon train had guaranteed the coming
winter would be more comfortable for them, and less so for the Yankees at
Fort Gibson. However, that was the only train they intercepted. The rapid
response of Williams' brigade and the coming of Major Foreman's regiment
demonstrated a growing quick response capability of northern troops, making such raids increasingly risky. The Confederate raid and subsequent narrow escape at Cabin Creek, proved to be the only successful one across the
Arkansas River in Indian Territory between 1863, when the Federals took
Fort Gibson, and the end of the war in April–May 1865.[34]

Chapter Twelve

Back to Arkansas: Final Campaigns, Promotion, Peace, and Transition

On September 22, General Thayer sent a message to Williams ordering him to keep his brigade at Fort Gibson until further notice.[1] Thayer had expressed dissatisfaction that the convoys from Fort Scott to Fort Gibson were without sufficient protection, compelling him to deploy regiments from Arkansas, leaving him without sufficient troops to counter local Confederate activity.[2] By positioning Williams at Fort Gibson, he could respond to needs from Cabin Creek south to Fort Gibson, an area in which Thayer considered highly vulnerable to enemy attacks. Williams' brigade did escort at least one large wagon train from Cabin Creek to Fort Gibson without any reported enemy attacks.[3]

Life in the brigade became mundane as the brigades' regiments went about re-provisioning, retraining, recruiting, and catching up administratively. Before and after Second Cabin Creek, recruitment was an issue for the brigade, especially the First Kansas, needing many replacements. The Regimental Order Book references many individuals, mostly officers, who were sent out on recruiting duty. Of course, there was guard duty and frequent scouting missions. Training and management issues took much of Williams' time. General Thayer at Fort Smith sent a flurry of messages to various commanders alerting to an enhanced level of concern on his part about enemy action. Confederate guerrillas killed Captain Benjamin Welch, commander of Company K, First Kansas Colored Infantry in a skirmish at Timber Hills, ten miles east of Cabin Creek, on November 19.[4]

Meanwhile, the War Department re-designated the First Kansas Colored Volunteer Infantry as the Seventy-Ninth United States Colored Troops. The Bureau of Colored Troops, established by the War Department in May 1863 to recruit and organize the black regiments in the army, directed the change. One part of that mandate was to designate all but a few regiments as United States Colored Troops. Thus, the First Kansas became the Seventy-Ninth USCT (new). The "new" tag meant that there was a previous Seventy-Ninth USCT disbanded, never mustered, or some similar fate. Apparently, a bureaucrat, reluctant to waste the number, achieved administrative stardom by appending the "new" tag.[5]

By January 1865, Federal armies held the initiative throughout the country. General Grant developed a strategy of coordinated offensives in the Eastern and Western Theaters of war. In the East, all resources focused upon destruction of General Lee's Army of Northern Virginia as it sought to defend Richmond and Petersburg. In the West, Federal resources were devoted to crushing Confederate forces that had returned to middle Tennessee, and driving a stake into the Deep South's heart as General Sherman's Army Group completed its march to the sea. Sherman's army then braced itself for a march through the Carolinas.[6] In the Trans-Mississippi Theater, Confederate General Sterling Price's fall campaign had been a disaster, culminating in the Battle of Mine Creek in Kansas on October 25, two days after his mauling at Westport, Missouri.[7] Price's campaign was the last major Confederate Civil War action in Arkansas and Missouri. Fallout from the blundering campaign lead to recriminations and political fragmentation within the Trans-Mississippi Confederate command structure.

In order to conduct major campaigns elsewhere, Grant pulled Federal resources from the Trans-Mississippi, leaving that theater with insufficient resources to continue major offensives against weakened Confederates. General Steele moved on, and a new Federal commander in Arkansas took responsibility for Union-occupied territory from the Mississippi River at Helena to Little Rock, and west to Fort Smith along the Arkansas River and beyond. Major General Joseph Reynolds, the new Union Commander in

Arkansas found himself stretched thin, with his command reduced from an overwhelming superiority to twenty-two thousand men, compared to forty thousand Confederates. He had insufficient resources to conduct major offensive campaigns against the Confederates, compelling him to conduct a strategic defense of his territory. He elected to conduct an active defense, using some of his forces to conduct raids into Confederate territory with the intention of keeping his enemy off balance. He also had the daily challenges of keeping the Arkansas River corridor open for critical logistics and communications support, foraging, apprehending deserters, and chasing bushwhackers.[8]

General Thayer, commanding the Frontier Division, to which Williams' Second Brigade was assigned, became alarmed about potential Confederate attacks, particularly in the vicinity of Fayetteville. He ordered Colonel Wattles at Fort Gibson to dispatch Williams and most of his brigade to Fort Smith, Arkansas on October 19, 1864. His directive tasked Williams "to march just as rapidly as his troops can stand it."[9] Still alarmed, on the next day, General Thayer ordered Colonel Wattles and his Indian Brigade to prepare to move from Fort Gibson to Arkansas on two hours' notice.[10]

In January 1865 two Confederate brigades, commanded by Colonel William H. Brooks, advanced to the Arkansas River with the mission of disrupting Union shipping. His rebel force attacked the Yankee garrison at Dardanelle, about eighty miles upstream from Little Rock on January 14. After an unsuccessful, four-hour, pitched battle the Confederates moved farther upstream another thirty miles to Ivey's Ford, near Clarksville. Their objective was to intercept a flotilla of four steamboats carrying supplies, soldiers, and refugees.[11]

On January 17, the steamers left Van Buren (near Fort Smith), en route to Little Rock. Some of them had as many as five hundred passengers and soldiers aboard. They were crowded aboard the riverboats in brutally cold weather. The river was crowded with floating ice, adding to the difficulty of navigation. As the flotilla neared Ivey's Ford, eighteen miles above Clarksville and twenty-five miles below Fort Smith, the Steamer *Chippewa*, leading the others by about a mile, came under fire from Confederate artillery, killing and wounding a number of passengers. In short order, the *Chippewa*—now in flames—beached on the south bank of the river. Confederate soldiers captured eighty-two Yankee prisoners and a large number of refugees. They plundered the boat of any valuables.[12]

The next steamboat, the *Annie Jacobs*, rounded a bend in the river, and before it could turn around, it too came under Confederate artillery and small arms fire. The senior military officer on board, Colonel Thomas Bowen of the Thirteenth Kansas Infantry, who was on military leave, took charge, ordering the steamer beached on the river's north bank and abandoned. Before he could get word upstream, the third boat, *Lotus,* came under fire, but also managed a north shore landing. Colonel Bowen used the troops from these boats to form a line along the north shore, and sent men upstream to warn the last boat, *Admiral Hines*. Bowen dispatched other messengers galloping to General Thayer at Fort Smith requesting James Williams and his brigade. He was contemplating moving all the troops to the south shore to take on the Confederates. He dispatched still more messengers rushing downstream for reinforcements. Later that night, he received unexpected help from a Union forage train with one hundred men who, as they moved in with their wagons, were making so much noise that the Confederates mistook them for artillery and pulled back. The next morning, on the eighteenth, he received more reinforcements from Clarksville when the *Admiral Hines* arrived. It was a bit of a windfall, for Colonel Bowen, as the *Admiral Hines* had not received an earlier message to proceed no farther.[13]

General Thayer received Bowen's dispatch on the nineteenth and immediately released Williams' brigade. Williams rushed his brigade twenty-five miles down the south shore of the river, headed east toward the Confederates. The next day, he reached a point on the river opposite Bowen and the grounded boats. The Confederates, thwarted by the sudden arrival of Williams' brigade, withdrew. Colonel Bowen rounded up the boats that were still seaworthy, put the passengers and troops aboard and moved carefully downstream. Williams' brigade paralleled them on the south bank, between the steamers and the potential Confederate threat. They arrived at Dardanelle two days later with no enemy contact. The boats then continued the rest of the way to Little Rock without incident. Bowen's quick response to the initial Confederate attack, and Williams' show of force on the south bank gave the Confederates enough incentive to call their damage to the boats a success, and return to Confederate territory.[14]

About a week later, there was a reallocation of resources within VII Corps in Arkansas. Brigadier General Salomon took over command of the First Division from General Thayer. Williams' brigade grew in size with the addition of new regiments. His command remained the Second Brigade, First Division, but now included six regiments:

Eleventh US Colored Infantry
Fifty-Fourth US Colored Infantry
Fifty-Seventh US Colored Infantry
Seventy-Ninth US Colored Infantry
112th US Colored Infantry
113th US Colored Infantry

He no longer had integral artillery, but could obtain attachments as needed. Even though these regiments, like most others, were weary so late in the war, his brigade numbers had now grown to more than thirty-six hundred men, nearly two-thirds of the troops in the First Division.[15]

On February 9, Williams took on a new mission: preserve order, e.g. martial law, north of the Arkansas River. This was to be a tough, but necessary, task. They had to carry out their mission in a southern state with a collapsed economy, low civilian morale, violent internal conflicts between pro-Union and pro-Confederate partisans, and a bleak future.[16]

Four days later, the news was better. President Lincoln promoted James Williams to Brevet Brigadier General, and directed he be assigned to serve with general officer responsibilities. This was a special privilege. Most brevet ranks, whether for service or gallantry in action, were honorary rank. Most officers who received brevet promotion never actually served in that grade.[17]

Williams snapped back to reality the next day with a written directive from General Salomon making him responsible for military security along the length of the north bank of the Arkansas River from Little Rock to Clarksville. This order combined his martial law responsibilities with military operations. The order included specific direction that Williams "assume charge of the entire picket line on the north side of the river, furnishing from the troops of your command such daily details as may be necessary to guard the same."[18]

An advantage of the combined civil and military security responsibility at that time was that there remained no question of source of jurisdiction when dealing with bushwhackers, other forms of insurgents, and regular Confederates troops. Williams was responsible for both. By this point, the war was winding down quickly. Planning was underway for an army of occupation, re-establishment of civil government, reconstruction, and demobilization of one of the largest armies in the world. Planning for accomplishing these missions in a ruined economy and social structure was an extraordinarily complex task, rife with pitfalls. Williams had his hands full.

The Civil War in Arkansas was stumbling to a close. Confederate General John Magruder took command of Confederate forces in Arkansas in February 1865. Assessing the strength of the Federal opposition and his own lack thereof, he went into a defensive posture. He built up his defenses, as did the bluecoats to his north. There was little else left to do. After the constant foraging of the two armies for nearly three years, the countryside was devastated and barren. Arkansas was on the brink of famine. Lawlessness prevailed, especially in the area between the two opposing armies. Bushwhackers attacked military and civilians indiscriminately without regard to their allegiance. Confederate deserters, growing exponentially in numbers, roamed the countryside. Remaining civil and military authorities remained in central and southern Arkansas worked impotently to restore order with greater application of capital punishment. Morale plunged even more in the spring, when the Confederate Congress elected to recruit and arm slaves for the Confederate Army. People railed in frustration with the hypocrisy of the government's giving slaves their freedom if they served, when the Confederacy fought to preserve slavery.[19]

General Robert E. Lee surrendered the Army of Northern Virginia to General Ulysses S. Grant at Appomattox Courthouse on April 9, 1865. The news reached central Arkansas on April 19. Panic was setting in. President Lincoln was dead. Confederate General Joseph E. Johnston surrendered the Confederate Army of Tennessee to General William Tecumseh Sherman April 26 at James Bennett's home near Durham Station, North Carolina. Confederate Lieutenant General Richard Taylor, son of former US President Zachary Taylor, surrendered his troops in Alabama, Mississippi, and east Louisiana to Union General E.R.S. Canby at Citronelle, Alabama. Federals captured Confederate President Jefferson Davis May 10. General Kirby Smith surrendered the Trans-Mississippi to General E.R.S. Canby May 26 at New Orleans. On June 23, Brigadier General Stand Watie surrendered his command at Doaksville, Choctaw Nation, in Indian Territory to Lieutenant Colonel Asa M. Matthews. Watie was the last Confederate general to surrender. The war was over.[20]

Figure 24   **Brigadier General James M. Williams, USA**

Williams assumed command of the Second Brigade, First Division of VII Corps in 1864, and received the stars of a brevet brigadier general in 1865. Promotion to brevet brigadier general, accompanied by a command in that grade was the high point in James Williams' Civil War career. Recruiting and commanding the First Kansas Colored Volunteer Infantry was his most gratifying experience. KANSAS STATE HISTORICAL SOCIETY PHOTOGRAPH.

The transition to peace took a few months. On June 26, Williams requested sixty days of leave to Washington, DC, to straighten out some of his records. When he resigned from the Fifth Kansas Cavalry, he failed to secure the proper receipts when he turned in the equipment with which he was furnished. Original records of those transactions were in Washington. The regiment lost its copies in combat. His leave was approved on the twenty-ninth, and he went on his way.[21]

Upon returning at the end of August, Williams found his brigade disbanded with the rapid mustering out of troops. He received assignment to command the post at Little Rock for his last month in the army. On October 1, 1865, Brevet Brigadier General James Monroe Williams, and the Seventy-Ninth US Colored Infantry Regiment (First Kansas Colored Volunteer Infantry) mustered out of the US Army at Pine Bluff, Arkansas. The army provided transportation home to Leavenworth, Kansas, where they assembled for their formal release.[22] Williams had been gone almost four years.

In the three years these men had served together, they formed an unbreakable bond of shared experience. They broke ground on abolition and civil liberties. They fought together, won and lost battles, and suffered high casualties. Deaths alone in the First Kansas Colored (with an original complement of approximately one thousand men) accounted for 170 combat deaths and 166 dead of disease—more than any of the other eighteen regiments from Kansas.[23] An enormous number of men suffered wounds of varying severity. They fought together in spite of the terrible risk of death or the penalties of capture. They established a reputation for bravery under fire. Their lives were irrevocably changed, and they had changed their country. The First Kansas Colored Infantry had a significant role in the Union victory in the Trans-Mississippi Theater of War.

After four long years, home was now a foreign place to Williams, as it was for most returning soldiers. Such a transition is difficult. Soldiers accustomed to intense pressure react differently to everyday situations than those who have not shared such experience. Some normally small stimuli can evoke disproportionally strong responses. Priorities change. People changed while their loved ones were away fighting, and did not know the ones who came back. Williams' wife and daughter changed. His little girl, who was only a small child of four when he left, had grown to a young lady of eight, and he barely knew her. His wife had learned to fend for herself, although being ten years his

Figure 25   **Black Troops Muster Out of the Army**

The black troops under Williams' command mustered out of the Army in October 1865 at Pine Bluff, Arkansas. With the end of the Civil War, and subsequent reduction in the volunteer army, the soldiers in Williams' brigade celebrated true freedom. Armed with the self-respect they earned as freedmen and soldiers, they looked forward to their future. LIBRARY OF CONGRESS IMAGE.

senior probably gave her an independence that came with maturity. Williams himself had been an idealistic abolitionist when he was involved with James Lane and became a Jayhawker. That experience changed him. Ideals change or even take on new meaning when confronted with reality. Combat on a greater scale, the horrors of war, and the heavy responsibilities of command had taken their toll. After such experiences at home and at war, people inevitably changed, and those who once were familiar became strangers.

Whatever happened, Williams embarked upon a campaign to obtain a commission in the regular (permanent) army. It was a daunting task. Over one million men mustered out of the army by the spring of 1866. It was necessary for the army quickly to reduce to a peacetime footing. Congress did not want to worry about the army; they were intent upon reconstructing political America. When, in July 1866, legislation finally passed establishing the peacetime structure of the regular army, its authorized strength was 54,302 officers and enlisted men, a reduction of 95 percent from wartime levels. By 1867, that would peak at 56,815. After that, and for the next two decades, the strength of the army would get progressively smaller.[24] By 1875, the strength of the army was 25,860, a further reduction of 50 percent in five years.[25]

Thousands of army officers, like Williams, found military life attractive for a variety of reasons. Some thrived on the risk and excitement of life on America's frontiers. Others found comfort in the structure. To some, it was a refuge from the problems and conflicts of domestic life. It also offered a job and steady, though limited, pay at a time when millions of veterans were flooding the job market. Nevertheless, for those many thousands of officers who sought commissions in the postwar army, there were few available. With so much competition, the decision-makers had to find reasons to deny applications.

Officers who held high rank during the Civil War found that the regular ranks were substantially lower and that, with few exceptions, brevet ranks had little or no impact. Thus, many who had been generals in the war found themselves at much lower grades, even as captains.

Obtaining a commission in the postwar army was as much or more a political process than one based upon merit. Candidates for commissions marshaled support from as many influential people as they could to influence the War Department process. Williams was no exception. Like the others, the endorsements to his application gave it the appearance of a petition. His endorsements included Governor Samuel Crawford of Kansas, who had commanded the Second Kansas Colored Volunteer Infantry, and Generals Blunt and Thayer. Other luminaries included several senators, various general officers, seventeen state senators, fifty-four state representatives, all members of the Kansas cabinet, a couple of Indian agents, and even a US Marshall.[26] There was one letter of dissent, written by J.M. Bowles, who had been Williams' one-time executive officer in the First Kansas. Bowles was court-martialed and dismissed from the army for corruption December 24, 1864, and obviously held a grudge against Williams.[27] In his letter, Bowles made allegations about Williams. After proper investigation, however, the allegations were disproved and appropriately noted on Williams' records.[28]

At some point in this process, Williams left Leavenworth, and took up residence in Washington, DC. He wrote a note to Secretary of War Stanton on August 1, 1865, commenting that he had forgotten to notify Stanton of his address change.[29]

The massive pile of correspondence finally paid off: James M. Williams was offered, and accepted, a commission as Captain in the Eighth US Cavalry on October 9, 1866. He received orders to join his regiment in San Francisco, California, where it was forming.[30] A new phase of his life was underway.

Chapter Thirteen

Indian Wars in the West with the Eighth Cavalry

US military needs did not fade with the closing of the Civil War. Indeed, national security challenges abounded. Fenians (Irish nationalists) caused strife north of the Canadian border, and were stirring unrest through brother Fenians in the United States. Emperor Maximilian, a French surrogate for Napoleon III in Mexico, was giving the American government a case of nerves, with the possibility of a European power on our border, and an ongoing Mexican civil war between Maximilian conservatives and the US-recognized Juarez government. Occupation duty during Southern reconstruction consumed a large proportion (about one-third) of the US Army. The western territories, a vast and rugged landmass larger than all the established states in the East, claimed army services where civil law enforcement was either inadequate or non-existent, and hostile Indians posed a threat to westward-bound settlers.

The onset of the Civil War had reduced the meager military presence in the West as most regular army units redeployed east to fight, leaving settlers exposed. The United States Army provided only two thousand men to garrison posts in the wartime West.[1] Volunteer militia backfilled some of the vacancies, but national needs took precedence.[2]

Over the course of the war, Federal and Confederate governments paid scant attention to the needs of the western territories. After the Confederate invasion and brief occupation of territorial Arizona and New Mexico faded into history, most of the opposing armies' attentions focused upon the Civil War. Conflicts with Indians, however, did not diminish just because the military presence abated. Southwestern Apaches, Comanche, and Kiowa saw conflicts between white men as an opportunity for exploitation. Indians found themselves with huge areas of rugged, western landscape devoid of military protection. Largely unopposed, they capitalized upon the opportunity by resuming raids on settlers. The settlers endured nearly four years of terror, convinced that the government had abandoned them.[3] The situation created a tremendous challenge for the postwar army: not only must it gain control of the Indians, but it must also restore credibility and confidence with settlers.

The postwar army was in a complicated bind when James Williams joined in the late 1860s. It had to staff more than two hundred widely separated posts with only a few hundred undermanned companies averaging about fifty men each. Traditional posts with entire regiments at one site were out of the question. Most of the new regimental missions required coverage of thousands of square miles. Consequently, a company, instead of regiment, became the combat element. Regimental commanders could go for long periods without seeing some of their companies.[4] Challenges to commanders seemed insurmountable.

Because of special duties, such as recruiting, court martial boards, a lag in filling vacancies, and sick absences, actual operational strength of the army hovered around 19,000 instead of the authorized 25,000. Present-for-duty strength of a postwar cavalry company, or troop, was usually 50–60 soldiers out of an authorized strength of 120. Senior officers in the War Department were frustrated by the congressional budgetary limits on manpower, with the army assigned such broad responsibilities. General Sherman, General-in-Chief of the Army after Grant's election to President, said, "such 'companies are ridiculous, compelling officers to group two and even four companies of soldiers together to perform the work of one.'"[5] The same problem existed in officer ranks, with some companies at times having one, or even no officers present for duty.[6] Consequently, whenever a mission emerged calling for what would be a full-strength company, two, and sometimes more companies had to be consolidated from far-flung posts to get the job done. The result was an army expensive compared to its size, because of transportation costs which more than offset the cost of providing more men per company. The army was powerless to contend with spending and manpower caps put in place by Congress.

Officers in the postwar army faced numerous obstacles to a military career. With a small and stagnant officer corps, the ranks of those with West Point commissions grew in relation to those either having civil appointments (as did the majority of Civil War officers), or officers appointed from enlisted ranks. Postwar legislation mandated 25 percent of officers come from the enlisted ranks. Officers with civil commissions had to have at least two years of wartime service to be eligible for regular army commissions. Pay for a lieutenant began at $117 per month, rising to $292 for a colonel. With the small army's seniority-based promotion system (as opposed to today's merit-based system), a lieutenant could expect to make it to major in twenty-four to twenty-six years (compared to about eleven in the modern army). A glut of senior officers hanging on for possible higher promotions further slowed the process.[7]

Williams and his contemporaries, scrambling for regular army commissions in 1866, either were unaware of, or naïvely disregarded how all this created a different army from the force of over a million men during the Civil War, which was purpose-driven, with a motivated cadre, and rich in resources. The postwar army of the frontier was much different. Western historian Robert Utley graphically and prophetically summed up the crushing weight of all these factors upon the officer corps into which Williams worked so hard to join: "As officers aged without advancement, their initiative, energy, and impulse for self-improvement diminished. Their concerns narrowed. They fragmented into hostile factions—staff and line, infantry and cavalry, young and old, West Point and Volunteer, Civil War veteran and peacetime newcomer." He wrote: "They bickered incessantly over petty issues of precedence, real or imagined insults, and old wartime controversies. . . . They preferred charges on the slightest provocation and consequently had to spend a preposterous share of their time on court-martial duty. They exploited every political connection in the quest for preferment." In examining the sense of this, he concluded, "It is true that the origins of military professionalism are found in this period. But it is also true that the parade ground of a two- or three-company post in the West defined the intellectual and professional horizons of most line officers in the postwar decades."[8]

Prolonged periods of isolation, boredom, and monotonous routines did little to provide a congenial or stimulating environment. The pace of promotions, stymied by the army's small size and the snail's pace of retirement by its most senior officers, only added to a growing perception of a bleak future. A surgeon (a class of officer not known for suppressing their opinions) indicated that while some of his fellow officers were gentlemen, many were "rascals and fools." He said, "Officers are jealous of rank, and in their hearts, I believe one half the army wishes the other dead."[9]

Enlisted men found similar issues with which to live. Pay ranged from thirteen to twenty-two dollars per month. They frequently went several months at a time without pay, until the paymaster, who rode a circuit, would arrive at their posts. Discipline was harsh, living conditions abominable.[10] Desertions were common. Army life on the frontier differed in many aspects from that depicted in motion pictures a century later.

Another irrepressible surgeon, at Fort Quitman, in western Texas described his post on the Rio Grande River some distance from El Paso, with clarity, characterizing stark conditions facing postwar soldiers in the Southwest:

> Fort Quitman is, as a whole, entirely unworthy of the name of fort, post, or station for United States troops. . . . The post was abandoned by the United States troops during the war, and not occupied again until the spring of 1868, when it was garrisoned by three companies of cavalry and one of infantry. . . . The country in every direction is a rolling sand prairie, covered with small stunted chaparral and mesquite bushes, and wild cactus which grow very high; beyond the prairie and within ten miles of the post at one point are steep rocky mountains, destitute of all vegetation. . . . The buildings are all adobe houses . . . now in a deplorable condition, entirely unfit for the accommodation of troops. Whenever it rains, which it does frequently during certain seasons of the year, officers, but more especially men in quarters and patients in hospital, are invariably subjected to a disagreeable and unhealthy wet and muddy bed. . . . It has been necessary, upon more than one occasion, to take the patients out of the wards during a rain and place them in tents.[11]

Conflict and confusion over how to deal with Indians further complicated army life on the frontier—there was no shortage of opinion. A new generation of postwar leaders reinvented army policy regarding treatment of Indians. Chief among them were generals Grant, Sherman, and Sheridan, whose opinions were far from unanimous. Grant, as army commander, did not believe all Indians were hostile. As president, he went a step further with his peace policy, advocating a number of benevolent strategies. He believed Indians should be allocated land, then be free to establish their own territorial governing structure. He delegated management of numerous Indian agencies to religious groups, including the Society of Friends (Quakers).[12]

One of the early strategies was to isolate all Indians from the flow of white migration. Major General John Pope, commanding the Department of the Missouri, believed this strategy, along with Christian education of Indians, would protect settlers, and likewise protect the Indians while preserving tribal identity. He was a proponent of consolidating widespread small garrisons into larger, more centralized posts in order to focus resources. He did recommend offensive action, until he could deem such a strategy was feasible.[13] A significant shortcoming of this strategy was that consolidation of the smaller units into larger posts would distance them farther from the settlers they were charged with protecting.

General William T. Sherman, as commanding general of the Army, in formulating an approach for the Sioux, advocated a harsh strategy "even to their extermination, men women, and children."[14] Major General Henry W. Halleck, commander of the Military Division of the Pacific, which included Arizona, was an adherent of the extermination policy.[15] General Philip Sheridan, who replaced Sherman, similarly favored an aggressive and unrelenting approach to the Indians, although he later became more moderate.[16] Diverging philosophies within ranks of the army contributed to a growing lack of focus.

The military leadership continuously clashed with civilian political advocates of a gentle approach. These were the Peace Commissions, appointed by President Andrew Johnson. The collision between their strategies, emanating from more genteel society in the eastern part of the country, and those of military, rooted in rugged lands of the west with scarce resources, played havoc with any kind of consistent approach to Indians.[17] As a result, Indians were constantly faced with a frustrating "good cop, bad cop" approach to relations with government representatives.

The Eighth United States Cavalry was one of eight white and two black cavalry regiments authorized by "An Act to increase and fix the Military Peace Establishment of the United States." The regiment was born at the Presidio of San Francisco on September 19, 1866 with activation of "Troop A." Eleven other troops mustered in the San Francisco area in subsequent months through February 1867.[18]

Williams' regimental commanding officer was Colonel (Brevet Major General) John I. Gregg. Gregg came from a well-known family in Pennsylvania. His grandfather was a United States senator; his cousin was a general officer in the Civil War; another relative had been governor; and his family owned a well-known iron business, which carried the Gregg name. General Gregg had a distinguished military record, having entered the army as a private during the Mexican War, rising to captain by war's end in 1848. After the war with Mexico, he was involved in his family's iron business. With the advent of civil war, Gregg accepted a commission as a captain. Within a year, he became a colonel and, for the next two years, commanded several brigades. He received a brevet to brigadier general in late 1864, and again to major general in spring of 1865. By war's end, he had commanded a cavalry division, and (briefly) the Union Cavalry Corps. He participated in several major campaigns, including Chancellorsville and Gettysburg and, to his good fortune, was wounded only once.[19] Gregg was a well-rounded officer who had proved himself an able and effective commander. Gregg and Williams would eventually meet and establish a friendship that would last for the remainder of their lives.

The regimental executive officer was Lieutenant Colonel (Brevet Major General) Thomas Devin. Prior to the Civil War, Devin, the son of Irish immigrants, painted houses and served as a part-time militia officer. During the war, he advanced to command both a regiment and a brigade. Brevetted brigadier general, he was in command of a division by the end of hostilities. After the war ended, Devin received a brevet to major general of volunteers for meritorious service. He was known as an abrasive, profane, hard-nosed, and aggressive cavalryman.[20]

Figure 26   Colonel (Brevet Major General) John Irvin Gregg, USA

General Gregg was grandson of a senator and a relative of a Pennsylvania governor. His cousin, David Gregg, also was a Union general. Gregg served in the Mexican war and, after a break in service, re-entered the Army during the Civil War as a captain in the Sixth Cavalry. Distinguishing himself in battle, he quickly found responsibilities as a regimental, brigade, division and, briefly, a corps commander. He remained in the regular Army after the war and assumed command of the new Eighth US Cavalry Regiment and District of New Mexico. He and James Williams became friends. National Archives and Records Administration photograph.

Figure 27   Lieutenant Colonel (Brevet Brigadier General)
Thomas Devin, USA

*Colonel Devin distinguished himself during the Civil War, was brevetted briga-
dier general and commanded at the brigade and division level. His civil war
service included the Battle of Gettysburg. After the Civil War, he remained in
the regular Army and was assigned as executive officer of the Eighth US Cavalry.*

When the regiment mustered into service, its troops deployed across a vast area of responsibility:

Regimental Headquarters, Camp Whipple, Arizona Territory.
Troop A, Camp Winfield Scott, Nevada.
Troop B, Camp Cadiz, California.
Troop C, Fort Vancouver, Washington Territory.
Troop D, Fort Walla Walla, Washington Territory.
Troop E, Fort Wapwai, Idaho.
Troop F, Camp Logan, Oregon.
Troop G, Camp Reading, California.
Troops H–M, Benicia Barracks, California[21]

The deployment of these understrength troops across a huge area of the western frontier embodied the difficulties faced by the army, and the myriad challenges of command in such circumstances.

Within a few months, Troops B, I, K, and L redeployed to Arizona. Other troops remained at stations in California, Oregon, Washington, Idaho, and Nevada.[22]

The authorized strength of the regiment on paper was approximately 660 men. Due to illness, desertion, and special detached duties, however, the regiment normally would have only 400 or fewer men present for duty. These few men were responsible for national security and civil protection over an area of 558,069 untracked square miles of what would become six different states.

Most men who joined the regiment did so from West Coast locations. Their number included men those who followed the gold rush to California, but struck it poor. Others were "wild characters who enlisted in the same spirit of adventure which led them to the frontier, and who could not generally adapt themselves to the restraints of a military life." Nearly 42 percent of them deserted before the end of 1867.[23] The lack of reliable service from these men only made the regiment's mission more difficult and exacerbated conflicts within each unit.

Others who joined were recruits transported to San Francisco by ship from eastern ports, across the isthmus of Central America over land, and by ship up the West Coast to California. James Williams was a passenger on one of those ships, with orders to report to the commanding officer of the Eighth Cavalry. Lieutenant Colonel Devin was also aboard, en route to the regiment, and in command of recruits. Williams and Devin did not hit it off. Williams was supportive of Devin in managing the troops but, as best as can be discerned from records, declined to take formal command of troops during the second stage of the journey, at a point when many men were ill with cholera. At that time, Williams was not yet an official member of the Eighth Cavalry. Upon arrival in California, Devin charged Williams for conduct unbecoming an officer for not assuming command. Williams stood trial by court-martial in San Francisco, resulting in acquittal February 9, 1867.[24] These events created hard feelings between Devin and Williams, particularly Devin's embarrassment for wasting army time and money over his accusations resulting in the court's conclusion that Williams was not guilty. Difficult conditions in the postwar army would continue to aggravate the conflict between these two men.

Chapter Fourteen

Campaigning: Fort Whipple, Arizona Territory

In 1867, General Gregg established Eighth Cavalry regimental head-quarters at Camp Whipple, Arizona Territory. Camp Whipple was outside the small community of Prescott, then the territorial capital. He went into Arizona to replace Colonel John Mason, commander of the District of Arizona. Arizona had been under jurisdiction of California's Union volunteers, filling the void left when Confederates pulled out in 1862, ending their brief occupation of the Confederate Territory of Arizona.[1]

The United States Congress established Arizona Territory, in its current configuration, in 1863. Union troops from California built Camp Whipple late in 1863 as a response to increased Indian activity in central Arizona. A month later, the new territorial governor of Arizona, John N. Goodwin, directed the establishment of a territorial capital near Camp Whipple. In May of 1864, the post—now designated Fort Whipple—relocated twenty miles southwest to more favorable terrain. Without missing a beat, Governor Goodwin moved the capital to a site near the new fort, planting a seed that grew into present-day Prescott.[2]

General Gregg and his Eighth Cavalry were to carry out their mission in the starkly beautiful, vast, rugged, and dangerous landscape known as "Apacheria." The area included Arizona, New Mexico, and western Texas in the United States and Sonora and Chihuahua in Mexico. Within the limits of Apacheria, there were several different tribes, some friendly, but most not. Apaches were predominant, but not identifiable as a single entity. There were many different subgroups of Apaches: Chiricahua, Mescalero, White Mountain, Tonto, Ojo Caliente, Warm Springs, and others. They all considered themselves Apaches, but because they lived in geographically diverse areas independent of each other, white men felt compelled to pigeonhole them in subgroups. There were Yuman Indians, also tagged as Apaches by the whites, but while ethnically related, some of them had no affinity for each other. These groups included Yumans, Yavapai, Walapai (or Hualapai), and Havasupai, all of which were sometimes clustered into the very loose category of Apache. Navajo Indians were a separate tribe, even though their language was similar to Apache.[3]

In May of 1864, when Fort Whipple and the territorial capital relocated, Fort Whipple was designated as the District of Arizona Headquarters for its central location and proximity to the new territorial capital. It was originally constructed as a rough stockade, with its outside walls forming a barrier from the savage foe. Contrary to popular history, the stockade style of construction was quite unusual, found in only the most dangerous and isolated forts. Later, in 1869, army soldiers tore down Fort Whipple's stockade, and built all new facilities. The result was much more desirable, with housing, barracks, and useful buildings.[4]

Fort Whipple's stockade, which composed much of the post when Williams arrived, was a palisade of vertical, unfinished pine logs with mud-filled crevices. Outer stockade walls doubled as walls for troop barracks, housing a cramped infantry company, officers' quarters, kitchen, bakery, guardhouse, and offices. A parade ground filled the stockade's center. Cavalry barracks added in 1867 by Eighth Cavalry troopers were a hundred yards downhill and away from the stockade. More spacious than stockade accommodations, they were log huts, each housing twenty men. Initially, as new Eighth Cavalry arrivals filled in, their huts had dirt floors, no windows, no bunks, and were heated with open fireplaces. Soldiers made improvements as time permitted. Mail service, frequently attacked or delayed by Indians, took two weeks from San Francisco to Fort Whipple, and twenty-five days from the East Coast.[5]

The country around Fort Whipple was hilly with many small valleys studded with pine trees. At a higher altitude, and north of lowland deserts in southern Arizona, the area around Camp Whipple enjoyed a pleasant climate, mild in spring and summer, rainy in fall, with occasional snow in winter.[6] Indians could be found in all directions from Camp Whipple.

Collisions between Indian and white cultures followed the same path as before the Southwest became part of the United States in 1848. Indians were fighting Spaniards and Mexicans long before turning their attention to the Americans. As American miners and settlers moved into the Southwest, pushing Indians out of their way, and little concerned with cultural issues, conflicts became increasingly violent. Mangas Coloradas, war chief of the Eastern Chiricahua Apaches, went on the warpath against whites at Pinos Altos in the mountains of southwestern New Mexico and in southeastern Arizona. Cochise, of the Central Chiricahua Apaches, reacted violently to a blundering army lieutenant, George N. Bascom, who, in February 1861, captured and falsely charged Cochise and five of his warriors with stealing a white man's six year-old stepson. Cochise escaped and took three of his own prisoners, whereupon Bascom hanged his Chiricahua prisoners, including Cochise's brother. Until then, Cochise had been on friendly terms with the whites. After that incident, the enraged chieftain embarked upon a bloodbath that cost an estimated five thousand American lives in just ten years. The United States reportedly spent $38 million to subdue the Apaches.[7]

These were clearly not the kind of Indians Williams encountered, and sometimes commanded, in the Civil War, who fought as soldiers on either side, and not on the warpath against whites. Camillo C.C. Carr, a retired brigadier general, who served with the Eighth Cavalry in Arizona said, "It might be truly said of them [Apaches] at any time, they have either just been hostile, are now, or soon will be."[8] General William Tecumseh Sherman, soon to be general-in-chief of the army, clearly expressed his frustrations with the Apaches in Arizona: "We fought one war with Mexico to take Arizona, and we should have another to make her take it back."[9]

Apaches in the Southwest differed from Plains Indians and other tribes confronting the army elsewhere in the country. They operated in small bands blending with the rugged terrain, employing hit and run tactics, both in combat, and in theft from settlers and the army.[10]

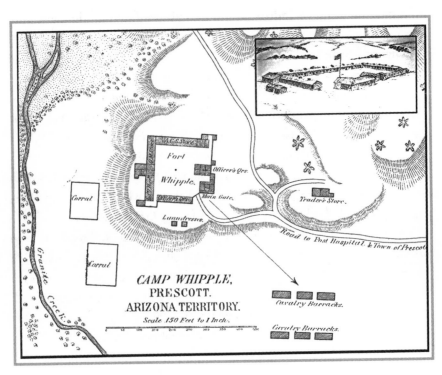

Figure 28   Plan of Fort Whipple, Arizona 1869

Initially built on a stockade pattern, Fort Whipple emerged as an open post without walls in the 1870s and afterward. As it became more permanent, the post assumed the designation of Fort Whipple. ILLUSTRATION FROM WAR DEPARTMENT CIRCULAR NO. 4: BARRACKS AND HOSPITALS, 1870. INSET FROM AUTHOR'S COLLECTION.

The most prevalent, hostile Indians close to Camp Whipple were the Yavapai, whose range spread from Prescott west to the Colorado River. Hualapai (Walapai) Indians claimed Arizona's northwest. Other hostile Indians, east of Camp Whipple, included the Tonto, Pinal, Sierra Blanca, and Coyotero Apaches.[11]

For much of the early years of the Civil War, when all the Federal troops were occupied in the east, settlers and miners in Arizona were left at the mercy of Indians. Confederate troops who occupied southern Arizona in 1862 were too few and too far away to be of any benefit to the small numbers of whites in central Arizona. After the Confederate withdrawal, the California Volunteers passed through, leaving little protection as their main body campaigned in southern Arizona and New Mexico. Hubert Bancroft, in his encyclopedic *History of Arizona and New Mexico*, cited a number of observations of the impact of military withdrawals from the territory:

> The arrival of the Cal. Column . . . found the country between the Colorado and Rio Grande a desolation marked by new-made graves. . . . The Apache marauders swept down . . . and carried death and destruction throughout. . . . The savages indulged in a saturnalia of slaughter, and the last glimmer of civilization seemed about to be quenched in blood. The horribly mutilated bodies of men, women, and children marked nearly every mile of the road to the Rio Grande.[12]

Early military efforts to coexist with Indians bore fleeting results. When Camp Whipple was originally established, Major Edward Willis of the California Volunteers successfully negotiated agreements with large numbers of nearby Indians. He further urged incoming whites to avoid conflicts with the Indians. Unfortunately, newly arriving government civilian officials employed different methods. While meeting with Indians, the bureaucrats made their armed escorts attack the Indians, killing twenty, prompting retaliatory attacks by Tonto and Yavapai Apaches throughout central Arizona. Subsequent organized responses to Indian war parties by local ranchers, California troops, and newly arrived postwar regulars killed over two hundred Indians. Remnants of the civilian population cringed for the next few years, seemingly abandoned by authorities.[13]

Williams arrived in Arizona in the spring of 1867. Initially, he was on Gregg's staff, without a command, but did not have to wait long to get into action and away from the hassles of headquarters. Early in April, Williams set out in command of a scouting mission with two troops of the Eighth Cavalry along the Verde River east of Prescott. After a reconnaissance of the river, they determined Indians were in the area, moving south and east, and proceeded to track them through the wild landscape. Newspaper accounts reported that a detachment of the Thirty-Second Infantry linked with the cavalry troopers shortly thereafter. The infantrymen had just engaged a large group of Yavapai Indians, killing three, and wounding more.[14] Army records of actions with Indians show an action on the same date, April 10, in which two troops of the Eighth Cavalry commanded by Williams engaged Indians, killing three.[15] These two events are probably the same.

Winding through remote canyons among sharp boulders and scrub brush, the soldiers (under Williams' command) doggedly pursued their prey. The jagged rocks tore at their horses. The terrain, for all its rugged beauty, was as much the enemy as the Indians. Robert Utley graphically described the joys of scouting the Arizona landscape: "Uncertain sources of water; the profusion of vegetation armed with thorns; and the snakes, scorpions, centipedes, tarantulas, and Gila Monsters." He quoted one officer's less than enthusiastic endorsement: "'I defy any one to make his way over this country without the aid of profanity. Many and many a time . . . I have come to some confounded cañon of piled-up rocks and slippery precipices, which would have been utterly impassable for myself and men if we had not literally cursed ourselves over.'"[16] On April 16, Williams' troopers finally discovered the Yavapai camp, attacked, and destroyed it. On the seventeenth and eighteenth, the combined force relentlessly tracked the Indians through the Black Mountains and Hell Canyon in the Verde River territory. Over the course of three days, the troopers and Indians engaged in four firefights; the Indians came up short each time. Fifty-three Yavapai warriors and one soldier died, bringing the mission to a close.[17] Arizona newspapers, starved for good news after years of Indian depredations, exploded. "Great Indian Killing," the *Arizona Miner* trumpeted. "Gen. Gregg at Work," and "54 Apaches Killed," were headlined, and significantly, "A New Order of Things."[18] The newspaper offered a clear message of the value of such news to the Prescott community, particularly commenting about Williams:

Prescott was much excited yesterday morning by the intelligence of two battles with the Apaches at Black Mountains had by Gen. Gregg's troops. . . . A report dated yesterday, from the General, to Governor McCormick, gives the following particulars: "Information of the presence of a large body of hostile Indians in Hell Canon having been received by the General. . . . Two companies of the 8th U.S. Cav . . . left this Post. . . . On the arrival of the command at the Canon a thorough reconnoisance [sic] of the vicinity was made, without discovering any indications of Indians. They had evidently retired in the direction of Black Mountains to the south east. Capt. J. M. Williams, 8th U.S. cav. with the two companies, was directed to scout accordingly. . . . From information, this morning received from Capt. Williams, it appears that on the 16th and 18th inst. two successful engagements were had with the Indians, in which 51 were killed and one wounded. . . . About sixty soldiers took part in these most successful fights, under Capt. Williams and Lieutenants Charles Hobart and Edmund Fetchet of the 8th Cav. and Lieut W. McK. Owens of the 32d Inf. Capt. Williams was colonel of a Kansas Cavalry Regiment [sic] during the war, and seems to be a man of great energy and courage. His conduct as well as of all the officers and men is spoken of as most creditable.[19]

A similar article in the same *Miner* issue restated the value of such news, and the hope it gave Arizona communities who had been hammered by Indian attacks for years. Inadequate numbers of (first) Confederate, and (later) Union troops stationed in Arizona during the Civil War were unable to keep Indians in check. Thus, any sign of forceful and proactive pursuit by the new postwar military regime earned enthusiastic accolades. The *Arizona Miner* article gushed that "General Gregg was noted in the Army of the Potomac, for bold and successful movements, and he has begun his administration here with vigor and gratifying efficiency. He has already had several scouting parties out, and has been in the field himself." The article went on to award verbal garlands to Williams: "The brilliant fight of Captain Williams, in which half a hundred Apaches were killed . . . reflects great credit both upon the General and Captain, and shows what determined men can do."[20]

The deaths of a number of Indians were only the first indication of Williams' successful mission. His accomplishments were soon multiplied when, shortly after his triumphant return, two hundred Yavapai came in to Fort Whipple seeking a peace agreement.[21]

Residents of Arizona had been frustrated because when the army did act, its actions were ponderous and inflexible, trying to use conventional methods of the recent Civil War to fight a guerrilla foe. Williams, on the other hand, having fought guerrillas in Missouri, knew how to strike fast. General Irvin McDowell, commanding the Department of California (which included the District of Arizona) was equally frustrated with his own forces. McDowell stated vigorously, "It is not so much a large body, but an active one that is wanted, one moving without any baggage, and led by *active, zealous* officers, who really wish to accomplish something, and who are able to endure *fatigue*, and *willing* to undergo great *personal privations*." Williams' actions in the Black Mountain engagements seemed to be just what McDowell had in mind.[22]

In a later article describing these engagements as "hand-to-hand," the *Arizona Miner* noted that Captain Williams gave specific credit to the non-commissioned officers, company commanders, and enlisted men for the mission's success.[23] That sort of public accolade for enlisted men had been lacking for some time in Arizona. Certainly, it went a long way in an environment of relentless hardship and danger to provide motivation and boosting morale.

Williams hit a strong positive chord with General Gregg, who in short order awarded him command of I Troop. Gregg penned a note to Williams before sending him on another scouting mission in June. He said, "In directing this movement of your command . . . I hope that you will be able to chastise the hostile Indians, and to give as good an account of them as you did [before]." He went on to write, "I hope . . . you will be able to bring them to bay. . . . I will not harass you with instructions which you may find impracticable, but leave you to exercise your own discretion." He closed, "I am sir very respectfully, J. Irvin Gregg, Bvt Brig Genl."[24] Williams had the kind of personality that thrived under leadership providing a substantial level of latitude.

The new scouting mission during June took Williams from Fort Whipple into the Hualapai country of northwestern Arizona. The Hualapai War lasted from 1866 to 1873. It need not have happened, however. The Hualapai had generally been on good terms with white men as far back as 1776 when they were briefly in contact with Spanish missionaries. Antagonistic relations with whites only began after the discovery of gold near their domain in 1863.[25] In 1866, Sam Miller, a prospector and mountain man, murdered Wauba-Yuba, one of the chiefs of the erstwhile peaceful Hualapai. Miller and Wauba-Yuba disagreed over some provisions Wauba-Yuba was trying to buy. Miller, with little or no provocation, blew a hole in Wauba-Yuba with his large caliber Hawkins rifle, abruptly ending the argument. Army troops chased down Miller, arrested him for murder, and turned him over to civil authorities. Miller went before a civilian grand jury in Prescott, which dismissed him, expressing its gratitude for his accomplishment. The event unleashed a bloody response from the relatively small tribe. The Hualapai assembled a force of 200–250 warriors and went on a rampage, killing dozens of whites, including many miners. The ferocity of the attacks was such that many of the miners in the area abandoned their claims and left.[26]

Williams' scout into Hualapai territory came on the heels of an earlier one in May resulting in a successful engagement with two hundred Hualapai Indians who attacked a way station at Beale's Springs in northwest Arizona, killing a number of whites. Williams' scout in mid-June was equally as successful, with an engagement at Truxton Wash, in the Yampai Valley, on June 14. The two scouts resulted in thirty-five Indian fatalities, with no army losses.[27] It prompted a comment in the *Arizona Gazette* of July 4, 1867: "Capt. Williams—This officer is evidently a fighter. Under the old order of things, he would certainly have been removed, and a muff put in his place. It is to be hoped, however, that hereafter activity and ability may not be considered to disqualify an officer for service in Arizona." The *Gazette's* tongue-in-cheek editorial staff did not appear to have a benign view of military support before the Eighth Cavalry arrived on scene.[28]

Williams and his men remained in the saddle, continuing their scout through the rugged Hualapai country. General Gregg, showing an enthusiasm for being with troops in the field, caught up with Williams on July 5 and rode on with him. They camped on July 9 at the base of Music Mountain, about 160 miles northwest of Camp Whipple, and 6 miles east of present-day Apache Junction, in the unforgiving mountainous terrain south of the Grand Canyon. That afternoon, Gregg, Williams, and eight enlisted men rode up the rock-strewn mountain to perform a visual reconnaissance of the next day's trek. Nearing the top of the mountain, they ran into a Hualapai ambush. In minutes, the mayhem was over; three Indians lay dead, and the rest scattered. The cavalry troopers did not escape unscathed; Williams and one of the soldiers were wounded.[29] Williams took two arrows in his side. Mounted on his horse and scrambling over the rocks after Indians, he was riding so fast with his pistol blazing that he never saw others hiding off the trail behind rocks. He later commented that he learned of their presence with the sensation of arrows stabbing into his side. One of the arrows penetrated a kidney; the other struck a vertebra. Continuing his mounted pursuit of the Indians, he jerked both arrows out, but the head of the one piercing his kidney stayed in and remained there for the rest of his life.[30]

Overtaken by pain and nausea, Williams landed in a heap after reining in his horse. His troopers gave him a drink, and helped him remount for the ride down the mountain. Four painful miles later, General Gregg, Williams, and the soldiers reached camp at the base of the mountain, where they laid Williams down on some blankets. General Gregg sent a courier to get an ambulance (wagon). After ten long days, the ambulance finally appeared, and began a long, rough trek back to the Fort Whipple hospital with their cavalry escort. Much of the route was across untracked country without benefit of so much as a wagon trail. For the next two months, Williams lay on a cot in the post hospital. He was in excruciating pain, unable to stand, and in need of morphine to sleep because of constant back spasms. Williams was again placed in an ambulance and subjected to a brutal ride of nearly four hundred miles to Drum Barracks, California (near Los Angeles), from there by ship to San Francisco, and another hospital. After further recovery, Williams was able to walk, but could not ride a horse, carriage, or streetcar.[31]

The news of Williams' wounds was met with significant public concern. The *Arizona Miner* expressed a sense of loss: "For some days, Capt. Williams was in critical condition," and later, "The recovery of Capt. Williams is a source of general satisfaction, as he has proven himself a fearless fighter, and a most energetic officer."[32]

Similar expressions of support came from the civilian community. A community meeting held on August 13 produced a resolution of thanks:

> Sir, At a large meeting of citizens of this vicinity held in Prescott last evening, the following resolution was unanimously adopted, Resolved, That we hereby express our thanks to Capt. J. M. Williams, and the brave officers, and soldiers of this command for the gallantry displayed by them in their recent conflicts with our common enemy.[33]

Major General Irvin McDowell, commanding the Department of California (which included Arizona), forwarded a comment about Williams in his annual report to the War Department, "[He] was badly wounded. I regret the loss of the services of this gallant and most effective officer."[34] He also had a letter sent directly to Williams expressing concern for Williams' welfare, particularly as initial reports indicated he had received mortal wounds. McDowell further commented how impressed he had been with Williams' success in fighting the Indians.[35]

General Gregg, who probably saved Williams' life at Music Mountain, nominated Williams for award of three brevet promotions, to major, lieutenant colonel, and colonel for "conspicuous gallantry." His nominations incorporated separate recommendations for the engagements in the Black Mountains, Yampai Valley, and Music Mountain.[36] Senator Edmund Ross of Kansas, in a letter to President Andrew Johnson, echoed Gregg's recommendation with his own that Williams receive a brevet to colonel.[37] Higher headquarters, possibly figuring that an award of three brevets was a bit much, consolidated the three recommendations into one, and awarded Williams a brevet promotion to major, effective July 9, 1867.[38]

Chapter Fifteen

Recuperation, a New Family, and Fort Selden, New Mexico Territory

While Williams' success against the Indians, and their success against him were transpiring, life went on. Some personal paperwork originated by Williams worked its way through the territorial legislature. Accordingly, the Fourth Arizona Territorial Legislature acted to grant Williams a divorce from his wife, Lydia, on September 23, 1867. No reason is stated, but there were obvious indicators that Williams and his wife did not enjoy a relationship when he returned home after an absence of nearly four years during the Civil War. He was evidently pursuing a different life after he mustered out of the army in October 1865, and immediately sought a commission in the regular army in the far west. In addition, during the interim, he took up residence in Washington, DC.[1]

In October 1867, three months after the ambush at Music Mountain, Williams began a period of recuperative sick leave and light duty that lasted for nineteen or twenty months. The recuperative sick leave extended over five months. Transitioning to light duty, his responsibilities included recruiting and court martial service. The purpose of such light duty was to provide time for recuperation and rehabilitation of soldiers that had been wounded or seriously ill. The light duty continued until June 5, 1869, when he returned to Arizona and resumed command of Troop I.[2]

He spent part of his recuperative leave in the Washington, DC area. While on leave, he met Mary Elizabeth Brawner, and they married on January 27, 1869. Mary Brawner was a remarkable woman with a lot of spunk—just the kind of person he needed to take up his reins. She was born on a small plantation in Port Tobacco, Maryland. Orphaned at the age of sixteen, she inherited the plantation and the slaves, becoming a ward of the court until reaching her majority. She sold the plantation in 1859 and moved to Baltimore where she worked as a live-in nanny. When she sold the plantation, she was offered a substantial amount of gold for the slaves; she refused the offer, however, and freed all of her slaves, professing a moral objection to slavery. She lived for a while on proceeds of the plantation sale, but the money quickly diminished in value in the inflationary wartime economy. By 1864, she was out of funds. Upon learning that the federal government was, for the first time, hiring women to work in the mint, she traveled to Washington. In spite of her glowing letters of recommendation from several dignitaries, the Governor of the US Mint turned her down because she had been a slave owner. Seeing her distress, he told her that her only possible chance was to seek a presidential waiver. Not dissuaded, she did just that. She hastened over to the White House, knocked on the door, and asked to meet President Lincoln. Lincoln, known to be receptive of job seekers, granted her an interview. Upon meeting him, she later related, "I stepped into the room which was a very large one and saw no one except a man sitting at a desk over in a far corner. He looked up, saw me and said, 'Well little girl what can I do for you?' and as he said it, he got up from the desk and I thought he would never stop getting up." She presented her letters of recommendation and explained her situation. After a brief conversation, Lincoln wrote a note to the Secretary of the Treasury on her behalf, and their meeting came to an amicable end. "He then rose, handed me the papers, and shook my hand. His fingers reached half way to my elbow." She landed the job, and worked there until she married James Williams in 1869.[3] She demonstrated the strength of character necessary to tolerate the privations of the life of an army wife on the frontier.

By June, Williams and his bride reached Fort Whipple. It is not certain how they made the trip. One popular route would have been retracing that which Williams originally took: by sea to Central America, across the isthmus, then by ship to California, and overland to Prescott. Another route would have been by rail to Colorado, the nearest railhead, then overland 750 miles on horseback or buggy. One Eighth Cavalry wife, Frances Boyd, chronicled her experiences along a similar route: she took a ship from New York to Panama, crossed the isthmus overland, and took another ship to San Francisco. She found the nearly two-month trip to be "delightful," and "exhilarating."[4] A remarkable trip overland from the East Coast was journaled by Eveline M. Alexander and published as *Cavalry Wife: the Diary of Eveline M. Alexander, 1866–1867*. Her journey originated twenty-five hundred miles east of Arizona. She had the luxury of traveling the last thousand miles with her husband's regiment as it moved west from Arkansas. Along the way, they made ten to twenty miles per day. The caravan had to deal with storms, floods, parched landscape, disease, and Indian raids. Her total journey took about three months. She concluded her most significant challenge was not the journey, but the transition to military posts with bare bones living conditions.[5]

Williams had been gone from Fort Whipple for well over a year. By the time he and Mary Williams arrived there, profound changes had taken place. Post reconstruction was well underway, providing pleasant living conditions surrounded by the beautiful mountains of northern Arizona. The rude stockade was gone, replaced by barracks, quarters, and buildings built of finished lumber. The nearby territorial capital was growing, and offered a congenial, but rustic community into which to introduce Mary Williams.

Earlier, in January 1868, while Williams was absent, regimental headquarters of the Eighth Cavalry moved to Churchill Barracks, Nevada, where General Gregg became commander of the District of Nevada. In Nevada, it soon relocated to Camp Halleck, where it remained for two years.

With General Gregg and the regimental headquarters away in Nevada, Lieutenant Colonel Devin became commander of the District of Arizona. Devin elected to pursue an aggressive campaign of relentless scouting against the Apaches. After forty-six patrols killed only thirty Apaches, Devin took on a strategy of going to the Apache reservations to convince the Indians to surrender those warriors known and labeled as murderers by the whites. The Indians, not kindly disposed to the idea of readily turning over some of their number to the likes of Devin, stared him down. Frustrated by his failure, Devin shut down the reservation and, consequently, prolonged the

Apache wars in Arizona. Other strategies by Devin's successors were little more successful.[6]

In response to growing Indian depredations further east, the regimental headquarters moved again in May 1870, this time to Fort Union, New Mexico. Most of the widely dispersed troops of the Eighth Cavalry also relocated to New Mexico forts. Regimental headquarters was initially at Fort Union, and later in Santa Fe. General Gregg became commander of the District of New Mexico. James Williams, his wife, and part of the regiment (including his troop of cavalry), relocated to Fort Selden, New Mexico. Fort Selden was in the southern part of the territory, about eighteen miles north of present-day Las Cruces.[7] The trek from Fort Whipple to Fort Selden, nearly five hundred miles, was not easy. The column of mounted troops, their wagons, and the meager household goods of the few families progressed at a snail's pace across the rocky, arid terrain, eating copious quantities of dust along the trail. A tense atmosphere surrounded the entire trip. Their route took them along the old main Butterfield Overland Stage Route through the Dragoon Mountains and Apache Pass into New Mexico. For decades, this had been the stronghold of Apache war chiefs Cochise, Geronimo and of their Chiricahua followers. Apaches had slaughtered hundreds of people along that route in recent years. Reports indicate that Cochise alone was responsible for the deaths of more than five thousand Americans in that region.[8]

Like Fort Whipple, Fort Selden was a relatively new post, but all similarity stopped there. Built in 1865, its purpose was to be a base camp for scouting missions sent out to reconnoiter fifteen thousand square miles of rugged, arid, and hostile territory. Their tasks were to protect settlers from Indians, chase rustlers, capture outlaws, escort the mail, protect travelers and wagon trains, and provide natural disaster relief.[9]

The post was situated on a low mesa of sandy and rocky desert about a half mile from the Rio Grande River, which made a gentle, lazy "S" curve, washing downstream from Colorado, through New Mexico, to Texas, and on to the Gulf of Mexico. The mesa sloped downward from northeast to southwest toward the river, providing good drainage and easy access to water. The site afforded a clear view about twenty miles east across a flat desert valley to the Organ Mountains, which jutted sharply upward, with a tight row of peaks resembling their namesake organ pipes. Closer by, across the river to the southwest, were the Robledo Mountains, sloping down to a ford across the river. Nearly two and a half centuries earlier, in 1598, Juan de Oñate led four hundred Spanish soldiers, settlers, and missionaries across the river at that ford, on the way up the valley into central and northern Nuevo México.[10]

The buildings of the fort consisted of adobe (sun-dried bricks from clay, dirt, and straw) walls and dirt floors. The roofs were made with a combination of wood vigas (strong, log roof beams) and smaller logs covered with dirt. Wood came from scrub cottonwood trees lining the banks of the river. The main part of the post was a quadrangle design, with a parade ground of sand in the center. Post headquarters, guardhouse, kitchen, storeroom, and bachelor officers' quarters were on the east side of the parade ground. Enlisted barracks (with bunk beds) and non-commissioned officer quarters formed the southern boundary. The western boundary was the post hospital, which had ten beds. Across the north perimeter of the parade ground were five sets of married officer's quarters, two duplexes, and one single set. Like other buildings at Selden, they were adobe. The officers' quarters had three rooms: a sitting room to the front and two small rooms to the rear. The kitchens were in small outbuildings in back. Floors were packed dirt. A porch with its roof made from brush graced the front of each set. Slightly offset to the northwest was the commander's quarters. Behind buildings on the east side, were adobe corrals. Soldiers obtained water by hauling tank wagons from the river to the fort.[11]

The weather was generally pleasant, due to the dry climate and an altitude of 4,250 feet above sea level. The summers were hot and dry, (with temperatures around a hundred degrees), and the winters were chilly (with the temperatures routinely below freezing at night). Average rainfall was seven inches per year.[12]

In the early days of the post, the nearest town was Doña Ana, a small village twelve miles south of the fort. Las Cruces, a dusty collection of adobe buildings, was about six miles farther. Franklin, Texas, (now known as El Paso), was sixty-seven miles downstream from Fort Selden, about two and a half days on horseback. The Mexican town of El Paso del Norte (today's Ciudad Juárez) lay just across the Rio Grande from Franklin. Close on the heels of troop occupation of Fort Selden, a cluster of adobe dwellings sprouted a couple hundred yards north. It picked up the name Leasburg. One author characterized it as "in most ways typical of parasitic communities that pop up wherever there are soldiers, usually faster than soldiers can pitch their tents." Leasburg had a small store, a saloon, and a number of whores.[13]

Fort Selden was strategically located alongside the main route from north to south in New Mexico, the old "Camino Real de Tierra Adentro," or Royal Road of the Interior, which linked the Spanish Colonial headquarters in Santa Fe with Mexico City. The portion of the Camino Real from the site of Fort Selden over eighty miles north to Socorro was the "*Jornada del Muerto*," or Journey of Death. The Jornada stretched across a dry, barren landscape, creating dramatic problems for the early travelers whose oxen made ten miles on a good day, a journey of more than a week without water. It got its name in 1680, during an Indian uprising against the Spanish settlers in northern New Mexico, when two thousand colonists and friendly natives attempted to escape down the Camino Real south to El Paso. Nearly six hundred of them died along the way. By Williams' time, it was, in comparison, a heavily traveled road, subject to frequent attacks from the Apaches.[14] The east-west trace of the old Overland Stage route passed south of Fort Selden. It was the main corridor from Texas through New Mexico and Arizona to southern California and the West Coast. Apache and bandit depredations along the Overland Stage route were a constant factor in life in the Southwest.

Fort Selden connected by the Overland road with Fort Cummings, about sixty-five miles to the west, and from there to points in Arizona. Silver City and nearby Fort Bayard, New Mexico were forty-four miles northwest of Fort Cummings, or 110 miles from Fort Selden. The intensity of Indian attacks on travelers along these routes made military protection mandatory.[15] Fort Cummings had a reputation as the "most dangerous point on the southern route to California." Indians, holdup men, and just plain bad guys killed approximately 425 people on a four-mile stretch of road near there, with some estimates running to twice that number.[16]

As usual, resources at Fort Selden were, in reality, less than the paper numbers. Authorization tables limited the strength of a cavalry company or troop to a hundred men by 1870. Reality was much different. A representative unit at Fort Selden while Williams was there, Troop C, Eighth Cavalry, averaged fifty-seven men assigned, and only forty-four present for duty. About 25 percent of the men were normally not available for duties because of sickness, special assignments, in confinement, or absent without leave (AWOL). Such numbers put a major crimp in the Eighth Cavalry's ability to patrol the endless country, and provide escorts along the most heavily travelled routes.[17] A photograph of Williams mounted astride his white horse (old western heroes

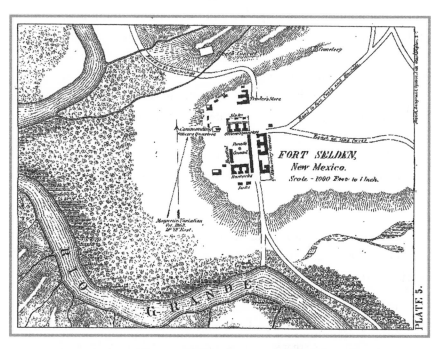

Figure 29   Plan of Fort Selden, New Mexico, 1869

Fort Selden was an open plan, with no exterior stockade walls. This was common practice with most of the forts in the West. ILLUSTRATION FROM *WAR DEPARTMENT CIRCULAR NO. 4: BARRACKS AND HOSPITALS,* 1870.

rode white horses), with Troop I mounted in formation behind him depicts approximately fifty men.

Although strategic in location, Fort Selden was isolated. It was 500 miles from the nearest railroad in Colorado, and 250 from the nearest telegraph in Santa Fe. Life at the post was difficult for the average soldier. Living conditions were abysmal in the adobe barracks. Dark, filthy, with inadequate air, infested with tarantulas, centipedes, and other critters. Their beds were bags of straw on wood frames. Most of the duty was mind-numbing, unrewarding, repetitive demeaning toil for no apparent purpose. Discipline was harsh at best, with brutal punishment for the most minor of offenses.[18]

The food was terrible, carrying a penalty for consumption or not. One soldier received a court-martial, confinement at hard labor for a month, and forfeiture of a month's pay for throwing a piece of bread in the mess hall. It is not difficult to conjure up reasons why he chose to throw it, rather than eat. Another soldier earned similar punishment when he asked for a second portion of bread, indicating a certain lack of intellect in wanting to eat the bread.[19]

Soldiers living in these conditions sometimes found innovative methods to combat the vermin that were a constant presence in their barracks. Bob Alexander, a notable western author provided a soldier's vivid description:

> The legs of the bedsteads were in good-sized tins containing water to prevent large red ants from crawling upon the beds. Overhead we nailed up rubber blankets, so that scorpions, centipedes, and tarantulas would slip off on to the floor, and be less likely to fall upon the sleeper. Rattlesnakes got into our store rooms and into any open boxes, or among blankets and clothing.[20]

On a sporadic basis, soldiers left the post on real missions, scouting for elusive Apaches. In spite of increasing Indian depredations, most soldiers never saw combat. Their chances of pulling a trigger in anger were slim. Even when encountering hostile Indians, engagements were quick, characterized by traditional Indian hit-and-run tactics. Indians rarely engaged in heavy combat.[21] The Indians were superb guerrilla fighters with many generations of experience. They fully understood a basic principle of combat: if you want to win, be the one to select the time and the place to fight.

Figure 30   Captain (Brevet Major) James M. Williams, Troop I,
Eighth US Cavalry

Williams is mounted in front of two ranks of cavalrymen. Williams' troop of cavalry, typical for the time, appears to have approximately 50–60 troopers out of an authorization of 100–120. KANSAS STATE HISTORICAL SOCIETY PHOTOGRAPH.

Figure 31   Fort Selden, New Mexico Barracks, ca. 1870

Looking south, toward the Robledo Mountains on the far side of the Rio Grande, this image depicts the enlisted men's barracks forming the southern structure of the quadrangle. COURTESY NEW MEXICO PALACE OF THE GOVERNORS PHOTO ARCHIVES (NMHM/DCA), 055039.

The days in a soldier's life dragged on in unending tedium, with little prospect for change. The average day in a soldier's life was almost a ritual.

Reveille	Sunrise
Stable Call	immediately after
Sick Call	7:15 a.m.
Breakfast Call	7:20 a.m.
Fatigue Call	7:50 a.m.
Grazing Call	8:30 a.m.
Guard Mount	8:45 a.m.
Water Mount	9:30 am.
Drill Mount	10:30 a.m.
Recall from Drill	11:30 a.m.
Recall from Fatigue, Dinner	12:00 m.
Sergeant's Call	12:00 m.
Fatigue Call	12:45 p.m.
Drill Call	1:00 p.m.
Recall from Drill	2:00 p.m.
Water Call	3:00 p.m.
Stable Call	4:30 p.m.
Recall from Fatigue	5:10 p.m.
Dress Parade and Retreat	5:45 p.m.
Tattoo	8:00 p.m.
Taps	8:30 p.m.[22]

The cluster of adobe hovels at Leasburg proved to be a constant source of problems for the command at Fort Selden, and entertainment for the soldiers. One of the post commanders at Fort Selden shared his dissatisfaction with Leasburg in a report to higher headquarters:

The inhabitants of this town or most of them have been a curse to this Post and the records of the Cemetery will show that some seven or eight of the soldiers of this Post have been murdered there, whether by the hands of thus respectable citizens or some of their comrades who were nearly crazy from the effects of the poisonous liquors sold them there I cannot say. . . . [At Leasburg are] established a few miserable buildings which are inhabited principally by liquor sellers, gamblers and prostitutes of the lowest class.[23]

The post surgeon wrote his own appraisal of Leasburg, echoing the previous quote: "The plague spot of the vicinity is the small settlement known as Leasburg, where prostitutes and bad characters congregate at times when the troops of the garrison have money. . . . All the venereal disease, which is by no means uncommon here, is directly traceable to this place."[24] It was an obvious conclusion, given that Leasburg was the only cluster of hovels within several miles. With only forty people, Leasburg was an efficient machine for separating soldiers from their money. Four bar-dancehall-whorehouse combinations operated around the clock. Six soldiers made the ultimate sacrifice in Leasburg barrooms, rather than at the hands of Apaches.[25]

Las Cruces, twelve miles downstream from Fort Selden, was a rapidly evolving cluster of adobe buildings with its share of saloons. It posed an attraction for soldiers seeking some diversity of entertainment. It was the scene of an occasional drunken brawl between soldiers, cowboys, desperados, and various others intent upon avoiding civilized society. Sometimes the pounding was excessive, and men died. On occasion, when combatants grew tired of bloody knuckles and having furniture broken over their heads, they resorted to gunplay.[26]

One of the more bizarre confrontations took place in the post commander's quarters at Fort Selden. Two lieutenants, enjoying the hospitality of their commander, but not paying close attention to the rules of etiquette, entered into a heated discussion. The conversation went in a direction where one can conclude the unit's upcoming picnic was not on the agenda. It seems that one of the lieutenants had a more than casual relationship with the other's wife, and both were inclined to settle their disagreement then and there. They squared off against each other, yanked out their six-shooters, and blazed away, killing each other. There is no record of the commander's opinion of their conduct.[27]

While protection of local citizens and travelers along the *Jornada del Muerto* was a paramount mission of the contingent at Fort Selden, they were occasionally dragged into civil strife. Politics played a major role. The old village of Mesilla, which had been capitol of the Confederate Territory of Arizona during the Civil War, was a hotbed of politics. One fine day, in August 1871, Democrat and Republican congressional candidates scheduled rallies on the same day in Mesilla's town plaza. Back East, political rallies were festive occasions with marching bands parading around the town, waving flags, making noise, and radiating good cheer. The idea was similar out West, but folks were armed and substantially rougher around the edges than their eastern cousins. Western whiskey tended to flow much more freely. There were a few dust-ups that morning, but nothing of consequence. Later, in the hot afternoon, with liquid fortitude cooking in their veins, the competing groups' noisy routes of march intersected. A Democratic newspaperman by the name of Kelly clubbed Republican John Lemon to death. Kelly's Irish luck terminated immediately when Felicito Arroyas y Lueras emptied his revolver into him. Then, an unknown participant reciprocated by whipping out his pistol and plugging Felicito. The melee became general in nature, with seven celebrants suffering fatal wounds in the first few seconds. Innocent bystanders, including one child, became mortal casualties. Rioting continued into the evening, with thirty or more wounded political partisans. Local peace officers were unable to cope, so someone sent for military help from Fort Selden. Lieutenant Colonel Devin mounted his trusty steed and charged in with two troops of the Eighth Cavalry. By the time the dust settled, as many as fifteen people lay dead, with many more wounded. Cavalry troopers bivouacked on Mesilla plaza until somber-attired morticians boxed up the dead, and lowered them into graves scraped from the rocky ground.[28]

As noted, desertions were high. They jumped even more when Congress reduced military pay after 1870. A private's pay—already about one-fourth that of a blacksmith, and way below that of a carpenter—was reduced from sixteen dollars per month to thirteen.[29]

As James Williams transitioned into Fort Selden, his life and priorities changed significantly. Before returning to duty at Fort Whipple, he had been on extended leave and light duty for two years in much more populated and attractive environs. He had taken on the concerns and responsibilities of a bride. He was approaching forty years of age, with little to show but the scars of three gunshot and two arrow wounds. The prospect of returning to frontier military duty, with little hope of a stable life in more congenial surroundings probably did not engender much enthusiasm. To that environment came a child, John. John Williams was born at Fort Selden in 1870.[30] Army life on the frontier likely became even more bleak for Mary Williams at that point.

Fort Selden, like most other frontier posts, experienced frequent changes in command, as well as changes in units. Some changes were due to a policy to rotate units from one locale to another to break up monotony. Monotony, however, was pretty much the order of things from one post to another. The policy had more negative than positive benefits. Significantly, units new to a post would take a substantial amount of time to learn their area of responsibility well enough to combat Indian problems. By the time they learned the law of the land, they would move on to the next post. Other changes in command were to rotate duties on the installation. Williams was the post commander at Fort Selden for a few months in 1870, which was about normal. In the thirteen-year period between 1865 and 1878, before the army temporarily closed Fort Selden, there were at least thirty different officers in command of the installation.[31]

Indian activity, which increased significantly in the late 1860s and early 1870s, prompted changes. Settlers and wagon trains were the Apaches' most popular targets. Picket posts were established halfway up the Jornada del Muerto, and in the pass through the San Andres Mountains, near San Augustine Springs, to the east of Fort Selden. That pass was one of the most dangerous places in southern New Mexico. Apache ambushes near San Augustine Springs resulted in dead travelers twelve times in a fifteen-month span between 1869 and 1870.[32]

Williams, suffering the after-effects of his wounds, went before a medical retirement board at Fort Leavenworth, Kansas from September through December of 1870. His request indicated that he was not particularly interested in getting out of the army, but rather wished to continue on active duty exempt from field service. Generals Gregg and Blunt, both present when Williams suffered his wounds, submitted affidavits verifying the records. Physicians on the board examined Williams, but without today's imaging and diagnostic equipment, were limited to peripheral external exams and poking about his body. The board concluded that although field duty and campaigning would cause him pain, he was still fit for duty, and would have to learn to live in constant pain.[33]

Williams returned in December. While he was gone, Lieutenant Colonel Devin had taken command of the post. Devin had overall command over Forts Bayard, Craig, Cummings, McRae, Selden, Stanton and Tularosa. As General Gregg was then responsible for all military units in the District of New Mexico, Devin was largely responsible for Eighth Cavalry operations, although still in the assignment of executive officer, and remaining under Gregg's chain of command. Gregg remained nominally in command of the Eighth Cavalry.[34] With Devin and Williams in such close quarters, their mutual dislike for each other was bound to escalate and boil over.

Figure 32   James and Mary Williams, Nurse, Baby John Williams 1870

This set of quarters, constructed of adobe, had three rooms. It was one of five sets of quarters on the north end of the post. A separate and larger set for the senior commanding officer was on the northwest corner. COURTESY OF KANSAS STATE HISTORICAL SOCIETY.

Chapter Sixteen

Fort Bayard, New Mexico Territory

Devin was responsible for resolving irregularities in accounts at various installations. Upon arrival at Selden, he summarily relieved the then post commander Major David Clendenin, making adverse record of his performance. Clendenin demanded a court of inquiry into "allegations against my integrity as an officer and a gentleman." One of the mandates given Devin was to clean up Fort Bayard, near Silver City in southwest New Mexico, which was apparently in a demoralized state. He opted to give the task to Williams, which was a bit out of synch given their poor relationship. He may have concluded that in spite of his dislike of Williams, he could expect positive results. He may have just wanted Williams away from him at Fort Selden; or he hoped the reassignment would ruin Williams' career. In any event, Williams left Fort Selden for Fort Bayard on March 21, 1871.[1]

Fort Bayard traced its origins to a camp established in 1863 by a troop of cavalry about 150 miles from El Paso in the mountains of southwestern New Mexico to protect settlers and the gold and silver miners from the marauding Apaches. In 1866, the 125th US Colored Infantry, a regiment of black, or "buffalo soldiers," established a more permanent camp. The site selected was about nine miles east of Silver City, ten miles southeast of the mines of Pinos Altos, and eight miles from the copper mines at Santa Rita. It sat astride the war trails over which the Apaches rode on frequent raids on all those sites. It formally became a post for stationing troops, and was designated Fort Bayard.[2] The post was named for Brigadier General George D. Bayard, killed at the Battle of Fredericksburg in the Civil War.[3]

Southwestern New Mexico was a beautiful, but geographically remote region. Tucked away between the Sierra and Santa Rita Mountains, Fort Bayard lay at an altitude of around six thousand feet. The climate was delightful, with four distinct seasons. Pine trees studded many of the mountains and valleys. With more than eleven inches of rain annually, and a moderate fifteen inches of snow, the site was not as arid and uncomfortable as Fort Selden.[4]

As commander of a troop of cavalry, Williams had many challenges. The site of the fort was raw; a few adobe and log huts clustered around the parade ground. There was a plan established for the fort, but accomplishments were limited. Construction of some permanent buildings was underway, but only in its infancy. Like most army forts, its plans did not include palisaded enclosure or any other form of stockade. The plan called for a rectangle of buildings around the parade ground, with open approaches and no protective fences or walls. Apaches tested the efficacy of the plan, when in 1867, just a year after its establishment, they counted coup by having a raiding party gallop through the center of the post before dawn one morning, ripping the night air apart with blood-curdling war whoops, and shooting up the site. They were gone before the sleepy troopers were able to grab their rifles and pants.[5] There had been earlier raids near the post, but never on it.[6] Their primary purpose had been to steal military livestock. Obviously the ride through the soldiers' home site was meant to be an insult and an Apache fraternity prank.

In the period leading up to Williams' arrival there had been a number of more serious depredations by the Apaches. At one point during the Civil War, when the Silver City area was officially part of the Confederate Territory of Arizona, Cochise and four hundred braves attacked the nearby town of Pinos Altos. A Confederate Army detachment of nine men, augmented by local miners fought them off in a pitched battle lasting five hours. In the early 1870s, Apaches killed and mutilated numerous miners and settlers near the fort, including six men killed taking supplies to the fort the month Williams arrived.[7]

Years later, the fort was finally complete: a rectangle eight hundred by five hundred feet, with adobe buildings. In 1871, when Williams arrived, only a few buildings, mostly storehouses, were complete. The hospital was complete as well, but the surgeon was unhappy because it did not meet minimal standards established by the surgeon general of the army. Accommodations for officers and men alike were conspicuously neither elegant nor sound. That same season, roofs of two soldiers' barracks collapsed.[8] The post surgeon reported, "The officers and men occupy temporary log huts, which are in bad condition." He was so dismayed with the quality of officers' quarters he made a point of reiterating, "The officers' quarters are in very bad condition."[9]

Soldiers stationed there were responsible for construction of the fort's buildings. Skill at such construction was only acquired only with long experience, sometimes not readily available. In 1872, the buildings could accommodate up to three hundred soldiers. The rudimentary buildings were either adobe or logs, with mud roofs, dirt floors, few windows, and teeming with vermin. The surgeon reported the buildings "rapidly decaying and becoming unfit for occupation."

Over the course of many more years, Fort Bayard would evolve into a first-rate installation, but not in Williams' time in the army.[10] Until permanent quarters were built in the late 1870s, accommodations were haphazard at best. The typical housing in which the officers lived before construction of permanent quarters were, at best, log hovels with dirt floors, dirt-covered viga roofs, and few, if any, windows. One lieutenant's wife noted when the strong summer storms rushed across the landscape; they nearly blew down the cabins. In heavy winds, soldiers had to open the front and back doors to allow the wind to pass through, and keep the cabins from collapsing. Unfortunately, that did not keep the accompanying rain out. She reported in a matter-of-fact tone, "It was therefore necessary, at such times, to mount on chairs or tables." She followed that comment with an observation that the viga roofs overlaid with mud constantly leaked and occasionally fell, at which time "the ladies always took refuge under umbrellas until after the storms subsided."[11]

One of the other officers in the Eighth Cavalry, First Lieutenant Frederick Phelps, provided a vivid first impression of the fort, and the accommodations he had as an officer. He wrote in his memoirs:

> The locality was all that could be desired; the post everything undesirable. Huts of logs and round stones, with flat, dirt roofs, that in summer leaked and brought down rivulets of liquid mud; in winter the hiding place of the tarantula and the centipede, and ceilings of "condemned" canvas; windows of four and six panes, swinging door-like, on hinges, (the walls were not high enough to allow them to slide upward) low, dark and uncomfortable.

Figure 33   Early House Built at Fort Bayard, New Mexico

The men of the Eighth Cavalry constructed this house between 1870 and 1872 for Sergeant Frank Eaton and his family. Although rudimentary, it represented the advancement of "civilization" in that part of Apacheria. COURTESY NEW MEXICO PALACE OF THE GOVERNORS PHOTO ARCHIVES (NMHM/DCA), 111667.

Figure 34   Fort Bayard Cavalrymen Training Horses for Combat

Just like cavalry troopers, horses also underwent combat training. These men are training their horses to go to the ground and remain there, providing protection and support for their riders. COURTESY OF THE NATIONAL ARCHIVES AND RECORDS ADMINISTRATION.

The primitive conditions and isolation of the post struck him. The nearest railhead was nearly seven hundred miles north at Kit Carson, Colorado (about ninety miles east of present-day Colorado Springs, near Cheyenne Wells). The only food available for the Phelps family was government rations. His house had the interesting feature of architectural diversity, depending upon the view. One wall was constructed of stones; one was adobe; one was of vertical pine logs; and one was built with slabs of wood obtained from a sawmill. His ceiling was canvas, set to catch the drippings of mud from the dirt and log roof. He had a floor of rough-hewn one-foot wide boards. His front door was two boards with a wood latch and leather hinges. The house had a single window with four permanently sealed glass panes.[12]

In the midst of a beautiful land, the Fort Bayard region was a slaughtering ground for many of the most infamous Apaches in history. Cochise, Mangas Colorado, Geronimo, and Victorio were all responsible for many deaths in the area of Fort Bayard, keeping the local populace constantly on edge. In one representative attack, Apaches captured three miners, hanged them from a tree by their feet over a fire, and burned them to death.[3]

Just as Leasburg became a stain on the landscape outside Fort Selden, so too, did the village of Santa Clara (later renamed Central City), near Fort Bayard. Demonstrating a liking for capitalistic enterprise, the residents of Santa Clara offered tried and true techniques of helping both soldiers and the army part with their money. Gambling, whores, and whiskey served as the means for removing the jingle from soldiers' pockets. Government contracts, even for legitimate goods and services, found their way into the hands of suddenly available merchants in the heretofore-unknown village. Santa Clara, just like any other place nearby a military installation, was bound to create headaches for the local commander. Drunkenness, fights, violations of off-limits policies, and soldiers falling in love with whores became guaranteed side effects of the Santa Clara pill.[14]

As a troop commander, Williams was responsible for doing all within his power to improve the living conditions of his soldiers. Building materials were scarce, and funds for their acquisition nonexistent. He was a soldier, and soldiers, never at a loss for ingenuity, have always managed to scrounge, beg, borrow, steal, and invent whatever is necessary to make life more comfortable. Williams sometimes looked to his counterparts at other installations as sources of materiel. One of the letters found in his records was from his

Figure 35   Apache War Chief Geronimo

Geronimo—one of the most famous of the Apache warriors to fight the US Army—was a respected leader. His braves kept travelers, miners, settlers, and soldiers on full alert for decades. Mangas Coloradas, Cochise, Geronimo, Victorio and other Apache warriors accounted for the deaths of thousands of Mexicans and Americans. PHOTOGRAPH COURTESY OF THE LIBRARY OF CONGRESS.

opposite number at Fort Cummings, New Mexico, May 28, 1872, illustrates how the soldiers' network worked and how scarce their resources were:

Dear Williams:

Many thanks for your pleasant letter received through the medium of Mrs. Vickey [?]. . . . The Bayard teams returned from Selden half an hour ago – will leave tomorrow morning. By them I send one keg of kraut and 18 pds of table salt. There is not a bit of ash or hickory at the post or I would gladly send it – I know Brewer has 3 or 4 old planks of ash – try him – if not try Slocum.[15]

Military missions went on and on. Conflicts with Apaches in Arizona were heating up, and spilling across the line into New Mexico. Troopers saddled up and set out on patrols, escorts, and other missions. The pressure of mission requirements were mounting as resources shrank. By the early to mid-1870s, the troop strength for the entire Territory of New Mexico was down to six hundred men.[16] Williams from time to time rode to Fort Selden and other posts on special duty (courts martial boards, etc.). He was on such duty at Tularosa in October 1871, and Fort Selden in February 1872. He led a patrol about two hundred miles north from Fort Bayard through Tularosa and back in May. In June, he was again in the field, this time on a lengthy scout through the Mogollon Mountains chasing Indians. The scout covered 368 miles, but was unsuccessful, as were most scouting missions. Regimental documents ("Returns") indicate that Williams' troop was in the field more than most of the other troops, which remained in garrison or on routine escorts.[17] These scouting missions frequented some incredibly beautiful, but hostile land. The deserts were arid wastes, and the mountains, reaching above ten thousand feet, were littered with boulders, and jagged rock outcroppings. To the north was the *Malpais*, or badlands, covered with volcanic rock, which could quickly cripple horses.

While on a scouting mission in the mountains, Williams' injuries finally caught up with him. He later reported, "On this scout in the mountains, my strength failed me and the horrible pain and spasms of my spine came back upon me and I was compelled to send for my buggy to take me into the post." His time on horseback was ending.[18]

In the fall of 1872, the conflict between Williams and Lieutenant Colonel Devin came to a head. These two officers, both with fine military records,

Figure 36   Troopers of Eighth Cavalry on Scouting Mission, 1871

This photograph depicts the rugged country that created obstacles to the Army, and sanctuary for the Apaches. COURTESY NEW MEXICO PALACE OF THE GOVERNORS PHOTO ARCHIVES (NMHM/DCA), 155008.

got off on the wrong foot in 1866, and their personalities clashed thereafter. Devin was pugnacious, aggressive, overbearing, and abrasive. Lieutenant Phelps, Devin's adjutant for three years, admired him, but acknowledged that he was a "grizzled, gray and iron-willed old man . . . a short, stout, Irishman with steel gray eyes, an explosive temper," and a "cruel, rasping sneer."[19] At one point when the army headquarters in Washington refused payment for some wood Devin purchased, Phelps said, "I have never seen a madder man, and have never heard more forcible language."[20]

Williams was straightforward, not terribly demonstrative, and displayed a quiet confidence. As a commander, he proved himself capable and trustworthy. In a combat environment, he proved himself fearless and aggressive. He chafed under overbearing supervision, and dug in his heels when pushed, tending to push back, sometimes unwisely.

It is likely that by the time Williams relocated to Fort Bayard, he had grown disillusioned with life in the frontier army. It certainly was not the wartime army in which he had thrived during the Civil War; nor was it a peacetime army. As previously noted, interpersonal conflicts, inadequate resources, terrible living conditions, no opportunity for advancement, and an elusive enemy were the realities of military life on the frontier. There seemed to be no unified purpose. Additionally, Williams' wounded back was causing chronic problems, which constantly reminded him of the retirement board's conclusion (back in 1870) that he should continue to do his full duty in pain.[21] This was not the career environment he envisioned, nor was it the way he expected to live with his new family. He was wearing down under the increasingly bleak prospects for the future.

In September 1872, Williams was acting commander of Fort Bayard in the absence of Lieutenant Colonel Devin, who was on detached duty in Santa Fe. Williams needed to expand a mess hall his troops used for various purposes. He noted that soldiers on punishment duty were fabricating adobe bricks nearby for use in construction of two rooms for a lieutenant and his wife, who were not at Fort Bayard at the time. Williams had his troops take a few hundred of the bricks. He instructed the officer supervising the soldiers to continue producing bricks. He also scrounged wood parts from a tumbledown hovel, and a window from an old unused structure. His troops built the adobe room, as was the common practice.[22]

Lieutenant Thomas Blair of the Fifteenth Infantry, also at Fort Bayard, was the post quartermaster. As such, he was responsible for the management of facilities, which included production of adobes. He was proud of the power that emanated from his job. Bypassing Williams, he wrote directly to District Headquarters in Santa Fe, narrating the incident, pointing out that the lieutenant whose house for which the adobes were destined had secured Devin's permission to have the adobe bricks fabricated. Blair stated that Williams' actions significantly delayed construction of the house. Blair acknowledged that he had approved Williams' request to take wood to be used in the project, but denied that he aided Williams in unauthorized use of the bricks, stating that he thought what Williams was doing was with permission.[23]

This was not the first disagreement Blair had with Williams; it appeared the two had a long-standing conflict. At one point, Blair accused Williams and another officer of gambling. Williams in turn filed charges against Blair for a false report. The court martial board acquitted Williams, and the animosity continued to simmer. Blair continued a checkered career, suspected at various times of stealing money from a unit safe, failing to report soldiers for desertion, and concealing court martial charges against another officer with whom he was friendly. Later, in 1876, gleeful at the death of General Gordon Granger, commander of the Fifteenth Infantry and the District of New Mexico, Blair set about courting the general's widow, marrying her in 1878. Shortly thereafter, authorities discovered that Blair had left a wife and two children in Scotland when he immigrated to America. He subsequently stood trial by court martial, was convicted, and thrown out of the army in 1879.[24]

Furious at learning about Blair's letter, Williams immediately dashed off a letter to the District Commander explaining himself. He related that he secured the bricks (fewer than Blair alleged) from the officer supervising the manufacturing detail, and instructed him to have the prisoners continue making bricks. The remaining bricks, he contended, were destroyed by a rainstorm that set in that evening, causing the construction delay, rather than the use of some of them for troop-oriented construction. Williams explained that he knew Devin had ordered the bricks made, but not that they were reserved for another officer's quarters. Annoyed that Blair had circumvented the entire chain of command by writing to District Headquarters, he commented that he had not received any complaints. Further, incensed that

Devin had to learn of the issue in the fashion he did, Williams pointed out that Devin did not leave any instruction regarding the adobes when he left. Williams bluntly said,

> I desire to state that no person would more cheerfully have carried out any instructions than the present post commander. Had any instructions on this or any other subject been delivered at the time of the departure of Col. Devin, but in the absence of any instructions I have, and shall continue so long as I have command of the Post to do what my judgment dictates, as for the best interest of the service and I trust that in so doing I may not be judged without a hearing and that I desired to be held in a strict account for my doings in the premises, but I would protest against this manner of transacting official business as being in violation of all the usages of the service and lacking in official courtesy.[25]

Devin did not buy Williams' side of the story. He demanded that Williams report to Santa Fe with an explanation. Their disagreement escalated, and Devin placed Williams in arrest on December 2, 1872.[26]

After all the brouhaha over the bricks, however, Devin charged Williams for another matter. He claimed that Williams had stolen and sold a carbine assigned to one of his soldiers, Private Michael Cornwall. Cornwall, a soldier in Troop I (Williams' command), deserted in March of 1872. When he deserted, the unit dropped from accountability all items for which Cornwall was responsible, declaring them stolen. This was routine. The charges against him included loss of a bridle, saddle, saddle blanket, his tent, and other articles, including his carbine. One week later, Cornwall turned himself in at Fort Craig, asserting that he had drunkenly wandered off on foot. How he managed to cross on foot more than one hundred miles of desert and mountains, and survive a trek through Indian country after one night of drinking never merited explanation. Nor was there any explanation why it took a week for him to sober up sufficiently to turn himself in.

Cornwall stood trial by court martial for desertion and theft. The trial resulted in a conviction of desertion, but not theft. A higher-level reviewing officer disallowed the finding of guilt, thus clearing Cornwall of all charges. When the paymaster confronted Cornwall with a bill for the items for which he was accused of stealing, he argued that because of his acquittal of all charges, he need not pay for what was missing, including his carbine. He claimed that Williams physically attacked him when he refused to pay. Devin ordered Williams to turn over the record book on weapons accounts, so that he could conduct an investigation. Williams insisted that he did not have the book. After much haggling over the status of the book, involving a number of people, Devin concluded that Williams was guilty of taking the weapon, and selling or disposing of it in some illicit way. He had Williams confined to his quarters, and forwarded a recommendation to District Headquarters asking that Williams be tried by court martial.[27]

Devin charged Williams with a shotgun blast of accusations, subjecting Williams to trial in Santa Fe. The charges included fraud, specifying that he sold government-owned corn on three occasions for a total of $153.71. That charge included two additional specifications that he sold flour as well. Another charge stipulated that he sold a government-owned carbine, and one hundred and twenty rounds of ammunition. The final charge included five specifications of conduct unbecoming an officer for requisitioning forage allowance for two horses, when he only had one in his possession.[28]

Williams was not Devin's only target. He relieved and court-martialed any number of other officers under his command. At the time of Williams' court martial, Devin in a long apoplectic tirade to the Adjutant General of the Army, vented his wrath about Williams and others under his command:

> This is the outlying Western Post of the Military Division of the Missouri, 1200 miles from Department Headquarters. . . . I have here some of the most incongruous elements in the service in New Mexico, that five officers are now in arrest at this Post awaiting action upon their trials before General Court Martial. . . . This state of things originated previous to my assignment. . . . I now propose to command and maintain discipline and compel obedience to my lawful orders if I have to place every officer at the Post under guard. I have important and responsible duties in addition to the command of Fort Bayard and have neither time nor inclination to parley with factious officers.

Devin closed his letter by confessing that he would continue to throw charge after charge at Williams until he could find one that stuck:

Capt Williams is the first officer of the Army under my command who has dared to disobey my positive order. He . . . must accept the legitimate consequence, renewed arrest and trial if acquitted on former charges.[29]

A court martial board of five senior officers was convened in Santa Fe. They found Williams innocent of all charges and specifications, except for the single charge of fraud for selling corn—the only charge he did not deny. Four of the five officers on the court martial board then recommended clemency on that conviction because Williams received no benefit from the fraud—he was using the money mostly to buy materials to construct a barracks building for his own troops. Subsequent to the board's conclusion, each level in the chain of command, all the way up to the War Department, reviewed the findings. The Judge Advocate General of the Army ultimately reviewed the legality of the trial process, and forwarded his comments to the Secretary of War for final signature. The Judge Advocate General concluded that the board's process was indeed legal. He also concurred with the officers on the board that the law made no allowance for motivation, and similarly supported their recommendation for clemency. The Judge Advocate General's review concluded:

> The transfer of corn of which accused is convicted under the first charge, was not denied by him. It is however shown that his forage [corn], which had been saved from the authorized allowance for the horses of his company, was exchanged by him for lumber with which to repair his own and his men's quarters, all of which were very dilapidated and insufficient. There is good reason to believe that these transactions, which took place fifteen months before his trial, were known to his commanding officer [Devin], who tolerated, if he did not expressly sanction, them. In view of the case, it is thought . . . that accused was innocent of any dishonest or corrupt purpose. . . . It is therefore advised that . . . the recommendation of four fifths of the court should be followed.[30]

Williams initiated a number of actions to exculpate himself to no avail. Devin, the post commander who preferred charges, refused to honor the recommendation for clemency. After a flurry of statements and correspondence flowed back and forth up and down the chain of command with no change in the outcome, Williams submitted his resignation from the army on March

29, 1873. The War Department accepted it a couple of weeks later. No sentence was ever imposed.[31]

Williams' resignation signaled an unsatisfactory end to a military career highlighted by extraordinary accomplishments, aggressive service in combat, and strong leadership, tempered by conflict with authority. He was frustrated and angry that his actions were interpreted differently than his intentions, and that his initiatives to provide for his men, though recognized at all levels up to the War Department, were brushed off by Devin. His experience in the post-war army had incorporated the all too common highs and lows of that era.

His twelve years in the army at a close, Williams moved on, looking to the future. His travels back and forth across America granted him unique experience and perspective, which gave him an advantage over most Americans of the time. The frontier was changing rapidly. Settlements spread across the landscape in spite of the fierce resistance of the Indians. The West represented opportunity, and Williams chose to exploit that opportunity. With high hopes for the next phase of his life, he gathered his family together and headed for Colorado.

Chapter Seventeen

Frontier Ranching, Congressional Accolades, and Redemption

Williams found opportunity in southern Colorado. He selected a site on the Santa Fe Trail, along the Purgatory River (also called Las Animas), about five miles northeast of the village of Trinidad. Trinidad was the gateway to the imposing Raton Pass through the Sangre de Christo Mountains separating Colorado from New Mexico. The constant flow of settlers along the Santa Fe Trail passed Williams' new home en route through the pass. The place where he settled became the village of El Moro, in Las Animas County.

The Purgatory River, on which Williams established himself and his family, had a name which was an ominous herald of southwest-bound settlers coming trip through the mountains. Its full name was "El Rio de las Animas Perdidas en Purgatorio," translated, "The River of Lost Souls in Purgatory"—a name dating back to the days of New Spain. The Spanish sent an infantry regiment from Santa Fe to link New Spain (New Mexico) to Spanish Florida. The regiment started late and wintered over at the present site of Trinidad. With the arrival of spring, the regiment set out on its journey, leaving all its camp followers (including women, children, and some men) behind. The Spanish soldiers, following a stream into a canyon, marched around a bend and out of sight, never to be seen or heard of again. Over time, with the advent of

French trappers into the region, the Purgatory evolved into "Le Purgatoire." American mountain men bastardized the name into "Picket Wire."[1]

For decades, the Santa Fe Trail had been the main route for thousands of soldiers, settlers, and others travelling to the southwest. It sliced across southern Colorado from Missouri and Kansas, through Bent's Fort and Raton Pass, into New Mexico, opening the way to Arizona and California. Raton Pass was a difficult passage through the mountains dividing Colorado from New Mexico. Indians, Spanish Conquistadors, mountain men, traders, soldiers and settlers used the rugged pass over the centuries. The pass opened to wagon traffic in 1821. General Stephen W. Kearny took his small army through the pass in 1846 en route to take New Mexico and California for the United States. Kearney's column included Colonel Alexander Doniphan and his regiment of mounted Missouri volunteers on their legendary expedition deep into Mexico. Later, when the Mexican war ended, and the vast lands of the Southwest were ceded to the United States, the flow of American settlers grew. The Trail had great strategic significance in the Indian Wars, providing logistical support for the dispersed installations throughout the Southwest.

Raton Pass was a rugged challenge to all those who transited southwest on the Santa Fe Trail. In 1846, during the Mexican War, Susan Magoffin and her husband, Samuel, were among a large contingent of commercial merchants whose column trailed that of Colonel Doniphan into New Mexico, and on to Chihuahua in Mexico. In her diary, she journaled their five-day crossing through the pass. According to her records, the travelers stopped to rest, feed their oxen on the Purgatory River, and repair damaged wagons just before starting into the pass.[2]

When the Magoffin party resumed their trek and moved into the canyon, the magnitude of their challenge became immediately apparent with a wagon turning over on a hillock, smashing against the rocks. As they continued, their progress was sufficiently frustrating that Magoffin commented they were "traveling at the rate of half mile an hour, with the road growing worse and worse." Later, they disconnected mules from their carriages and had men manhandle carriages across the rocks instead. It took a dozen men to steady wagons on the boulder-strewn trail. On that day, they traveled "six to eight hundred yards during the day." Ultimately, they completed the slow and difficult transit through the pass and made it to their destination.[3]

Later, in 1866, "Uncle Dick" Wootton improved the trail through the pass, creating a passable trail. He then charged a toll for those crossing his road: 25 cents per person, $1.50 per wagon, 5 cents per head of cattle. Indians transited free. Travelers were much happier, the time reduced dramatically, and Uncle Dick made a fortune.[4] Concurrently, the volume of travelers increased.

Eveline Alexander, wife of Colonel Jonathan Alexander, was a latter-day version of Mrs. Magoffin. Seventeen years after the Magoffins, she noted in her 1866 diary that Wootton's road included wooden bridges that crossed the same creek fifty-seven times. Their transit time was reduced by more than half. Nevertheless, they still had to contend with stampedes, wild weather, and other difficulties.[5]

Before entering the pass, travelers like the Magoffins and Alexanders would pause, resting their animals, and preparing for the next stage of their journey. The prairie before the entrance to the pass was an excellent site for grazing and refreshing. Recognizing economic opportunity, this was exactly where Williams chose to put down roots.

Similarly, other migrants from "the states" into "the territories" found the nearby area on the Colorado side of the pass attractive to settle down. Thus emerged the town of Trinidad on the banks of the Purgatory River, and the front range of the Rocky Mountains. One of the first recorded settlers there was Gabriel Gutiérrez, who stopped to graze his sheep in 1859. Felipe Baca arrived about the same time, left for Denver and returned to settle.[6] Albert Archibald and his brother, Ebenezer, followed the Bacas and built the first house in 1860. By the next year, the population had expanded to twenty, and the race was on. By 1870, shortly before Williams entered the picture, the population was 4,276, and it doubled each decade thereafter through the 1890s.[7] In spite of the numbers, Trinidad was a long way from today's bustling town. Another veteran of the Eighth Cavalry, George Raper, passed through there in 1870 en route to his assignment in New Mexico. He described Trinidad as a "few scattering adobe shanties down near the river."[8]

Williams' selection of the El Moro site was logical. He was next to a ready source of water with the Purgatory River. His ranch occupied a large expanse of fertile grazing land on the Santa Fe Trail with a growing flow of settlers, posing a potential source of revenue. His location was convenient to the growing community of Trinidad, five miles away. Trinidad was the seat of Las Animas County, and as such would draw in folks that represented a buying public. Williams took advantage of the land and entered into the cattle business as a rancher. Not wasting any time, he established a general store, catering to the westward bound travelers on the trail. The store carried the elegant name, "J.M. Williams, Dealer and Jobber in Dry Goods, Clothing, Groceries and Crockery."[9] His land was a great place for travelers to refresh their livestock, re-provision their wagons from his general store, and prepare themselves before moving on through Raton Pass. In short order a tiny village emerged, getting its own post office.[10]

Ranching initially boomed for Williams. In the middle 1870s, tens of thousands of cattle—many of them Williams' own—grazed across the landscape around El Moro. But not everything was easy. Ute Indians, who had been resettled from northern New Mexico to southern Colorado, targeted settlers in the area well through the 1870s, with their last uprising in 1879. Utes had been resettled from northern New Mexico to southern Colorado between 1873 and 1877. Historically, they had resisted reservation life, asserting their rights to roam the land and hunt freely. Government response was measured, even to the 1873 treaty that secured their promise "to go to Colorado 'after a while.'"[11] Although there is no specific record of an attack upon Williams and his family, the stress of watchfulness would have extracted a price on their peace of mind.[12] In the late 1870s, a grasshopper plague laid waste the grazing land, which drastically reduced the number of cattle his land could support. In the same period, there was a national economic recession, further impacting Williams' business.[13]

Winter weather sometimes played havoc with business. Williams wrote a letter to a customer in January of 1878, noting that winter storms and extreme cold had prevented him from gathering sufficient steers, apparently to fulfill an order. He indicated that unless the weather broke, he would have to wait until the spring roundup to get as many steers as needed.[14]

El Moro was little or nothing when Williams arrived, just a pleasant prairie with a great view of nearby fourteen-thousand-foot peaks. It invited a pleasant country existence for Williams and his family. Soon, however, two factors created significant changes there in the late 1870s: railroads and coal. There was coal in Las Animas County, lots of coal. This coal was especially desired for its high quality and easy access (near the surface). It was discovered in 1848, when an officer of the Army's US Topographical Engineers, Major W.H. Emery, spotted ants picking small pieces of coal, and putting them around

Figure 37   Site of Williams' Ranch and General Store on Santa Fe Trail

This photograph, taken in 2010, shows the open space in southern Colorado. James Williams established his cattle ranch and general store here on the Santa Fe Trail, next to what became the village of El Moro. This view looks south to Trinidad, at the base of the mountain in the distance. The front range of the Rocky Mountains is to the right, or west. The Santa Fe Trail enters Raton Pass between the Rockies and to the right of the mountain in the photograph. Author's Collection.

their holes. He looked around, and noted lumps of bituminous coal scattered across the landscape. His observation led to the discovery of a thirteen hundred square mile coalfield immediately below the surface. Ultimately, the area around El Moro would produce six to seven thousand tons of coal daily.[15]

Nothing much happened with the coalfield, however, until the railroad arrived in 1878. The Denver and Rio Grande Railroad and the Santa Fe Railroad were in all out corporate warfare to get to the mineral deposits throughout Colorado and their attendant profits. The competitors fought viciously as they extended into the mountains to get rights to transport gold, silver, lead, and other minerals. About the time Colorado was admitted to the Union in 1876, the railroads pursued the coal trade in the northern part of the new state (1876). Then, casting their attention south, they looked at two prizes, coal in Las Animas County, and the route through Raton Pass. In 1878, the Denver and Rio Grande Railroad pushed its way into El Moro, and, together with its subsidiary, the Colorado Coal and Iron Company, began to mine coal and to build massive coke ovens for processing. The industrial ovens were soon belching smoke around the clock. Overnight, the population of El Moro jumped from a handful of people to eight hundred, almost all laborers for the coal company and the railroad roundhouse. At the same time, the Santa Fe Railroad beat the Denver and Rio Grande to Trinidad and Raton Pass. The fight between the railroads was at times bloody throughout Colorado. Finally, Jay Gould, the railroad magnate, mediated a solution, which divided the state into operating regions for each company.[16]

The advent of coal mining and railroads changed Williams' environment dramatically. His quiet, rural world turned upside down. Further, railroads played a role in withering away traffic on the Santa Fe Trail, cutting into revenues at the general store. At the same time, the cattle industry took a downturn in Colorado. Fences forever shut down the open range that cattlemen had enjoyed for a decade or more. Cattlemen were also smothered by the rapidly growing sheep industry. From 1870 to 1880, the number of sheep raised in Colorado grew from twenty thousand to more than two million.[17] Williams looked at the future for himself and his family in El Moro. He now had four sons ranging from newborn Robert Lincoln Williams to his oldest son, John, nearly ten years old. He made the decision to capitalize on the new boom, and chase other opportunities. He sold his land, cattle, and store, and moved into Trinidad in 1879.[18]

Figure 38   Mary Brawner Williams and Son, Robert L. Williams, 1879

Mary Brawner Williams gave birth to their fourth (and last) son, Robert Lincoln Williams in 1879, at Trinidad Colorado. Robert's elder brothers were John, James, and George. AUTHOR'S COLLECTION.

By then, Trinidad was bustling and growing rapidly. The population was around five thousand, with nearly seventeen thousand in the county.[19] It was a town of well-known and notorious characters. Kit Carson had been a regular until his death in the late 1860s. Bat Masterson was Trinidad's marshal in the 1880s and his good friend Doc Holliday frequented the streets. Charles Goodnight and Oliver Loving, the most famous of the Texas cattlemen, had driven their thousands of longhorns through the Trinidad area in the heyday of cattle on the plains. The Prairie Land and Cattle Company, holding sixteen million acres of land between Pueblo and Amarillo based its headquarters in Trinidad. The Atchison, Topeka and Santa Fe Railroad supported coal-coking plants in Trinidad, and had pushed through Raton Pass. The Denver and Rio Grande had finally extended its terminus from El Moro to Trinidad. Covered wagons continued to roll through the town, the creaking of the wheels and raucous yells of their passengers punctuated by the crack of bullwhips.[20]

Williams built a large, three-story house in Trinidad for his family. A newspaper article described it as a "Second Empire Revival style building, located at the southeast corner of West First and South Beech streets . . . the largest known extant adobe building in the city of Trinidad." As befitted a man now labeled "pioneer," Williams built the house on a hillside only one block off Main Street, the town's commercial center. The building's third floor consisted of a mansard roof and gabled windows. Wood shutters, doors, trim, and a second-floor balcony graced the façade of the building. The house, like many others, seemed to be a work in progress. A local newspaper noted on November 1, 1882, that Williams was "remodeling the house, putting in a couple bay windows. The Major will have one of the finest residences in town."[21] A competing paper carried its own story on November 9, "The 'Williams House' on the hill having been completed presents a very improved appearance, proving that the major is fully up with the times regarding a handsome residence."[22]

In 1882, Williams started a lumber and sawmill business in Trinidad, as well as a lumber business in Lamar. His Lamar business was over 130 miles distant, and proved to be too much strain for Williams. He sold it four years later, in 1886. His health was deteriorating and, in 1887, he sold his businesses in Trinidad, and retired. The old arrow wounds in his back were becoming increasingly painful and debilitating. He was frequently unable to move around outside his own room, and was often bed-ridden.[23]

Figure 39   James Williams' House, Trinidad, Colorado

This house was the largest adobe structure in Trinidad when it was first built in 1879. The house—photographed in 2010—is still in use today. AUTHOR'S COLLECTION.

Williams converted part of his huge home into a boarding house in 1888.[24] Partially disabled, and with a potentially uncertain future for his family if they remained in Trinidad, Williams placed his house up for rent in 1889.[25]

In 1890, at age sixty-seven, he packed up his family and relocated to Washington, DC, finding circumstances more comfortable for his family.[26] His oldest son, John (by then twenty years old), remained in Trinidad as an employee of Colorado Coal and Iron Company.[27]

In June 1890, Williams received a letter which provided an enormous boost to his morale. It emanated from a meeting of veterans of nine black regiments. It included the text of a resolution celebrating the military service of black men in all wars from the Revolution through the Civil War, in particular noting the men of the First and Second Kansas Colored Volunteer Infantry Regiments, and First Independent Battery of Light Artillery. It recognized Williams' leadership and command of the Seventy-Ninth Colored Infantry, and the other regiments in his brigade. The resolution commended his actions in Washington to secure recognition and legislative support for black veterans.[28]

That October, Williams made a special trip to Leavenworth, Kansas to attend a Grand Army of the Republic (G.A.R.) reunion of the regiments and brigade he commanded in the Civil War. Crowds of veterans gathered in the town to welcome him in grand style on October 7. The *Leavenworth Times'* headlines trumpeted his return to Kansas,

> A REUNION, A Perfect Love Feast Held at G.A.R. Hall. Colonel J. M. Williams Arrives in the City and Draws a Big Crowd, Especially Among the Colored People – They Think More of Col. Williams Than of Any Man Living To-day – He Was Besieged All Day – A Big Gathering at the G.A.R. Hall Last Night – A Big Demonstration – Music and Speaking and Applauding – Col. Williams, Col. Anthony, Col. Gilpatrick and Others Make Ringing Speeches – Resolutions Passed – Refreshments.[29]

The newspaper noted that since Williams' move to Washington, he had used his time on behalf of the men who had served under his command during the Civil War. Williams was the central feature of the newspaper on that day. "The occasion of the gathering was the arrival in the city yesterday of Col. J. M. Williams, who during the late war was brigadier general of the colored regiments of Kansas, Arkansas and Missouri." The newspaper presented him as a prodigal son, reporting that he was "well known throughout [that] section of the country," and that his "brilliant war record and achievements [made] him beloved by all who were under his command."[30]

All day long, former soldiers barraged Williams with greetings. That evening, a brass band led a large contingent of veterans with Williams in their midst through the streets of Leavenworth as they marched on Garfield Hall for preliminary meetings and conferences. Afterward, they continued to the G.A.R. Hall, where the reunion was in full swing. As they neared the building and a huge crowd of its celebrants, the band swung into "Marching Through Georgia." A roar went through the crowd, greeting Williams and the other dignitaries. As they took their seats on the stage, the group of dignitaries with Williams included his old friend, Captain William Matthews, for whom Williams had secured a commission in 1862, making him one of the first black commissioned officers in the army. William D. Kelly, a veteran of the Fifty-Fourth Massachusetts Infantry called the session to order at 8:00 p.m. An election of G.A.R officers was held, and Captain Matthews elected chairman.

Matthews then took charge of the meeting, and greeted the distinguished guests. He recognized Williams as the first commander of black troops, with the First Kansas Colored Volunteer Infantry. He also recognized Samuel Crawford as commander of the Second Kansas Colored Volunteer Infantry (and former governor of Kansas), and Crawford's successor, Colonel James H. Gilpatrick of the Eighty-Third US Colored Infantry. Matthews detailed the triumphs of those regiments, and then formally introduced Williams as a speaker. The introduction elicited a roar from the crowd and an ovation lasting more than a minute.[31]

Williams began his speech by pointing out that when he recruited the First Kansas Colored Volunteer Infantry, skin color was not an issue with him; all he wanted was "someone who could whip the enemies of the government of the United States." He recalled that for many opposed to building the regiment; skin color was an issue, particularly some local governmental authorities. He continued, "I believe to-day there are four indictments against me on file in the court house for enlisting colored troops. I consider them papers of honor. . . . They undertook to arrest me, but I did not fear them. I would do it again." It was an emotional moment for him as well as his former comrades. "I am so proud to meet so many of these men who took up their muskets in the war; and of those who started in with the old First Kansas regiment and went through with me." Then, he focused upon the quality of the men with whom he served:

On investigating the records of the war department I came upon the records of the different regiments in the United States service. I found that there is not on file in the war office the records of a single regiment that begins with the record of the old First Kansas. The records there show that you lost more men in proportion to the number enlisted, than any regiment in the United States service of any color. The records show that you lost more men in a single engagement in proportion to the number enlisted than any regiment in the United States service. . . . There is nothing in the whole world in referring to any engagement that begins to compare with the action of the First Kansas Regiment at Poison Springs. . . . There was nothing that so impressed me as that engagement when I rode down the line. In that engagement 46 per cent of your men were either killed or wounded; and still that line was as perfect as when first formed. Not a single man had fallen back one foot. . . . There is nothing in history, not only in the history of the recent war, nothing in modern history, nothing from Thermopylae to Appomattox which show the spirit which was shown by the First Kansas regiment on that day.[32]

He went on to discuss his discovery that there was no record of the Battle of Island Mound in the War Department. Seemingly, that was because it had taken place before the regiment formally mustered into Federal service. He was able to correct that oversight. When he concluded with an expression of his thanks for the honor of being at the meeting, there was a loud and long ovation. His speech was followed by many others, and the applause for them was just as enthusiastic. A resolution presented to the assembly honoring the commander, officers, and men of the First Kansas Colored, recognized their honor "of being in the van and influencing the immortal Lincoln in bringing about the freedom of our race." The resolution singled out for praise Senator C.K. Davis of Minnesota, and Representative O.B. Thomas for their role in presenting legislation to benefit black soldiers.[33] The events in the G.A.R. Hall that night, thirty-five years after the Civil War, likely brought a lump to the throat of many an old soldier.

That year, 1890, continued to be a huge boost for Williams. The G.A.R. reunion was heartwarming, while simultaneously another momentous event was shaping up to cap Williams' life. Earlier in the year, General Gregg,

Williams' regimental commander in the Indian Wars, and New Mexico District Commander, went before the Committee on Military Affairs of the US Senate, supporting an effort to have Williams' military record cleared, and to provide him a pension. He tendered a letter, pointing out Williams' exemplary service in the Civil War and the Indian Wars. In it, he cited examples of special consideration granted to several of the most senior general officers at the end of the Civil War, noting that Williams served the country for more years than they had. He wrote, "If there were any special reasons why any or all of a number of officers who within the last few years have been appointed and placed on the retired list should have been so appointed . . . the same special and particular reasons exist in stronger force in the case of Captain Williams.[34]

Gregg went on to cite Williams' contributions in the Indian Wars. He said, "Of Captain Williams's services and their value to the country I can speak intelligently . . . and I have no doubt but his operations definitely settled the Indian question in that part of Arizona." He went on to say that the Indians "never recovered from the stunning blows he dealt them, nor have they since molested that portion of the Territory."[35]

The Committee on Military Affairs reviewed the entirety of Gregg's letter, Williams' military record, and the proceedings of the court martial that led to his resignation. They summarized his service thus:

> During his volunteer service, Colonel Williams received four gunshot wounds, and had three horses shot under him; and his conspicuous gallantry, with the conscientious discharge of duty in connection with the organization, discipline, and command of this colored regiment, at a time when the performance of such duty carried with it a degree of approbrium now difficult to appreciate, secured him a brevet of brigadier-general of volunteers, and upon the enlargement and reorganization on of the regular Army, after the close of the rebellion, an appointment as captain of the Eighth Cavalry.
>
> The promise which Captain Williams gave as a volunteer officer was more than confirmed by his career in the regular service. He proved himself one of the most efficient of the Indian fighters on the frontier, winning encomiums from his superiors, and a major's brevet conferred, in engagements with Indians. [36]

222   ★   James M. Williams

The Committee concluded that "Captain Williams was the victim of . . . legalized injustice." They noted that the charges against Williams emanated from "an officer, who was afterwards dishonorably dismissed the service for infamous crimes clearly proven."[37] They further remarked that Williams' "sentence was never carried into effect, but was left for months to hang over the head of this gallant officer . . . until, smarting under the outrage of such legalized injustice, he resigned." The Committee's final recommendation was the passage of Senate Bill 1037, to restore James Williams' rank and award him a pension.[38] The bill passed. Accordingly, it required the re-commissioning of Williams as a Captain of Cavalry on January 7, 1891, signed by President Benjamin Harrison on January 12, 1891, and Williams was retired with a pension.[39] With his name and reputation restored, he was vindicated.

After that, life passed quietly for Williams. He was a participating member of the Military Order of the Loyal Legion of the United States (MOLLUS)—a predecessor organization of the Military Officer's Association of America (MOAA)—but kept a low profile.[40]

Even in retirement, and with physical limitations, Williams could not pass up one more opportunity to get involved in history-making events. On April 16, 1898, he penned a letter to the Secretary of War, General Russell Alger, offering his services in the brewing conflict between the United States and Spain. He indicated that he hoped for a negotiated peace, but if the parties could not secure peace, and the matter descended into a war, he said, "In case of an appeal to arms for the settlement of the controversy, I desire to offer my services to the Government of the US." He was well intentioned, but the conduct of the Spanish-American War played out without his assistance as an aging, disabled former soldier.[41]

James Monroe Williams died on February 15, 1907 in Washington, DC. His death certificate notes that a primary cause of death was kidney failure—possibly related to wounds he suffered in Arizona in 1867 and the arrowhead that remained in this kidney. The Military Order of the Loyal Legion of the United States conducted ceremonies at his home in Washington. Afterwards, Troop G, Thirteenth Cavalry escorted the cortege through the city to Arlington National Cemetery, where he was buried with full military honors. He was survived by his wife, Mary Elizabeth (Brawner).[42]

Figure 40   The Mission Continues

US Cavalry on Scout. Troopers from Fort Bayard move out on patrol. Arizona, Southwestern and Borderlands Collection, courtesy University of Arizona Libraries, Special Collections.

Chapter Eighteen

Conclusion

Like Theodore Roosevelt's "Man in the Arena," James Monroe Williams was the man on the ground when American history happened. He was not a spectator. Wherever he was, and whenever the muses of history needed a catalyst, he made it happen. He did so as a Jayhawker in the days of the antebellum conflict over slavery as it played out across the landscapes of Kansas and Missouri. He led his Jayhawking team into the first year of the war commanding them as a company of cavalry. Undeterred by social or political concerns, he stepped across the ethnic line ahead of his peers, recruiting and leading a regiment of escaped slaves who became outstanding infantrymen, amassing an enviable combat record. He went toe-to-toe, never backing away from a fight with an implacable Southern foe who might have been a neighbor before the Civil War. He led regiments and a brigade into battles involving black men, white men, and Indians in a theater of war not yet understood by most historians. He led postwar cavalrymen in Southwestern deserts and mountains in brutal campaigns against Apaches, Yavapai, and Hualapai. Afterward, he settled as a rancher and business man on a rugged and unforgiving frontier at the foot of the Rocky Mountains. Even as an old man debilitated by wounds, he volunteered to fight the Spanish in Cuba and the Philippines. His story is worth telling because it spans so many different aspects of American history in which he was personally involved every step of the way. He made a difference.

He shaped history just as much as it shaped him. An affirmed abolitionist, he supported the underground railroad, participated in the Kansas Free-State movement, recruited and led a regiment and, later, a brigade of former slaves in the crusade to re-unite the country and abolish slavery. He led his men to victories in the Trans-Mississippi Theater of war, which gave them dignity, pride, and value as soldiers and citizens. He and his soldiers earned the respect of their enemies. His legacy is that of the leaders of his time.

In spite of his extensive experience and contributions, no one has taken a comprehensive look at James Williams and written his story. His name appears in many books, but never as the central character. Many formal histories make mention of Williams, even as a child on the New York and Wisconsin frontiers. Edwin Bearss, the iconic Civil War historian, wrote of the "important role Williams and his regiment and later his brigade played in the war . . . a man who played a significant role in our nation."[1] Robert Utley, distinguished historian of the Indian Wars, in *Frontier Regulars*, praised Williams as one of few officers "skilled in guerrilla warfare and as perfectly tuned to the natural environment as the Apaches."[2] Dan Thrapp, author of *The Conquest of Apacheria*, lauded Williams as "one of the most successful Indian fighters of the period."[3] Williams and the First Kansas Colored appear in histories written about the general experience of black soldiers in the Union army, but most only do so in passing. Williams and the regiment emerge from time to time in various Civil War journals and magazines. There are numerous primary sources of information about Williams, ranging from local histories to the National Archives. No one, however, has tapped into these resources to produce a single biography until now. Few biographies exist of other such men whose personal experience incorporated westward migration, Civil War, Indian Wars, and frontier settlement. Williams' story is unique.

The First Kansas Colored Volunteer Infantry Regiment was his entire world from 1862 until 1865. Williams recruited, trained, and led the regiment before it was legal to do so. He commissioned black officers before it was legal to do so. He risked arrest and imprisonment by doing so. Having the courage of his convictions, he risked his life in battle to make change.

The First Kansas Colored Infantry was special. They were in the vanguard of black regiments. They stand out as both the first black regiment to fight under the same command as white men, and the first non-white regiment to fight against non-white regiments. They fought many engagements against uneven odds, facing almost certain death, or at least slavery, if captured. They earned the respect of white soldiers around them, even their enemies. Most importantly, they made a difference in the outcomes of their campaigns and battles.

The First Kansas Colored Volunteer Infantry made history, yet no one has authored a nonfiction book about their history either. A number of outstanding authors have included the First Kansas in books and articles, though, which have contributed greatly to this book. Chris Tabor published a study of the regiment's first battle at Island Mound in October 1862, near Butler, Missouri.[4] It is a single publication and an excellent analysis of a historically significant event, which was only one of many such events in the regiment's three-year history. Peripheral to his analysis, he included commentary about other events in the history of the regiment, but a complete history of the regiment still needs telling.

It is possible that that some of the absence of books and memoirs specifically about the First Kansas Colored may be a function of the fact that the vast majority of the soldiers in the regiment, being former slaves, were illiterate. As such, their writing of soldier narratives did not keep pace with their compatriots in other Northern regiments, such as the Fifty-Fourth Massachusetts. Certainly, the regiment's genesis west of the Mississippi River kept it from getting the attention and publicity afforded other regiments in the East. Its turn will come.

Williams' actions showed that he loved and cared for his soldiers, even to the extent of publishing guidance about being careful with their pay, a new experience for former slaves. He fought for them to be paid, and to be paid equally. He exposed himself to arrest and prosecution when he shielded his men from oppressive civil government and law enforcement. After he was carried from the field with three gunshot wounds at Honey Springs, the first question he asked of General Blunt when he came to visit Williams in the hospital was an inquiry about how his men did in the battle. He stayed on the firing line with his men in the heat of the Confederate onslaught at Poison Spring. He knew his men formed an extraordinary regiment. The 1890 reunion with his fellow veterans at Leavenworth was a high point in his life.

James Williams' story in antebellum Kansas, specifically the time from 1856 to 1861, provides significant perspective and insight to the years of "Bleeding Kansas." Abolitionist groups in New England underwrote many of the northerners who flooded into Kansas seeking to prevent its admission to the Union as a slave state. Idealistic purposes, the possibility of excitement, or good old-fashioned capitalistic opportunism drove others, like Williams. He arrived in Leavenworth when it was a boomtown, established a business, started a family, and, equally as fast, involved himself in the Free-State movement. He displayed his deep committment when writing of his role in the recovery of "Old Kickapoo." He said, "I hope Free Kansas may forever keep it as a memento of the triumph of the "Free State Boys" over those who would blacken the soil with the curse of African Slavery." Together with future general William Tecumseh Sherman, he risked his life rescuing an escaped slave from Missouri Border Ruffians. He educated his men, trained them as soldiers, led them in battle, treated them with dignity, and gave them America.

Historically, there are legions of stories about Border Ruffians and Bushwhackers running amok amongst the well-meaning settlers of Kansas. The feud between Kansas and Missouri was, however, along the lines of "an eye for an eye." Kansas Jayhawkers raided into Missouri and pro-slavery enclaves within Kansas as often as Missourians did in Kansas. There are fewer of those stories. Williams commanded one such Kansas organization under the purview of James Henry Lane. He found the action to be exciting, providing transition into command of a company in the Fifth Kansas Cavalry during the first year of the Civil War.

James Williams boldly recruited and raised a black regiment. He was a "volunteer," not a regular army officer. He had no formal military training. He learned how to command, administer, organize, and train his regiment on the fly and from a manual, figuratively firing a pistol with one hand, grasping his manual in the other, with his saber clenched in his teeth. The majority of his men were illiterate, and strangers in a white world. Nevertheless, he got the job done—he had his men in combat even before their training was complete. He did not come close to the description noted earlier that characterized him as a commander selected for the ease with which he could be politically controlled. Instead, he "proved to be an independent military leader who strongly advocated for the rights and abilities of his men."[5]

His tactics were neither complex nor elegant. When attacked, he counter-attacked. He formed his men to meet enemy formations. He effectively employed infantry, cavalry, and artillery together. His enemy outnumbered him more often than not; regardless, he also defeated his enemy more often than not. The enemy defeated him only when overwhelming odds were in their favor. No matter how bleak the circumstances, he never ran from a fight.

Williams led his unusual regiment in an unusual theater of war. He fought alongside and commanded Indian and white units as well as his own black regiments. He fought against Confederate Indians and their white allies. His alter egos were a Cherokee brigadier general, Stand Watie, of the Confederate Indian Brigade, and a Confederate colonel, Charles DeMorse of the Twenty-ninth Texas Cavalry.

His Indian opposition came from different tribes, with differing perspectives, including Cherokee, Creek, Choctaw, and Chickasaw. While Williams was engaged in that form of war, the Indians themselves, especially the Cherokee, were undergoing a brutal Civil War within the larger Civil War. Thus, Federal Cherokees fought Confederate Cherokees.

As a brevet brigadier general, Williams commanded one of the few black brigades in the Union Army. His brigade had as many as six black infantry regiments under his command, as well as white artillery units. Some of these regiments, especially his own First Kansas Colored Infantry (re-designated as the Seventy-Ninth Colored Infantry), experienced combat well before the vast majority of black regiments mustered into service.

Williams experienced the dramatic transition from the Civil War to the Indian Wars in the West, in an army with 95 percent fewer soldiers. Operations took place in an environment wildly rugged and deadly in its own right. His enemies were elusive, and fought their battles hit-and-run style rather than toe-to-toe. They were wily, brave, and strong-willed. The small army's security mission covering vast areas of the country forced the fragmentation of regiments into small, widely dispersed enclaves. The transition was difficult, stressful, and sometimes hostile. Most of the officers in the postwar army, including Williams, had held much higher rank in the Civil War, and commanded large numbers of troops. Adapting to the new reality was difficult. The army itself evolved into a new culture, however, and somehow got the job done

Williams' early success in battles with the Indians of Arizona brought him accolades and a brevet promotion. Higher command credited him with eliminating the Indian conflict in the region of Arizona in which he operated. However, after recuperating from two arrow wounds, and bringing a new bride into the mix, his perspective changed. The camaraderie of the Civil

War was missing. The cohesiveness and sense of purpose was no longer there. Petty bickering and political infighting were routine, and Williams experienced them from all angles. Although he had a close relationship with his regimental commander, Williams never got along with the executive officer. Williams' experience was characteristic, and while fighting with Indians was exciting fodder for pulp novels and later in motion pictures, much of frontier military life was far from the popular image. Williams was disillusioned.

Just as in the Civil War, he took pains to improve the lot of his soldiers. Like other leaders through the ages, he scrounged, begged, borrowed, and misappropriated property to improve the lot of his soldiers. He stretched and broke rules wherever necessary to get the job done. Another officer, seeking recognition, noted Williams' acts, and reported him. The resulting legal action against Williams added to his dissatisfaction with the frontier army and led to his resignation.

Williams experienced life on the western frontier as a pioneer and settler. He was a rancher in the waning days of the open range and Santa Fe Trail. He was a merchant and entrepreneur. He raised a family in the Rocky Mountain West. He built up his ranch and cared for his family on the open range and under the threat of attack from Ute Indians.

Nineteenth-century America was a land of strong-willed citizens, and Williams was definitely one of them. He was not particularly demonstrative, but had a personality and drive that inspired confidence and placed him in leadership roles. He did not travel in large circles of friends, but his friends were loyal. He did not have a close relationship with James Lane, but they apparently had great respect for each other. Lane demonstrated his confidence in Williams by selecting him, instead of more senior and experienced officers, in command of a company and, later, a regiment. Lane's contacts with President Lincoln in protecting Williams as a regimental commander ratified that respect. His correspondence with Williams was straightforward and uncomplicated, reflecting confidence. General Blunt showed substantial confidence in Williams by placing Williams' regiment in the center of the line against the Confederates at Honey Springs. His praise of Williams was effusive, and his support continued beyond the Civil War. General Gregg, commander of the Eighth Cavalry, shared a friendship with Williams that lasted until late in their lives. He always gave Williams autonomy in command. He saved Williams' life while fighting Indians. And decades later, he went to extreme measures in going to the United States Congress to clear Williams' name.

Williams was a decisive, independent thinker. He was willing to commit himself, and did not back away from his commitments. He backed up his commitments with actions, even if it meant risking his life. He was aggressive—he never dodged a fight—but at the same time, he was literate, articulate, and devoted to his family. He was an American in every sense of the word.

America came of age in the nineteenth century. It was not a smooth transition—the events of those times tested its mettle as a nation—but it emerged proudly. James Williams was an integral part of that process, reflecting the events of national history, and his contributions made a difference. An understanding of his role opens a valuable window into the heart of the nation, providing a glimpse of one kind of person who helped to lead the country through difficult times.

Appendix

Senate Report 1002
51st Congress, 1st Session

IN THE SENATE OF THE UNITED STATES

May 15, 1890 – Ordered to be printed.

Mr. Davis, from the Committee on Military Affairs, submitted the
following
REPORT
(To accompany S. 1037)

The Committee on Military Affairs to whom was referred the bill (S.1037) authorizing the placing of the name of James M. Williams upon the retired list of the U.S. Army, with the rank of captain of cavalry, have examined the same and report:

The army record of James M. Williams, late captain of the Eighth Cavalry, shows he entered the volunteer service in July, 1861, as captain of the Fifth Kansas Cavalry, and served therewith until September, 1862, when he accepted an appointment as lieutenant-colonel of the First Kansas Colored Volunteers—afterwards the Seventy-ninth United States Colored Troops;

that he was promoted to be colonel of that regiment and served therewith until May, 1864, when he took command of a brigade, retaining such command until near his muster out in October, 1865.

His record in the volunteer service was exceptionally good. He was among the first to approve the policy of utilizing the colored men as troops on the Union side and giving them the opportunity, by displays of courage and self-control, to demonstrate their fitness for the freedom that awaited them and the higher duties of citizenship with which they were to be invested. He enlisted, equipped, and mustered into service the First Kansas Colored Volunteers, which afterwards became distinguished as the Seventy-ninth Colored Troops. While in command of this colored regiment it participated in engagements at Cabin Creek in June [July], 1863, at Honey Springs in July, 1863, and at Poison Springs April, 1864, in which last action 40 per cent of the men engaged were killed and wounded, and 22 per cent were left dead on the field. Of an action at Elk Creek, C.N., in which the regiment was engaged July 17, 1863, General Blunt, in his official report thus speaks.

> Much credit is due to all of them for their gallantry. The First Kansas Colored particularly distinguished itself; they fought like veterans, and preserved their line unbroken throughout the engagement. Their coolness and bravery I have never seen surpassed; they were in the hottest of the fight, and opposed to Texas troops twice their number, whom they completely routed. One Texas regiment (the Twentieth Cavalry) that fought against them went into the fight with 300 men and came out with only 60. It would be invidious to make particular mention of anywhere all did their duty so well.

General [John] McNeil, on assuming command of Fort Smith, Ark., November 2, 1863, bears the following testimony to the thoroughness of the drill and discipline of this regiment:

> On Saturday, I reviewed the First Arkansas Infantry Volunteers, First Colored Infantry Kansas Volunteers, and Rabbi's[sic] Battery. The negro regiment is a triumph of drill and discipline and reflects great honor on Colonel Williams, in command. Few volunteer regiments that I have seen make a better appearance. I regard them as first-rate infantry.

During his volunteer service, Colonel Williams received four gunshot wounds, and had three horses shot under him; and his conspicuous gallantry, with the conscientious discharge of duty in connection with the organization, discipline, and command of this colored regiment, at a time when the performance of such duty carried with it a degree of opprobrium now difficult to appreciate, secured him a brevet of brigadier-general of volunteers, and upon the enlargement and reorganization of the regular Army, after the close of the rebellion, an appointment as captain of the Eighth Cavalry.

The promise which Captain Williams gave as a volunteer officer was more than confirmed by his career in the regular service. He proved himself one of the most efficient of the Indian fighters on the frontier, winning encomiums from his superiors, and a major's brevet conferred, according to the army record, "for conspicuous gallantry displayed in engagements with Indians on the Verde, Arizona, April 19 and 17, in Yampa, Valley, June 14, 1867, and near Music Mountain, Arizona, July 9, 1867." In this latter action Captain Williams was wounded with two arrows, the head of one of which he still carries. The other injured his spine, which confined him in hospital and on nominal duty nearly two years, and from the effects of which he has never recovered. The injury to his spine has seriously affected his nervous system, producing nervous prostration, and by wrecking his health, has incapacitated him from gaining a livelihood by work. He was undergoing treatment for these wounds when the law permitting retirement, which expired in 1868, was still in force; and it was recommended to him by his superiors that his condition not merely justified, but required him to take advantage of its provisions. He had, however, faith in his recuperative powers, and believing that he would recover, declined to be retired. He was able to return to duty, but finding he could not again endure the fatigues and privations of frontier service, he afterwards made and unsuccessful application for retirement; and following this failure, and under the circumstances hereinafter detailed, he resigned.

A system like the military, which is founded upon unquestioning obedience, becomes of necessity technical in its spirit and administration, with little chance for equity to modify the strict letter of regulations and law; and while it fosters the noblest, permits the exercise of the most ignoble qualities of human character. During the closing years of his service, Captain Williams was the victim of this permissory and legalized injustice. In 1871, while stationed at Fort Bayard, N.Mex., Captain Williams allowed the forage savings of his company to be applied to the purchase of lumber and other materials which were needed for reconstruction and repair of quarters that were dilapidated and unfit for shelter and use. The rebuilding and repair occurred under the eye of the commanding officer of the post, and remained unquestioned for more than a year, when an officer, who was afterwards dishonorably dismissed the service for infamous crimes clearly proven, discovered a technical irregularity on the part of Captain Williams, and preferred charges against him. These were made the subject of a court-martial; and while it was proved that the repairs were needed, were judiciously executed, and that the forage funds were economically and honestly applied to such purpose, yet it was shown that there had been a carelessness of detail involving a technical violation of an act of Congress. The committee's judgment upon the transaction is sustained in an official review of the case by Judge-Advocate-General Hold, in which he says:

> The transfer of corn of which accused is convicted under the first charge (the only charge under which there was conviction), was not denied by him. It is, however, shown that this forage, which had been saved from the authorized allowance for the horses of his company, was exchanged by him for lumber with which to repair his own and his men's quarters, all of which were very dilapidated and insufficient. There is good reason also to believe that these transactions, which took place fifteen months before his trial, were known to his commanding officer, who tolerated if he did not expressly sanction them. In this view of the case, it is thought while the unauthorized disposition made by accused of public property under his charge clearly constituted and offense under the fraud act of March 2, 1863, which denounces all such acts without reference to the motive prompting them, yet that accused was innocent of any dishonest or corrupt purpose.

The sentence of the court-martial upon the facts detailed above, which, reviewed by the highest judicial officer connected with the War Department, showed that the transaction conferred a needed benefit to the troops under Captain Williams's charge, and concerning which, in the language of such reviewing officer, "accused was innocent of any dishonest or corrupt purpose," was, that Captain Williams –

Be dismissed and cashiered the service, and refund to the United States the sum of $153.71 and be confined at such place as the proper authority may direct, until such time as the sum of money aforesaid shall be refunded, and that the crime, place of abode, name of the accused, and the sentence of the court martial be published in the Las Cruces Recorder, Santa Fé New Mexican, and the Leavenworth Times;

thus surrounding what was at most a technical, and might even be termed a virtuous, violation of law, with all the opprobrium and disgrace which can be made to attach to the willful commission of an infamous crime. This sentence was never carried into effect, but it was left for months to hang over the head of the gallant officer, whose nervous system was shattered by years of suffering from his wounds, until smarting under the outrage of such legalized injustice, he resigned. This case is exceptional in its meritorious features.

The committee call attention to the following letter, addressed by Col. J.I. Gregg, U.S. Army, retired, to the chairman of the committee; and following the suggestions of Captain Williams's regimental commander, as well as the conclusions which are sustained by the record in the case, they report the bill favorably, and recommend its passage.

Washington, 2025 G st., January 9, 1890

Sir: I notice that a bill has been introduced into the United States Senate, and referred to the military committee for report, to appoint James M. Williams, of Trinidad, Colo., late a captain in the Eighth United States Cavalry, a captain in the Army and to place him on the retired list.

I believe this is not only a proper bill to be passed, but a bill that simple justice to a gallant and meritorious officer, disabled in the service of the country, demands be passed without a dissenting vote.

If there were any special reasons why any or all of a number of officers who within the last few years have been appointed and placed on the retired list should have been so appointed, or if there is any special reason why the pending bill to appoint General J. C. Fremont a major-general in the Army and place him on the retired list should pass, the same special and particular reasons exist in stronger force in the case of Captain Williams.

In the cases of General Pleasanton, general Averill, and General Rosecrans, they each left the Army immediately after the close of the war of the rebellion for other reasons than disability occurring in the line of duty. Captain Williams, who entered the volunteer service at the beginning of the rebellion, remained in it until the war ended and then accepted a commission in the regular service of the United States tendered him for his valuable services. In this capacity he continued to render to the country most valuable services against hostile Indians in Arizona, in which he received the disabling wounds which have rendered his life on of prolonged suffering, almost entirely unfitting him for the successful prosecution of any kind of active business.

Captain Williams came under my command in February, 1867, and from that time until he received the wounds from which he is still suffering he was constantly in the field, active, energetic, judicious, and efficient.

Of Captain Williams's services and their value to the country I can speak intelligently, as they were rendered in obedience to my orders and partly under my personal supervision, and I have no doubt but his operations definitely settled the Indian question in that part of Arizona. They never recovered from the stunning blows he dealt them, nor have they since molested that portion of the Territory.

The official reports of Captain Williams's superior officers, to which I respectfully call your attention, ought to be alone sufficient to secure for him favorable consideration and action on his application.

The one special or particular reason why Captain Williams's bill for appointment and retirement ought to be favorable considered is the he declined to make application to be retired in 1868 when there is no question but that he would have been placed upon the retired list, but hoping that he might recover sufficiently to enable him to perform further service he, after a long period, returned to his command. Finding, however, himself unable to perform all the duties incident to his position, he made, in 1870, an application to be retired, which was not favorably acted upon by the board of officers. After his application to be placed upon the retired list, to which he was undoubtedly entitled by every rule of justice, Captain Williams remained in the service for one or two years, but being unable to perform all the duties incident to his position he tendered his resignation rather than continue to draw pay for services he could not render.

There can not be any doubt Captain Williams was entitled to and could have been placed upon the retired list in 1868, and his declining to take advantage of this opportunity ought not now be made to operate to his prejudice. I sincerely hope the committee will find sufficient merit in this case to warrant them in bringing in a most favorable report, and that Captain Williams may speedily be placed in the position, he should have been in more than twenty years ago.

Respectfully,

J. Irwin Gregg
Colonel, U.S. Army, Retired
The Chairman Committee on Military Affairs
United States Senate

Notes

Introduction

1. United States, War Department, General Order 97, *J.M. Williams, Col, 1 Kan. Colored Vols. Appointed to be Brigadier General by Brevet in the Volunteer Force, Army of the United States, effective February 13, 1865, Washington, D.,* 26 May 1865.

2. Lewis County Historian Office (New York), "Williams (Absalom)," Genealogical record, Absalom Williams family, Lowville, New York, n.d.

3. Dorothy K. Duflo, *Lowville,* Images of America, with a foreword by Charlotte M. Beagle (Charleston: Arcadia, 2009), 7.

4. Ibid., 41.

5. Franklin B. Hough, *A History of Lewis County in the State of New York from the Beginning of Its Earliest Settlement to the Present Time,* (Albany: Munsell & Rowland, 1860), 148.

6. Lewis County, New York, *Grantee Index, Lewis County, New York, Liber P,* p. 289-291; *Grantor Index, Lewis County, New York, Liber I,* p. 146; *Liber S,* pp. 330, 484; *Liber U,* p. 72. Absalom Williams sold more land than he bought, according to records. As he settled in Lowville approximately twenty years before his first recorded purchase of land, it is likely that he obtained his first acreage before the county established formal records

7. *Census of the State of New York for the Year 1825,* Town of Lowville, Lewis County, New York," New Horizons Genealogy, accessed May 2, 2010, http://www.newhorizons genealogicalservices.com/1825-census-ny-lewis-lowville.htm.

8. Henry P. Johnson, ed., *The Record of Connecticut Men in the Military and Naval Service during the War of the Revolution 1775-1783* (Clearfield: Connecticut Historical Society, 1997), 177.

9. Hough, 299-302.

10. New York, "List of Claims to the State of New York for Arms and Clothing Provided by Individual Members of the State Militia, No. 15106," *Index of Awards on Claims of the Soldiers of the War of 1812* (Albany: New Adjutant General's Office, 1880), 540.

11. Alexis De Tocqueville, *Democracy in America,* translated by Henry Reeve, Vol. 1 (New York: D. Appleton, 1904), 81.

12. A. Judd Northrup, "Slavery in New York: A Historical Sketch," *State Library Bulletin: History*, No. 4 (May 1900), 292, 294, 299.

13. Michael L. Lanning, *Defenders of Liberty: African-Americans in the Revolutionary War* (New York: Kensington Press, 2000), 82.

14. Daniel W. Howe, *What Hath God Wrought: The Transformation of America, 1815–1848* (New York: Oxford University Press, 2007), 136–137.

15. Albert Clayton Beckwith, *History of Walworth County Wisconsin*, Vol. 1 (Indianapolis: B.F. Bowen & Co., 1912), 353.

16. Wisconsin, General Land Office Records, Southeastern Wisconsin, accessed 2 May 2010, http://searches.rootsweb.com/cgi-bin /wisconsin/wisconsin.pl.

17. United States Census Bureau, *1850 Census*, accessed November 21, 2009, http://www.ancestry.com.

18. *Who Was Who in America*, Vol. 1 (Chicago: Marquis, 1950).

19. Ibid.

Chapter 1

1. Anna E. Arnold, *A History of Kansas* (Topeka: State Printing Plant, 1914), 46–48.

2. Nicole Etcheson, *Bleeding Kansas: Contested Liberty in the Civil War Era* (Lawrence: University Press of Kansas, 2004), 29.

3. William G. Cutler, *History of the State of Kansas* (Chicago: A.T. Andreas, 1883), accessed May 12, 2010, http://www.kancoll.org/books/cutler/.

4. H. Miles Moore, *Early History of Leavenworth City and County* (Leavenworth: Sam'l Dodsworth Book Co., 1906), 18.

5. Ibid., 26.

6. "Milwaukee Kansas Aid Society Beaten all to Pieces," *Daily Sentinel* (Milwaukee, Wisconsin), 22 April 1856; "Great Meeting at Market Hall, 'The Wrongs of Kansas,' Speech of Colonel Lane," *Republican Sentinel* (Beaver Dam, Wisconsin), 25 May 1856; *Fountain City Herald*, (Fond du Lac, Wisconsin), June 10, 1856.

7. *Leavenworth City Directory and Business Mirror for 1859–60* (St. Louis: Sutherland and McEvoy, 1859), 151; *Leavenworth City Directory and Business Mirror for 1860–61* (St. Louis: Sutherland and McEvoy, 1860), 52; *Leavenworth City Directory and Business Mirror for 1863–64* (St. Louis: Sutherland and McEvoy, 1863), 162; *Leavenworth City Directory and Business Mirror for 1865–66* (St. Louis: Sutherland and McEvoy, 1865), 170.

8. Frank W. Blackmar, ed., *Kansas: A Cyclopedia of State History, Embracing Events, Institutions, Industries, Counties, Cities, Towns, Prominent Persons, etc.*, Vol. 3. (Chicago: Standard Publishing Co., 1912), 125.

9. Nicole Etcheson, *Bleeding Kansas: Contested Liberty in the Civil War Era* (Lawrence: University Press of Kansas, 2004), 53–61.

10. James Denny and John Bradbury, *The Civil War's First Blood: Missouri, 1854–1861* (Boonville, Missouri: Missouri Life, 2007), 7.

11. Jay Monaghan, *Civil War on the Western Border 1854–1865* (Lincoln: University of Nebraska Press, 1955), 57–58; Sara T.L. Robinson, *Kansas: Its Interior and Exterior Life*

(Boston: Crosby, Nichols and Company, 1856), 243; Etcheson, 10; William Earl Parrish, *David Rice Atchison of Missouri, Border Politician* (Columbia: University of Missouri Press, 1961), 200.

12. Monaghan, *Civil War on the Western Border*, 58.

13. Cutler, *History of the State of Kansas;* "Cool Things—Old Kickapoo Cannon," Kansas State Historical Society, accessed November 10, 2011, http://www.kshs.org/p /cool-things-old-kickapoo-cannon/10234; Debra Graden, "January in Local History," Leavenworth County Historical Society and Museum, accessed 10 November 2011, http://skyways.lib.ks.us/genweb /leavenwo/library/JANUARY2.htm. In addition to these, there are a number of other slight variations on the central theme of the story, with no change in the outcome.

14. Williams to F.G. Adams, August 18, 1884, BGA (B-Williams), Topeka: Kansas State Historical Society, Topeka.

15. Judy Tharp, "A Story from Platt County, Missouri: 'Old Kickapoo,'" *The Border Star*, Nov–Dec, 2007; reprint, *The Missouri Unionist, Newsletter of the Department of Missouri—Sons of Union Veterans of the Civil War*, Vol. 2, No. 2 (December 2007), 16.

16. "Old Kickapoo Cannon," Kansas State Historical Society, accessed May 5, 2010, http://www.kshs.org/cool3/oldkickapoo.htm; Mary Ellen Hennessey Nottage, "Cannons, Spinning Wheels, and a Train: A History of the Museum Collection," *Kansas History*, Topeka, Kansas: Kansas State Historical Society, Vol. 7 (Spring 1984), 76–78.

17. Arizona State Archives, *Arizona Territory, House Bill No. 12: An Act to Divorce James M. Williams from the Bonds of Matrimony Heretofore Contracted with Lydia E. Williams, Late Lydia E. Francis*, approved September 23, 1867; United States Census Bureau, *1860 Census*, Leavenworth, Kansas; Family Search—"Family History and Genealogy Records, Family Group Record: Parents and Siblings, Lydia Francis Williams," accessed May 2, 2010, http://www.familysearch.org/eng/default.asp.

18. *Leavenworth Land Record Index*, Vols. 84–85, Leavenworth, Kansas, courtesy Leavenworth Public Library.

19. William H. Ward, ed., *Records of the Members of the Grand Army of the Republic with a Complete Account of the Twentieth National Encampmen*t (San Francisco: H.S. Crocker & Company, 1886), 417; William Tecumseh Sherman, Memoirs of *General William T. Sherman* (Bloomington: University of Indiana Press, 1957), 140–143.

20. Steven E. Woodworth, *Manifest Destinies: America's Westward Expansion and the Road to the Civil War* (New York: Alfred A. Knopf Publisher, 2010), 221.

21. Ian M. Spurgeon, *Man of Douglas, Man of Lincoln: The Political Odyssey of James Henry Lane* (Columbia: University of Missouri Press, 2008), 2.

22. Etcheson, *Bleeding Kansas*, 71.

23. Ibid.

24. Ibid, 82.

25. Monaghan, *Civil War on the Western Border*, 38–43.

26. Ibid., 76–77.

27. Bryce Benedict, *Jayhawkers: The Civil War Brigade of James Henry Lane* (Norman: University of Oklahoma Press, 2009), 18.

28. Monaghan, *Civil War on the Western Border*, 38–43.

29. Ibid., 43.

30. Spurgeon, *Man of Douglas*, 98.

31. Monaghan, *Civil War on the Western Border*, 74–76.

32. Ibid, 88.

33. Charles Robinson, *The Kansas Conflict*. (New York: Harper & Brothers, 1892), 305.

34. Moore, *Early History of Leavenworth City and County*, 166.

35. Denny and Bradbury, *The Civil War's First Blood*, 55–61.

36. The Jayhawk is a mythical bird with many legends surrounding its origins. It is reputed to be a cross between a blue jay, and a hawk, their attributes making it a quarrelsome egg sucker. It has been described as a bird that lives off other birds, is capable of fighting off bushwhackers, and flies backwards when necessary. Kirke Mechem, "The Mythical Jayhawk," *Kansas Historical Quarterly* (Topeka, Kansas: Kansas State Historical Society, February 1944, 1-5), accessed February 20, 2010, http://www.kancoll.org/khq/1944/44_1_mechem.htm.

37. Albert Castel, *Civil War Kansas: Reaping the Whirlwind* (Ithaca: Cornell University Press, 1958; reprint, Lawrence: University Press of Kansas, 1997), 43.

38. Leverett W. Spring, *Kansas: the Prelude to the War for the Union* (Boston: Houghton, Mifflin, 1885), 170.

39. Benedict, *Jayhawkers*, 41. The practice of electing officers differs substantially from today's process of formal training of officers through such channels as the US Military Academy at West Point, Reserve Officer Training Corps (ROTC), and Officer Candidate Schools (OCS). Leadership, strategy and tactics, and technology, more than popularity, drive the need for today's officers.

40. "Another Skirmish at Harrisonville," *New York Times*, July 30, 1861; Benedict, *Jayhawkers*, 47.

41. Castel, *Civil War in Kansas*, 32.

42. "When Kansas Became a State," *Kansas Historical Quarterly*, Topeka: Kansas State Historical Society 27, No. 1 (Spring 1961), 1–21.

43. Ibid.

44. Etcheson, *Bleeding Kansas*, 226–227.

45. *US Constitution*, Article I, Section 6, Paragraph 2.

46. Castel, *Civil War in Kansas*, 47–49.

47. Benedict, *Jayhawkers*, 34–35.

Chapter 2

1. The number of regiments reported to be in Lane's Brigade varied from three to eight, depending upon the source. All these regiments existed, but whether or not they were all in the brigade is questionable.

2. Castel, *Civil War in Kansas*, 50.

3. Benedict, *Jayhawkers*, 42–43.

4. Castel, *Civil War in Kansas*, 89–90; Howard Mann, "True Tales of the Tenth Kansas Infantry: Excitement at Alton Prison," accessed February 20, 2010, http://www .civilwarstlouis.com/Gratiot/tenthkansas2.htm.

5. W.S. Burke, *Official Military History of Kansas regiments during the War for the Suppression of the Great Rebellion* (Leavenworth: Kansas: Heritage Press, n.d.), 139.

6. Ibid., 151.

7. Ibid., 160.

8. US National Archives and Records Administration, *Compiled Service Records, Records of the Adjutant General's Office, 1780–1917, RG 94, Williams, James M.* (Washington, DC, n.d.), Hereafter noted as Williams Service Records.

9. Benedict, *Jayhawkers*, 45.

10. Ibid., 46.

11. Ibid.

12. Ibid., 47.

13. Ibid., 48.

14. Joseph Trego, *Diary, 1861–63*. Microfilm MS 1008. Kansas State Historical Society.

15. *History of Vernon County, Missouri* (St. Louis: Brown & Co., 1887), 288, 390–391; John C. Moore, *Confederate Military History of Missouri*, (Pensacola: eBooksOnDisk .com), 55–56, 151; Albert Castel, *General Sterling Price and the Civil War in the West* (Baton Rouge: Louisiana State University Press, 1996), 230–231.

16. Benedict, *Jayhawkers*, 70.

17. Castel, *Civil War in Kansas*, 52.

18. Benedict, *Jayhawkers*, 73.

19. Ibid., 74.

20. Ibid., 76.

21. Burke, *Kansas Regiments*, 108.

22. William F. Creitz, *Civil War Diary* (Topeka: Kansas State Historical Society), accessed May 4, 2010, http://www.griffingweb.com/captain_creitz's_diary.htm.

23. Benedict, *Jayhawkers*, 69, 90–91.

24. Castel, *Civil War in Kansas*, 53.

25. Richard Sunderwirth, ed., *"The Burning" of Osceola, Missouri* (Independence, Missouri: Two Trails Publishing, 2009), 53.

26. William F. Zornow, *Kansas: A History of the Jayhawk State* (Norman: University of Oklahoma Press, 1957), 109.

27. Ibid., 99–100.

28. Donald L. Gilmore, Civil War on the Missouri-Kansas Border (Gretna: Pelican Publishing, 2006), 134–135; Benedict, *Jayhawkers*, 98–107; Castel, *Civil War Kansas*, 54–56; Sunderwirth, 108–152.

29. Sunderwirth, *Burning of Osceola*, 250–251.

30. Ian M. Spurgeon, *Man of Douglas Man of Lincoln: the Political Odyssey of James Henry Lane* (Columbia: University of Missouri Press, 2008), 206.

31. Duane Schultz, *Quantrill's War: The Life and times of William Clarke Quantrill* (New York: St. Martin's Griffin, 1996), 187.

32. Benedict, *Jayhawkers*, 155–156.

33. Charles Robinson, *The Kansas Conflict* (New York: Harper & Brothers, 1892), 439–440.

34. Ibid., 438–439.

35. Benedict, *Jayhawkers*, 158–159.

36. *War of the Rebellion: A Compilation of the Official Records of the Union and Confederate Armies*, 128 vols. and atlas (Washington, DC: Government Printing Office, 1881-1901), Series 1, Vol. 8, 449. Hereafter noted as O.R.

37. O.R., Series 1, Vol. 8, 615. Lane's Brigade was never assigned a numeric designator. Formed early in the conflict, it merely carried his name, similar to the process used by Confederate units. It was disbanded before it could be fitted into the overall structure of the Federal Army. Another example in Kansas was Hopkin's Battery, which went for a year without a numerical designation. This reference in the O.R. is the only one specifically referring to Lane's Brigade (Kansas).

38. Ibid., 208–210. This reference cites General Order 26, dated February 28, 1862 from General Hunter's headquarters. Williams' personnel files maintained at regimental level do not coincide, depicting his company being in the Third Regiment of Kansas Volunteers continuously from July 12, 1861 until December 31, 1861, and in the Fifth Kansas Cavalry Regiment thereafter. *The History of Vernon County, Missouri*, p. 288 places Williams in Montgomery's regiment on August 28, 1861 at Ball's Mill. The War Department AGO summary depicts him in the Fifth Kansas Cavalry from July 12, 1861 until discharge on September 4, 1862, to accept appointment with US Colored Troops (Williams Service Records). The *Report of the Adjutant General of the State of Kansas, Vol. 1, 1861–1865* (Chicago: Bulletin Co-operative Printing Company, 1867), 329, places Williams in Company F, Fifth Kansas Cavalry for the entire period from his muster on July 12, 1861 to his resignation on May 15, 1862 to accept appointment as lieutenant colonel, First Kansas Colored Volunteer Infantry. Some of this confusion is derived from the absorption of the Third Regiment into the Fifth, blending their histories. Given Williams' respect for Montgomery, it is safe to say Williams spent some time under his command.

39. Burke, *Kansas Regiments*, Index (n.p.).

40. Ibid., 109.

41. Albert Castel, "Civil War Kansas and the Negro," *The Journal of Negro History*, Vol. 51, No. 2 (Apr 1966), 126–127.

42. Williams Service Records.

43. Ibid. Interestingly, there are a number of entries in Williams' records that suggest either clerical ineptness in his regimental headquarters, or a quest to make him look bad. He is noted as being absent without leave (AWOL), and a deserter. Over time several corrections to those entries were made, some as late as 1866, 1872, 1879, and 1891. The corrections also change the date of his muster out of the regiment, probably to account for his time.

44. Ibid.

Chapter 3

1. Benedict, *Jayhawkers*, 237–238.
2. Williams Service Records.
3. O.R., Series 3, Vol. 2, 959.
4. "General Orders No. 2, Office of the Recruiting Commission," *Smoky Hill and Republican Union* (Junction City, Kansas), 6 September 1862.
5. Roger D. Cunningham, "Welcoming 'Pa' on the Kaw: Kansas's 'Colored' Militia and the 1864 Price Raid," *Kansas History* 25 (Summer 2002), 97.
6. United States, *Congressional Globe*, 37th Congress, 2nd Session, 15 January 1862, 334–336; United States Constitution, Article 1, Section 6.
7. O.R., Series 3, Vol. 2, 294–295.
8. Ibid., 311.
9. Ibid., 312.
10. Ibid.
11. Chris Tabor, *The Skirmish at Island Mound, Mo.: the First Battle Fought by an African-American Regiment during the Civil War* (Butler, Missouri: Bates County Historical Society, 2001), 6.
12. Benjamin Quarles, *The Negro in the Civil War* (Boston: Little Brown, 1953; reprint, New York: Da Capo Press, 1989), 126.
13. Joseph A. Walkes, "Captain William D. Matthews: Freemason, Leavenworth, Kansas," *The Phlaxis* 14 (4th Quarter, 1987), 3–8, 29. Roger D. Cunningham, "Douglas' Battery at Fort Leavenworth: the Issue of Black Officers during the Civil War," *Kansas History* 23:4 (Winter 2000-2001), 200-217. Walkes and Cunningham disagree about Matthews' place of birth. Walkes believes it is Washington, DC, and Cunningham believes it is Caroline County, Maryland.
14. Tabor, *Skirmish at Island Mound*, 7; Cunningham, "Douglas' Battery," 206. Cunningham identifies a third black officer—Lieutenant Henry Copeland—also not allowed to muster into Federal service with the regiment. However, a Lieutenant Henry Copeland in Company D appears on rosters of the regiment when designated First Kansas Colored Volunteer Infantry, and later as the Seventy-Ninth US Colored Infantry. That being the case, it is logical to conclude the Henry Copeland was white.
15. Quarles, *Negro in the Civil War*, 9.
16. Ibid.
17. O.R., Series 3, Vol. 2, 445.
18. Albert Castel, *Civil War Kansas*, 93.
19. Dudley Taylor Cornish, *Kansas Negro Regiments in the Civil War* (Topeka: Kansas Commission on Civil Rights, 1969), 7–8.
20. Ibid., 8.
21. Burke, *Kansas Regiments*, 407–408.
22. Lane to Williams, October 9, 1862, Kansas State Historical Society.
23. John H. Stearns, "Interesting Reminiscences of Colored Troops Who Probably Saved Mound City from the Fate of Lawrence," *Linn County Republic*, 31 January 1902. Hereafter noted as Stearns Reminiscences.

24. N.P. Chipman, "Excerpt from Coln. N.P. Chipman to General [Samuel R. Curtis], 16 Oct. [1862], C-46 1862, Letters Received, ser. 2593, Dept. of the MO, RG 393 Pt. 1 [C-104], in *Freedom, A Documentary History of Emancipation, 1861–1867, Series II, The Black Military Experience*, Ira Berlin, ed. (Cambridge: Cambridge University Press, 1982), 70–72.

25. Castel, "Civil War Kansas and the Negro," 151.

26. Ibid.

27. Ethan Earle, *Account Book of Ethan Earle* (Mss C 4911), R. Stanton Avery Special Collection Dept., New England Historic Genealogical Society.

28. Ibid.

29. John David Smith, "Let Us All Be Grateful That We Have Colored Troops That Will Fight," *Black Soldiers in Blue, African American Troops in the Civil War Era*, ed. John David Smith (Chapel Hill: University of North Carolina Press, 2002), 37.

30. Thomas W. Higginson, *Army Life in a Black Regiment* (Mineola, NY: Dover Publications, 2002); Smith, "Let Us All Be Grateful," 37.

31. Ibid.

32. O.R., Series 1, Vol. 53, 744.

33. Earle, *Account Book*, 18.

Chapter 4

1. "Missouri Digital Heritage Collections," accessed May 29, 2010, http://cdm.sos .mo.gov/cdm4/document.php?. Bushwhacker is a term applied to guerrillas operating out of Missouri after the beginning of the Civil War. These were the same type of people as the Border Ruffians, but came from more far-flung areas than just the border counties. Thomas Livingston was a well-known bushwhacker in southwest Missouri. He led a loosely organized battalion with a reputation of barbaric cruelty, known as "thieves and robbers," notorious for "arson, murder, and robbery." "[H]e often refused to take or release prisoners. Livingston preferred murder over capture, and he was known to shoot unarmed or wounded soldiers at point blank range."

2. Stearns Reminiscences. The Marais des Cygnes is also known as the Osage River. One of the more significant historical reports of this engagement, in *The Rebellion Record*, Vol. 6, edited by Frank Moore (New York: G.P. Putnam, 1863), refers throughout as the Osage. Another report in the same volume, however, refers to it as the Marais des Cynes. The confusion arises from the fact that the Marais des Cygnes, rising in Kansas, is the primary tributary of the Osage, which is the primary tributary of the Missouri in the state of Missouri.

3. Tabor, 2.

4. O.R., Series 1, Vol. 53, 455–458, Report of Major Richard Ward, First Kansas Colored Infantry, October 29, 1862.

5. O.R., Series 1, Vol. 53, 455–456.

6. Tabor, *Skirmish at Island Mound*, 10.

7. Ibid. Tabor describes the mounds: "The undulating topography is dotted by mounds that range in size from small knolls to large hills. These mounds are the result

of the underlying rock strata, primarily limestone, eroding at a slower pace than the surrounding countryside."

8. *O.R.* Series 1, Vol. 53, 456. Ward reported estimates of seven to eight hundred men. Chris Tabor noted an estimate of four hundred or more made by Seaman, and commented on multiple estimates of two to six hundred. It was common for official reports to exaggerate enemy strength in order to create greater credence in friendly leaders. Certainly, if Colonel Cockrell was in fact seeking to combine multiple Confederate forces into one command for a raid on Mound City, it is logical to conclude that his command numbered several hundred.

9. Matt Matthews and Kip Lindberg, " 'Shot All To Pieces' The Battle of Lone Jack, Missouri, August 16, 1862," *North and South*, Vol. 7, No. 1 (January 2004), 56–72.

10. Sidney Jackman, *Behind Enemy Lines: The Memoirs of Brigadier General Sidney Drake Jackman*, CSA, ed. Richard L. Norton (Springfield Missouri: Oak Hills Publishing, 1997), 78.

11. United States, Congress, Senate, Committee on Claims. *Elkanah Huddleston*, Report Prepared by Senator Willey, 41st Cong., 3d Sess., 1871, Report No. 332, 1.

12. Tabor, *Skirmish at Island Mound*, 11. Chris Tabor's book is the only comprehensive detailed research that has been ever been conducted on the fight at Island Mound. Mr. Tabor is a former resident of Butler, and is deeply involved in Civil War history activities in that area. The O.R. has only one report (Major Ward), and there is no Confederate account of the engagement. The State of Missouri recently acquired part of the battle site as an historic park.

13. "Affairs in the West: A Negro Regiment in Action – The Battle of Island Mounds – Desperate Bravery of the Negroes – Defeat of the Guerrillas – An Attempted Fraud," *New York Times*, November 19, 1862; O.R. Series I, Vol. 53, 456. The timing in Ward's report conflicts with the newspaper account, which was allegedly written in first-person by an on-site correspondent. The New York Times article reports that the request for reinforcements went out the first night that the Union troops were at the Toothman Farm. Ward's report indicates that the plea for help went out during the second night. The outcome was not affected by the difference in reports. The First Kansas handled the problem without help.

14. Ibid., 11.

15. Stearns Reminiscences.

16. *O.R.* Series I, Vol. 53, 456.

17. *New York Times*, November 19, 1862.

18. As Williams and Seaman worked to recruit troops for the regiment during the Island Mound expedition, Williams had already formed his new soldiers into separate companies, but Seaman did not as yet have enough men to warrant that stage of organization.

19. Tabor, *Skirmish at Island Mound*, 13–14.

20. Ibid., 15–16.

21. Ibid., Appendix B.

22. Stearns Reminiscences.

23. Roger McKinney, "Battle of Island Mound marked first time blacks fought in Civil War combat," *Joplin Globe*, July 30, 2011.

24. Burke, *Kansas Regiments*, 409.

25. Tabor, *Skirmish at Island Mound*, 16, Appendix B; Stearns Reminiscences.

26. *O.R.* Series 1, Vol. 53, 456.

27. Frank Moore, ed., *The Rebellion Record: A Diary of American Events*, Vol. 6, Document 19 (New York: G.P. Putnam, 1863), 52–54.

28. Dudley Cornish, *The Sable Arm: Black Troops in the Union Army, 1861–1865* (Lawrence: University Press of Kansas, 1987), 76–77.

29. Ian M. Spurgeon. *Man of Douglas*, 234.

30. Tabor, *Skirmish at Island Mound*, 17.

Chapter 5

1. Williams to Blunt, November 24, 1862, Kansas State Historical Society.

2. Noah Andre Trudeau, *Like Men of War: Black Troops in the Civil War 1862–1865* (New York: Little Brown, 1998; reprint. Edison, New Jersey: Castle Books, 2002), 19.

3. Ibid, 20.

4. Ibid, 19–20.

5. Grafton to "My Dear Wife," January 10, 1863, Kansas State Historical Society.

6. Six companies mustered in January, and the remaining four in May.

7. There is much quibbling and competition for bragging rights over which was first. There is room for several. Certainly, Colonel Thomas W. Higginson's First Regiment of South Carolina Volunteers was first in one category. General Butler's two regiments of Louisiana Native Guards had a legacy that stretches well back—they originally offered their services to the Confederate army before the fall of New Orleans (we won't count that). The Fifty-Fourth Massachusetts, famous for their sacrifice at Fort Wagner, received ample publicity that provided credibility to black soldiers. They were, after all, the first black regiment raised in the north, east of the Mississippi.

8. Joseph T. Glatthaar, *Forged in Battle: the Civil War Alliance of Black Soldiers and White Officers* (Baton Rouge: Louisiana State University Press, 2000), 178.

9. John David Smith, "Let Us All Be Grateful," 28.

10. O.R., Series 1, Vol. 43, 604.

11. Bryce D. Benedict, "Kansas' Colored Btry Fought in Civil War," *Plains Guardian*, Vol. 43, No. 2, February 1998.

12. Reynard to R.C. Anderson, March 10, 1863, Topeka: KSHS, Williams Collection.

13. Carney to Lincoln July 19, 1863, Kansas State Historical Society.

14. *Leavenworth Times*, October 8, 1890.

15. Williams Service Records. His regimental service record says he was thirty-two. He was actually thirty.

16. Trudeau, *Like Men of War*, 91–92.

17. Ibid., 254.

18. Edwin Redkey, ed., *A Grand Army of Black Men: Letters from African American Soldiers in the Union Army 1861–1865* (New York: Cambridge University Press, 1993), 230.

19. Joseph Glatthaar, *Forged in Battle: the Civil War Alliance of Black Soldiers and White Officers* (Baton Rouge: Louisiana State University Press, 2000), 171–172.

20. Ibid., 255.

21. Cornish, *Kansas Negro Regiments in the Civil War*, 8–10.

22. Ibid.

23. Blackmar, ed., *Kansas: a Cyclopedia of State History, Vol. 2, 160.*

24. O.R., Vol. 22, Pt. 1, Chapter 34, 320–322.

25. William A. Dobak, *Freedom by the Sword: The U.S Colored Troops, 1862-1867* (Washington, D.C.: Center of Military History, U.S. Army, 2011), 234–235.

26. O.R., Series I, Vol. 22, Pt. I, 329–332.

27. Ibid., 321–322; *Report of the Adjutant General of Kansas, 1861–65* (Topeka, 1896; reprint, n.d.). Livingston reported to General Price he only used sixty-seven cavalrymen in the attack. Major Ward reported three hundred. It seems reasonable from what happened, and the engagements in the immediate vicinity and time frame, that Livingston probably had at least 150–200 men with him.

28. Ward reported sixteen dead and five captured; Livingston reported twenty-three blacks and seven whites killed, and an unstated number of prisoners. Wounded were not reported.

29. John Livingston, Jr., *Such a Foe as Livingston: The Campaign of Confederate Major Thomas R. Livingston's First Missouri cavalry Battalion of Southwest Missouri* (Wyandotte, OK: Gregath Publishing Company, 2004), 91. Livingston claimed his men killed twenty-three black men from the First Kansas.

30. O.R. Vol. 22, Pt. 1, Chap. 34, 322.

31. *Kansas Regiments*, 410.

32. John Hacker, "Jasper County Park to Commemorate Rader Farm Massacre," *Carthage Press* [Missouri], November 16, 2009. Quote is from a comment by Jasper County historian Steve Weldon at dedication.

33. *Kansas Regiments*, 410.

34. Ibid.

35. Livingston to Williams, May 20, 1863; Regimental Order Book, 79th United States Colored Infantry, Regimental and Company Books of Civil War Volunteer Union Organizations, compiled 1861–1865; Records of the Adjutant General's Office, Record Group 94; NARA, Washington, DC. Hereafter Regimental Order Book, 79th United States Colored Infantry.

36. Williams to Livingston. May 21, 1863; Regimental Order Book, 79th United States Colored Infantry.

37. Williams to Livingston, May 26, 1863, Regimental Order Book, 79th United States Colored Infantry.

38. Livingston to Williams, May 27, 1863, Regimental Order Book, 79th United States Colored Infantry.

39. *Kansas Regiments*, 410.

40. John Hacker, "Jasper County Park to Commemorate Rader Farm Massacre," Comment by Jasper County Historian Steve Weldon.

Chapter 6

1. Ralph Jones and Mike Adkins, *The Battle of Honey Springs: A Clash of cultures in the Indian Territory* (Oklahoma City: Oklahoma Historical Society, 1993), 4.

2. Alvin M. Josephy, Jr., *The Civil War in the American West* (New York: Random House, 1991), 323–332; Clarissa W. Confer, *The Cherokee Nation in the Civil War* (Norman: University of Oklahoma Press, 2007), 53–56, 59–66; Whit Edwards, of the Oklahoma Historical Society summed up the numbers: "At war's end, 14 percent of the Indian population in Indian Territory were orphans, another 16 percent were fatherless children, and 33 percent of the populations were widows. The Five Tribes were more destitute than at the time of their arrival." Whit Edwards, Foreword to *Civil War in the Indian Territory*, by Steve Cottrell (Gretna: Pelican Publishing, 1998), 10.

3. Watie would later be promoted to brigadier general, the only Indian on either side to achieve that grade. He was the last Confederate general officer to surrender to the Union at the end of the Civil War.

4. Kenny A. Franks, *Stand Watie and the Agony of the Cherokee Nation* (Memphis: Memphis State University Press, 1979), 14–18.

5. Wiley Britton, *The Civil War on the Border: A Narrative of Military Operations in Missouri, Kansas, Arkansas and the Indian Territory during the Years 1863–65, Based upon Official Reports and Observations of the Author*, Vol. II (New York: G. P. Putnam's Sons, 1899), 3. Hereafter Wiley Britton, *Civil War on the Border*.

6. Ibid., 17.

7. Grant Foreman, *Down the Texas Road: Historic Places along Highway 69 through Oklahoma* (Norman, University of Oklahoma Press, 1936), 11, 25, 40.

8. Wiley Britton, *Civil War on the Border*, 37–38.

9. Ibid., 74–76.

10. Phillips to Blunt, May 9, 1863, O.R., Series 1, Vol. 22, Part 2, 279–277.

11. Ibid., 80–86.

12. Wiley Britton, *Memoirs of the Rebellion on the Border, 1863* (Chicago: Cushing, Thomas & Co., 1882; reprint, Lincoln: University of Nebraska Press, 1993), 315–316.

13. Blunt to Schofield, O.R., Series I, Vol. 22, Pt. 2, 895.

14. Blunt to Williams, June 18, 1863, Kansas State Historical Society.

15. Steele to Cooper (2 messages); Steele to Cabell (2 messages), June 29, 1863, O.R., Series 1, Vol. 22, Pt. 2, 893–895.

16. Williams to Phillips, O.R., Series 1, Vol. 22, Pt. 1, 379–381.

17. Foreman to Phillips, O.R., Series 1, Vol. 22, Pt. 1, 382.

18. Williams to Phillips, O.R., Series 1, Vol. 22, Pt. 1, 379–381.

19. Ibid.

20. Ibid.

21. Ibid.

22. Wiley Britton, *Memoirs of the Rebellion, 1863,* 323.

23. Williams to Phillips, O.R., Series 1, Vol. 22, Pt. 1, 379–381.

24. Wiley Britton, *Memoirs of the Rebellion, 1863,* 324.

25. Whit Edwards, *The Prairie Was on Fire: Eyewitness Accounts of the Civil War in the Indian Territory* (Oklahoma City: Oklahoma Historical Society, 2001), 59.

26. "Spirited Actions Not in History," The *National Tribune,* Washington, DC, 1November 1883.

27. Wiley Britton, *Civil War on the Border,* 100.

28. Wiley Britton, *Memoirs of the Rebellion,* 314.

29. Wiley Britton, *Civil War on the Border,* 115.

30. Moonlight to Williams, June 18, 1863, Williams Service Records. Moonlight, as General Blunt's Chief of Staff was conveying a direct order to Williams directing him not to assume command of the varied units moving with the wagon train, telling him, "your forces will not be united for the purpose of escorting the train and you assume command as the ranking officer, but comply with previous orders issued you."

Chapter 7

1. Britton, *Memoirs of the Rebellion,* 342–343.

2. Robert Collins, *General James G. Blunt: Tarnished Glory* (Gretna: Pelican Publishing, 2005), 141–142.

3. Livingston, 115, 117–118.

4. President Davis to Governor Flanagin, July 15, 1863, O.R., Series I, Vol. 22, Pt. 2, 932.

5. Wiley Britton, *The Union Indian Brigade in the Civil War* (Kansas City, Missouri: Franklin Hudson Publishing Company, 1922), 271.

6. Annie Heloise Abel, *The American Indian in the Civil War 1862–1865* (Cleveland: A.H. Clark Co., 1919; Reprint, Lincoln: University of Nebraska Press, 1992), 287.

7. Jess C. Epple, *Honey Springs Depot: Elk Creek, Creek Nation, Indian Territory* (Muskogee, Hoffman Printing Co., 1964), 5.

8. Ibid., 61.

9. Abel, *American Indian in the Civil War,* 288.

10. Kip Lindberg and Matt Matthews, " 'To Play a Bold Game:' The Battle of Honey Springs," *North and South* 6, No. 1 (December 2002): 61–62.

11. Wiley Britton, *Civil War on the Border,* 116.

12. Ibid., 117.

13. O.R., Series 1, Vol. 22, Pt. 1, 461–462.

14. Ethan Earle, *Account Book of Ethan Earle.*

15. Ibid.

16. Blunt to Schofield, July 26, 1863, O.R., Series I, Vol. 22, Pt. 1, 447–448

17. Ibid.

18. Britton, *Union Indian Brigade,* 276–277.

19. Ibid.

20. Bowles to Judson, July 20, 1863, O.R., Series I, Vol. 24, Pt. 1, 449–451.

21. Ibid.

22. Ibid.

23. Ibid.

24. Britton, *Union Indian Brigade*, 285.

25. John Grady and Bradford Felmly, *Suffering to Silence: 29th Texas Cavalry, CSA Regimental History* (Quanah, Texas: Nortex Press, 1975), 93.

26. Ibid.

27. Blunt to Schofield, July 26, 1863, O.R., Series 1, Vol. 22, Pt. 1, 447–448.

28. Whit Edwards, *Eyewitness Accounts*, 69.

29. Ibid., 70.

30. Patrick Minges ed., *Black Indian Slave Narratives* (Winton-Salem: John F. Blair, 2004), 123–125.

31. Whit Edwards, *Eyewitness Accounts*, 69.

32. Abel, *American Indian in the Civil War*, 290.

33. Robert M. Utley, *The Indian Frontier of the American West 1846–1890* (Albuquerque: University of New Mexico Press, 1984), 75.

34. Ethan Earle, *Account Book of Ethan Earle*.

35. General Order 61, August 11, 1863, Regimental Order Book.

36. Britton, *Union Indian Brigade*, 286–287.

37. Blunt to Schofield, August 27, 1863, O.R., Series I, Vol. 22, Pt. 1, 597–598; Britton, *Union Indian Brigade*, 290–291.

38. Blunt to Schofield, September 3,1863, O.R., Series I, Vol. 22, Pt. 1, 601–602.

39. Wiley Britton, *Civil War on the Border*, 209–210.

40. Williams Service Records.

41. Ethan Earle, *Account Book of Ethan Earle*.

42. Ibid.

43. Collins, *General James G. Blunt*, 164–167.

44. Mark K. Christ ed., *"All Cut to Pieces and Gone to Hell:" The Civil War, Race Relations, and the Battle of Poison Spring* (Little Rock: August House Publishers, 2003), 12–13.

Chapter 8

1. Edwin C. Bearss, *Steele's Retreat from Camden and the Battle of Jenkins' Ferry* (Little Rock: Pioneer Press, 1966; Reprint, Little Rock: Eagle Press, 1990), ix–xi.

2. Ibid., Union General Frederick Steele should not be confused with Confederate General William Steele, previously mentioned.

3. John C. Waugh, *Sam Bell Maxey and the Confederate Indians* (Abilene, Texas: McWhiney Foundation Press, 1998), 53.

4. Michael J. Forsyth, *The Camden Expedition of 1864 and the Opportunity Lost by the Confederacy to Change the Civil War* (Jefferson, North Carolina: McFarland & Co., 2003), 39–43.

5. Gary D. Joiner, *One Damn Blunder from Beginning to End: the Red River Campaign of 1864* (Wilmington, Delaware: Scholarly Resources, 2003), 38–41.

6. Ibid., 42.

7. Earle, *Account Book of Ethan Earle;* O.R., Series 1, Vol. 34, Pt. 1, 759–60.

8. Daniel Sutherland, "1864: 'A Strange, Wild Time,'" in *Rugged and Sublime: The Civil War in Arkansas,* Mark K. Christ, ed., (Fayetteville: University of Arkansas Press, 1994), 111.

9. Albert Castel, *General Sterling Price and the Civil War in the West* (Baton Rouge: Louisiana State University Press, 1996), 3–6.

10. Thomas A. DeBlack, "An Overview of the Camden Expedition," in *"All Cut to Pieces and Gone to Hell:" The Civil War, Race Relations, and the Battle of Poison Spring,* Mark K. Christ, ed. (Little Rock: August House Publishing, 2003), 15.

11. Campbell to Cloud, O.R., Series I, Vol. 34. Pt. 1, 759–760.

12. Sutherland, "1864: A Strange, Wild Time," 111.

13. Steele to Grant, March 18, 1864, O.R., Series I, Vol. 34, Pt. 2, 646.

14. Sutherland, "1864: A Strange, Wild Time," 112.

15. Ibid., 113.

16. Britton, *Union Indian Brigade in the Civil War*, 359.

17. Sutherland, "1864: A Strange, Wild Time," 114.

18. Marmaduke to Price, O.R., Series 1, Vol. 34, Pt. 1, 824–825.

Chapter 9

1. Ira Don Richards, "The Battle of Poison Spring," *Arkansas Historical Quarterly*, Vol. 18, No. 4, 339.

2. Ibid., 340.

3. DeBlack, "Overview of the Camden Expedition," 20.

4. Richards, 340.

5. Edwin C. Bearss, *Steele's Retreat From Camden and The Battle of Jenkins' Ferry* (Little Rock: Eagle Press of Little Rock, 1990), 1.

6. Henry to Meigs, May 12, 1864, O.R., Series I, Vol. 34, Pt. 1, 680.

7. A squadron of cavalry consists of two or more companies of cavalry.

8. L.A. Thrasher Statement, O.R., Series 1, Vol. 34, Pt. 3, 237.

9. Bearss, *Steele's Retreat*, 4.

10. Williams to Whitten, April 24, 1864, O.R., Series I, Vol. 34, Pt. 1, 743.

11. Bearss, *Steele's Retreat*, 6; Henry to Meigs, May 12, 1864, O.R., Series I, Vol. 34, Pt. 1, 680.

12. Williams to Whitten, April 24, 1864, O.R., Series I, Vol. 34, Pt. 1, 743.

13. Bearss, *Steele's Retreat*, 8.

14. Ibid., 744.

15. Mitchell to Williams, April 20, 1864, O.R., Series I, Vol. 34, Pt. 1, 747.

16. Bearss, *Steele's Retreat*, 21.

17. Ibid.

18. Williams to Whitten, April 24, 1864, O.R., Series I, Vol. 34, Pt. 1, 744; Charles Grear, "Gano's Brigade: A History of the Fifth Texas Cavalry Brigade, 1863–1864" (M.A. Thesis, Texas Tech University, 2001), 50.

19. Ibid.

20. Marmaduke to Price, O.R., Series 1, Vol. 34, Pt. 1, 825.

21. Ibid., 826.

22. Ibid.

23. Waugh, *Sam Bell Maxey*, 14.

24. Grear, "Gano's Brigade," 24–25.

25. Marmaduke to Price, O.R., Series 1, Vol. 34, Pt. 1, 826.

26. Williams to Whitten, April 24, 1864, O.R., Series I, Vol. 34, Pt. 1, 744.

27. Ibid.

28. Bearss, *Steele's Retreat*, 25–26.

29. Buck and ball was an ammunition charge to soldiers' muskets that included a large bullet (ball) and three buckshot, fired at once.

30. DeMorse to Ochiltree, April 21, 1864, O.R., Series I, Vol. 34, Pt. 1, 847.

31. Britton, *Civil War on the Border*, 286.

32. DeMorse to Ochiltree, April 21, 1864, O.R., Series I, Vol. 34, Pt. 1, 847.

33. Gregory J.W. Urwin, "Poison Spring and Jenkins' Ferry: Racial Atrocities during the Camden Expedition," in *All Cut to Pieces and Gone to Hell: The Civil War, Race Relations, and the Battle of Poison Spring*, ed. Mark K. Christ (Little Rock: August House Publishers, 2003), 117.

34. Ernest Wallace, *Charles DeMorse: Pioneer Statesman and Father of Texas Journalism* (Paris, Texas: Wright Press, 1985. First published 1943 by Texas Tech Press), 149.

35. Charlean M. Williams, "The Battle of Poison Spring," in *The Old Town Speaks: Recollections of Washington, Hempstead County, Arkansas; Gateway to Texas 1833 Confederate Capital, 1863* (Houston: Anson Jones Press, 1951), 91–92.

36. Williams to Whitten, April 24, 1864, O.R., Series 1, Vol. 34, Pt. 1, 745; *Britton, Civil War on the Border*, 286.

37. "From the Front," *The New Era* (Fort Smith, Arkansas), May 7, 1864. Grady and Felmly, *Suffering to Silence*, 122.

38. Williams' report indicates that his troops repelled two attacks from the Confederates; Ward reports three; General Marmaduke made no such reference; Colonel DeMorse acknowledged he had been repulsed, but did not say how many times. Historian Wiley Britton noted three on the front line, and a fourth on the Eighteenth Iowa. Either Williams or Ward was probably correct.

39. Bearss, *Steele's Retreat*, 31.

40. DeMorse to Ochiltree, April 21, 1864, O.R., Series I, Vol. 34, Pt. 1, 847.

41. Duncan to Williams, April 21, 1864, O.R., Series I, Vol. 34, Pt. 1, 751.

42. Britton, Civil *War on the Border*, 290.

43. Bearss, *Steele's Retreat*, 35.

44. Price to Boggs, O.R., Series 1, Vol. 34, Pt. 1, 781.

45. Frank Marshall White, "Mark Twain Amused," *New York Journal*, June 2, 1897. In response to a newspaper report that Clemens had died, Clemens commented that, "The report of [his] death was greatly exaggerated." It was actually his brother who had died.

46. Williams to Whitten, April 24, 1864, O.R., Series I, Vol. 34, Pt. 1, 745–746.

47. Bearss, *Steele's Retreat*, 41.

Chapter 10

1. Williams to Whitten, April 24, 1864, O.R., Series I, Vol. 34, Pt. 1, 746.

2. Ward to Williams, April 20, 1864, O.R., Series I, Vol. 34, Pt. 1, 751.

3. Gregory J.W. Urwin ed., "We cannot treat Negroes . . . as Prisoners of War," in *Black Flag over Dixie: Racial Atrocities and Reprisals in the Civil War* (Carbondale: Southern Illinois University Press, 2004), 135.

4. Ibid.

5. Britton, Civil *War on the Border*, 291.

6. Urwin, "We Cannot Treat Negroes . . . as Prisoners of War," 215.

7. Urwin, "Poison Spring and Jenkins' Ferry," 125.

8. Charlean Williams, *The Old Town Speaks*, 91.

9. Bearss, *Steele's Retreat*, 37.

10. Charles Grear, "Red and White Fighting the Blue: Relations between Texans and Confederate Indians," in *The Seventh Star of the Confederacy: Texas during the Civil War*, War in the Southwest Series, No. 10, ed. Kenneth W. Howell (Denton, Texas: University of North Texas Press, 2009), 175.

11. Anne J. Bailey, "Was There a Massacre at Poison Spring?" in *Military History of the Southwest*, Vol. 20, No. 2, (Fall, 1990), 164.

12. Ibid, 167.

13. Howard C. Westwood, "Captive Black Union Soldiers in Charleston: What to Do?" in *Black Flag Over Dixie: Racial Atrocities and Reprisals in the Civil War*, ed. Gregory J.W. Urwin (Carbondale, Illinois: Southern Illinois University Press, 2004) 35.

14. Cornish, *Sable Arm*, 161–162.

15. Howard C. Westwood, "Captive Black Union Soldiers in Charleston: What to Do?" in *Black Flag Over Dixie: Racial Atrocities and Reprisals in the Civil War*, ed. Gregory J.W. Urwin (Carbondale, Illinois: Southern Illinois University Press, 2004), 41.

16. John D. Smith, "Let Us All Be grateful That We Have Colored Troops That Will Fight," in *Black Soldiers in Blue: African American Troops in the Civil War Era*, ed. John D. Smith (Chapel Hill, North Carolina: University of North Carolina Press, 2002), 46.

17. Ibid., 47.

18. George S. Burkhardt, "No Quarter! Black Flag Warfare 1863–1865," *North and South*, Vol. 10, No. 1 (May 2007), 15.

19. Alan Axelrod, *The Horrid Pit: The Battle of the Crater, the Civil War's Cruelest Mission* (New York: Carroll and Graf Publishers, 2007), 183–185, 215, 217; Thomas D. Mays, *The Saltville Massacre* (Fort Worth: Ryan Place Publishers, 1995), 58–60.

20. Ibid.

21. Henry to Steele, April 19, 1864, O.R., Series I, Vol. 34, Pt. 1, 682–683.

22. Bearss, *Steele's Retreat*, 57.

23. Ibid., 76–77.

24. Ibid., 55.

25. Britton, *The Indian Brigade in the Civil War*, 360.

26. Britton, *Civil War on the Border*, 295–296.

27. Ibid., 296–311.

28. Burke, *Kansas Regiments*, 429–430.

29. Urwin, "Poison Spring and Jenkins' Ferry," 144.

30. Bearss, *Steele's Retreat*, 169, 174–175.

31. S.O.32, HQ. Frontier Division, Department of Arkansas, Little Rock, May 7, 1864; Williams Service Records.

Chapter 11

1. O.R., Series 1, Vol. 34, Pt. 4, 609.

2. S.O. 147, District of the Frontier; S.O. 43, 2nd Brigade, Frontier Division, 14 September 1864; Regimental Order Book, 79th United States Colored Infantry; Regimental and Company Books of Civil War Volunteer Union Organizations, compiled 1861–1865; Records of the Adjutant General's Office, Record Group 94; NARA, Washington, DC.

3. Steven L. Warren, *Brilliant Victory: The Second Civil War Battle of Cabin Creek, Indian Territory* (Wyandotte, Oklahoma: Gregath Publishing, 2002), 18–20.

4. Castel, *General Sterling Price and the Civil War in the West*, 196, 203.

5. Wiley Britton, *The Civil War on the Border*, 244–245.

6. Barker to Adjutant General, September 20, 1864, O.R., Series I, Vol. 44, Pt. 1, 771–772.

7. Urwin, "Poison Spring and Jenkins' Ferry," 146.

8. Gano to Maxey, September 23, 1864, O.R., Series I, Vol. 44, Pt. 1, 788–789.

9. Gano to Cooper, September 23, 1864, O.R., Series I, Vol. 44, Pt. 1, 788–789.

10. Barker to Adjutant General, September 20, 1864, O.R., Series I, Vol. 44, Pt. 1, 771–772.

11. Ibid.

12. Ibid.

13. George W. Grayson, *A Creek Warrior for the Confederacy: The Autobiography of Chief G. W. Grayson*, The Civilization of the American Indian Series, ed. W. David Baird (Norman: University of Oklahoma Press, 1988), 96.

14. Warren, 25.

15. *Report of the Adjutant General of the State of Kansas, 1861–1865. Vol. 1.* (Topeka, Kansas: The Kansas State Printing Company, 1896), 594.

16. Ibid., 29.

17. Ibid., 30.

18. Ibid.

19. Hopkins to Thomas, September 25, 1864, O.R., Series I, Vol. 41, Pt. 1, 769–771.

20. Double-quick, or double time (as it is known today), is a trot of roughly 180 steps per minute. It can be physically debilitating over long distances in hot, humid weather with a heavy backpack and musket.

21. Warren, *Brilliant Victory*, 31.

22. Grayson, *Creek Warrior for the Confederacy*, 100.

23. Jennison to Hampton, September 22, 1864, O.R., Series I, Vol. 41, Pt. 1, 774.

24. Ibid., 772.

25. Johnson to Morris, September 20, 1864, O.R., Series I, Vol. 41, Pt. 1, 775.

26. Ibid.

27. Warren, *Brilliant Victory*, 37–40.

28. Ibid., 39–43.

29. Epple, *Honey Springs Depot*, 46.

30. Williams to Blair, September 20, 1864, O.R., Vol. 41, Pt. 1, 765.

31. Foreman to Williams, September 20, 1864, O.R., Series I, Vol. 41, Pt. 3, 267.

32. Williams to Blair, September 20, 1864, O.R., Vol. 41, Pt. 1, 765.

33. Foreman to Wattles, September 20, 1864, O.R., Series I, Vol. 41, 766.

34. Charles D. Grear, "Cabin Creek: the One and a Half Million Dollar Raid," *North and South*, Vol. 11, No. 6 (December 2009), 30.

Chapter 12

1. Thayer to Williams, September 22, 1864, O.R., Series 1, Vol. 41, Pt. 3, 300.

2. Thayer to Halleck, September 22,1864, O.R., Series 1, Vol. 41, Pt. 3, 300.

3. Blair to Thayer, September 24, 1864, O.R., Series I, Vol. 41, Pt. 3, 352.

4. *Report of the Adjutant General of the State of Kansas, 1861–1865. Vol. 1*, 594.

5. General Order No. 143, May 22, 1863; Orders and Circulars, 1797–1910; Records of the Adjutant General's Office, 1780s–1917; Record Group 94; National Archives.

6. Carl Moneyhon, "1865: 'A State of Perfect Anarchy,'" in *Rugged and Sublime: The Civil War in Arkansas*, Mark Christ, ed. (Fayetteville, Arkansas: University of Arkansas Press, 1994), 145–146.

7. John Spencer ed., *Thunder on the Plains: 140th Anniversary of the Battle of Mine Creek* (Topeka: Kansas State Historical Society, 2004), 3.

8. Moneyhon, "'A State of Perfect Anarchy,'" 147–148.

9. Thayer to Wattles, October 19, 1864, O.R. Series I, Vol. 41, Pt. 4, 107–108.

10. Thayer to Wattles, October 20, 1864, O.R., Series I, Vol. 41, Pt. 4, 108–109.

11. Moneyhon, "A State of Perfect Anarchy," 150.

12. Jayme Millsap Stone, "Brother Against Brother: The Winter Skirmishes Along the Arkansas River, 1864–1865," in *Civil War Arkansas: Beyond Battles and Leaders*, eds. Anne J. Bailey and Daniel E. Sutherland (Fayetteville: University of Arkansas Press, 2000), 207.

13. Bowen to Levering, January 24, 1865, O.R., Series I, Vol. 48, Pt. 1, 14–16.

14. General Orders No. 18, 25 January 1865, Headquarters District of Arkansas, Confederate States Army, O.R., Series I, Vol. 48, Pt. 1, 16–17.

15. Reynolds to Christenson, February 6, 1865, O.R., Series I, Vol. 48, Pt. 1, 756.

16. General Order 10, Headquarters, First Division, VII Corps, February 9, 1865, Kansas State Historical Society.

17. Williams Service Records; Roger Hunt ed., *Brevet Brigadier Generals in Blue* (Gaithersburg, Maryland: Olde Soldier Books, Inc., 1990), 676.

18. Ibid.

19. Moneyhon, "'A State of Perfect Anarchy,'" 150–158.

20. Ibid.

21. Williams to Adjutant General US Army, June 26, 1865; Headquarters, Department of Arkansas, June 29, 1865, Special Order No. 153, Kansas State Historical Society.

22. Headquarters, Department of the Missouri, October 12, 1865, Special Order No. 72, Kansas State Historical Society.

23. Report of the Adjutant General of the State of Kansas *1861–1865. Vol. 1.*, xlv.

24. Robert M. Utley, *Frontier Regulars: The United States Army and the Indian, 1866–1891* (New York: Macmillan Publishing, 1973. Reprint. Lincoln: University of Nebraska Press, 1984), 13.

25. John A. Church, "Army Reduction," *The Galaxy*, Vol. 21, No. 2 (February 1876), 260.

26. Williams Service Records.

27. "Military Art and Science," *The United States Service Magazine* (1865): 188.

28. Ibid.

29. Ibid.

30. Ibid.

Chapter 13

1. John A. Hawgood, *America's Western Frontiers: The Story of the Explorers and Settlers Who Opened up the Trans-Mississippi West* (New York: Alfred A. Knopf, 1972), 289.

2. William A. Ganoe, *The History of the United States Army*, Revised Edition, (Cranbury, New Jersey: Scholar's Bookshelf, 2006), 298–299.

3. Michael Hughes, "Western American Indians during the American Civil War, 1861–1865," *Journal of the Indian Wars* 1, No. 3 (2000): 76.

4. Utley, *Frontier Regulars*, 16.

5. United States Secretary of War. Annual Report (1881): House Executive Document No. 1, Pt. 2, 47th Cong., 1st sess, Vol. 2 (Serial 2010), quoted in Utley, *Frontier Regulars*, 16.

6. Utley, *Frontier Regulars*, 17.

7. Ibid., 18–20.

8. Ibid., 21–22.

9. Sherry L. Smith, *The View from Officers' Row: Army Perceptions of Western Indians* (Tucson: University of Arizona Press, 1990), 5.

10. Ibid., 22.

11. United States War Department, Surgeon General's Office, *Circular No. 4: Barracks and Hospitals* (Washington, DC: December 5, 1870), 230–232. Hereafter noted as *Barracks and Hospitals*.

12. Robert Wooster, *The Military and United States Indian Policy 1865–1903* (Lincoln, Nebraska: University of Nebraska Press, 1988; reprint, 1995), 45.

13. Ibid., 114–115.

14. Ibid., 119, quoting correspondence between Sheridan and Sherman in 1866.

15. Ibid., 127.

16. Ibid., 48–49.

17. Ibid., 119, 121, 122.

18. Charles M. O'Conner, "The Eighth Regiment of Cavalry," in *The Army of the United States: Historical Sketches of Staff and Line with Portraits of Generals-in-Chief*, ed. Theophilus Rodenbough (New York: Maynard, Merrill, & Co., 1896), 268.

19. John H. Eicher and David J. Eicher, *Civil War High Commands* (Stanford: Stanford University Press, 2001).

20. "Obituary, Gen. Thomas C. Devin," *New York Times*, April 5, 1878, 5.

21. O'Conner, "Eighth Regiment of Cavalry," 269.

22. Ibid.

23. Ibid.

24. Devin to Adjutant General, January 26, 1873; Williams Service Records. Devin wrote a letter for the record, including three pages on the court martial of 1867, which resulted in acquittal. The only official mention of this court martial anywhere in the NARA file of Williams' service records is a hand-written, two-sentence entry on the margin of a summary of Williams' service dated March 1, 1890. The marginal notation is dated March 3, 1890.

Chapter 14

1. O'Conner, "Eighth Regiment of Cavalry," 269.

2. Hubert H. Bancroft, *The Works of Hubert Howe Bancroft, Volume XVII: History of Arizona and New Mexico 1530–1888* (San Francisco: The History Company, 1889), 521–522.

3. Dan L. Thrapp, *The Conquest of Apacheria* (Norman: University of Oklahoma Press, 1967), vii–xii.

4. David Alexander, *Arizona Frontier Military Place Names 1846–1912*, Revised Edition (Las Cruces, New Mexico: Yucca Tree Press, 2002, 151–152.

5. *Barracks and Hospitals*, 457–458.

6. Ibid.

7. Gordon Cortis. Baldwin, *The Warrior Apaches: A Story of the Chiricahua and Western Apache* (Tucson: Dale Stuart King, 1965), 32.

8. Camillo C.C. Carr, "The Days of Empire—Arizona, 1866–1869," in *The Struggle for Apacheria*, Vol. 1, *Eyewitnesses to the Indian Wars 1865–1890*, ed. Peter Cozzens (Mechanicsburg: Stackpole Press, 2001), 19.

9. Thomas E. Farish, *History of Arizona*, Vol. 3 (San Francisco: Filmer Brothers Electrotype Co., 1918), 222.

10. Bill Yenne, *Indian Wars: The Campaign for the American West* (Yardley, Pennsylvania: Westholme Publishing, 2006), 253.

11. John Mason, quoted in Thomas E. Farish, *History of Arizona*, Vol. 5 (San Francisco: Filmer Brothers Electrotype Co., 1918), 186. Brevet Brigadier General Mason was Gregg's predecessor in Arizona.

12. Bancroft, *History of Arizona and New Mexico*, 502.

13. Donald E. Worcester, *Apaches: Eagles of the Southwest* (Norman: University of Oklahoma Press, 1979), 100–103.

14. *Arizona Miner* (Prescott), April 20, 1867, courtesy of Sharlot Hall Museum, Prescott, Arizona.

15. US Army Adjutant General's Office. *Chronological List of Actions, &c., With Indians, January 1, 1866–January 1891.* US Army Center of Military History, US Army Military History Research Collection, n.d.

16. Utley, *Frontier Regulars*, 171–172.

17. Yenne, *Indian Wars*, 136.

18. *Arizona Miner* (Prescott), April 20, 1867

19. Ibid.

20. Ibid.

21. Ray Brandes, *Frontier Military Posts of Arizona* (Globe, Arizona: Dale Stuart King, Publisher, 1960), 77.

22. Utley, *Frontier Regulars*, 192–173.

23. *Arizona Miner*, July 13, 1867.

24. Gregg to Williams, June 9, 1867, Williams Service Records.

25. Thomas R. Mcguire, "Walapai," in *Handbook of North American Indians*, Vol. 10, *Southwest*, ed. Alfonso Ortiz, gen. ed. William Sturtevant (Washington: Smithsonian Institution, 1983), 26–28.

26. Thrapp, *Conquest of Apacheria*, 39–40.

27. Ibid., 58.

28. *Arizona Gazette*, July 4, 1867.

29. Thrapp, *Conquest of Apacheria*, 58.

30. Personal Statement of J.M. Williams, Pension Application, Williams Service Records.

31. Ibid.

32. "Indian Outrages," *Arizona Miner*, July 27, 1867, courtesy of Sharlot Hall Museum, Prescott, Arizona.

33. Bigelow to Williams, August 13, 1867, Williams Service Records.

34. McDowell to Fry, September 14, 1867, "Report on Expeditions against the Indians," in Thomas E. Farish, *History of Arizona*, Vol. 3 (San Francisco: Filmer Brothers Electrotype Co., 1918), 255.

35. John H. Foster to JM Williams September 13, 1867. Foster was General McDowell's aide de camp, writing the letter as instructed by McDowell. Williams Service Records.

36. Extracts from G.O. 33, HQ, Dept. of California, May 30, 1867; and G.O. 49, HQ, Dept. of California, September 13, 1867, issued by General McDowell, commending Williams were included in Williams' file, along with a reference to The Official Army Register of 1898, p. 324, documenting the award of the brevet; Williams Service Records.

37. E.G. Ross to the President, November 21, 1867, Williams Service Records.

38. Extracts from G.O. 33, HQ, Dept. of California, May 30, 1867; and G.O. 49, HQ, Dept. of California, September 13, 1867, issued by General McDowell, with a reference to The Official Army Register of 1898, p. 324, documenting the award of the brevet; Williams Service Records.

Chapter 15

1. *House Bill No. 12, An Act to Divorce James M. Williams from the Bonds of Matrimony Heretofore Contracted with Lydia E. Williams, Late Lydia E. Francis*, 4th Territorial Legislative Assembly of Arizona, September 23, 1867.

2. Williams Service Records.

3. Williams–Harrower Family Bible, "Narrative on the Life of Mary Elizabeth Brawner Williams."

4. Frances Anne Mullen Boyd, [Mrs. Orsemus B. Boyd, pseud.] *Cavalry Life in Tent and Field*, introduction by Darlis A. Miller (New York: J. Selwin Tait and Sons, 1894; Reprint, Lincoln: University of Nebraska Press, 1982), 24.

5. Eveline M. Alexander, *Cavalry Wife: The Diary of Eveline Alexander, 1866–1867*, ed. Sandra Myers (College Station: Texas A&M University Press, 1977).

6. Worcester, *Apaches: Eagles of the Southwest*, 110; Bancroft, *Works of Hubert Howe Bancroft*. In citing this situation in his 1889 *History of Arizona and New Mexico*, who? provides the same narrative and conclusions, but noted 114 Indians killed. Nevertheless, the outcome was unchanged.

7. O'Conner, "Eighth Regiment of Cavalry," 269–270.

8. Thrapp, *Conquest of Apacheria*, 19.

9. Alan J. Holmes, *Fort Selden 1965–1891: The Birth, Life, and Death of a Frontier Fort in New Mexico*, New Mexico Centennial History Series (Santa Fe: Sunstone Press, 2010), 11.

10. Marc Simmons, *The Last Conquistador: Juan de Oñate and the Settling of the Far Southwest*, Oklahoma Western Biographies, Vol. 2, ed. Richard Etulain (Norman: University of Oklahoma Press, 1991), 103.

11. *Barracks and Hospitals*, 237–238.

12. Ibid.

13. Ibid.

14. Sally Bickley, "Jornada Del Muerto—90 Miles of Hell," accessed May 12, 2010 http://www.southernnewmexico.com/ Articles/Southwest/JornadadelMuerto-90mileso.html.

15. The adobe ruins of Fort Selden still remain today as the Fort Selden State Monument. The site includes the adobe walls of most structures, an interpretive center and museum, walking paths with interpretive signs describing the buildings, vintage photos of the buildings, and a bronze statue of a buffalo soldier (black cavalrymen from the Ninth Cavalry, which served there at various times). There are frequent reenactment events held there, inviting the public to view life on the frontier. The Fort Selden State Monument is located just off Interstate Highway 25, approximately eighteen miles north of Las Cruces, New Mexico.

16. Bob Alexander, *Desert Desperados: the Banditti of Southwestern New Mexico* (Silver City, New Mexico: Gila Books, 2006), 26.

17. Holmes, *Fort Selden 1965–1891*, 37.

18. Utley, *Frontier Regulars*.

19. Holmes, *Fort Selden 1965–1891*, 40–41.

20. Alexander, *Desert Desperados*, 27.

21. Don Rickey, *Forty Miles a Day on Beans and Hay* (Norman: University of Oklahoma Press, 1963), 272.

22. Timothy Cohrs, "Fort Selden, New Mexico," *Palacio*, 1973 m 79 (4), 19.

23. Timothy Cohrs and Thomas J. Caperton, *Fort Selden, New Mexico: Fort Selden State Monument* (Santa Fe: Museum of New Mexico, 1983), 14.

24. Ibid.

25. Alexander, *Desert Desperados*, Ibid.

26. Bob Alexander, *Sheriff Harvey Whitehill: Silver City Stalwart* (Silver City, New Mexico: High Lonesome Books, 2005), 156.

27. Cohrs, "Fort Selden," 25.

28. Ibid, 25; Bob Alexander and Jan Devereaux, "Trumpeting Elephants & Kicking Asses: Republicans vs. Democrats, New Mexico Style," *True West* 57/2 (January/February 2010) 26–31.

29. Ibid., 20.

30. United States Census Bureau, 1880 Census, accessed 21 November 2009, http://www.ancestry.com.

31. Holmes, *Fort Selden 1965–1891*,147–150.

32. Cohrs, *Fort Selden*, 23.

33. Williams Service Records, Jackson to Townsend, December 14, 1870,.

34. *Fort Selden State Monument General Management Plan*, Appendix 4: Historical Summary (Santa Fe: New Mexico Department of Cultural Affairs, 2004) 74.

Chapter 16

1. *Fort Selden State Monument General Management Plan*, 75.

2. Don Lusk, "Fighting Post," *New Mexico Magazine*, June 1936, 25.

3. Daniel C.B. Rathbun and David V. Alexander, *New Mexico Frontier Military Place Names* (Las Cruces, New Mexico: Yucca Tree Press, 2003), 12.

4. *Barracks and Hospitals*, 240.

5. Hart, *Old Forts of the Far West*, 170.

6. Neta Pope and Andrea Jaquez, *The Fort Bayard Story: 1866–1869* (Silver City, NM: Andrea Jaquez, 2011), 24–26.

7. Herbert Hart, *Old Forts of the Far West* (Seattle: Superior Publishing Co., 1965), 171–172.

8. Pope and Jaquez, *Fort Bayard Story*, 15.

9. *Barracks and Hospitals*, 240–241.

10. Hart, *Old Forts of the Far West*, 170.

11. Mrs. Orsemus B. Boyd [Frances Anne Boyd], *Cavalry Life in Tent & Field* (New York: J. Selwin Tait and Sons, 1894; reprint, Lincoln: University of Nebraska Press, 1982), 216.

12. Frederick E. Phelps, "Memoirs" (Unpublished), Rio Grande Collection, New Mexico State University Library, Las Cruces, New Mexico, 2007, 1–2. Segments of these memoirs were later published in four quarterly issues of the *New Mexico Historical Review* in 1950.

13. Ibid., 171.

14. Alexander, *Desert Desperados*, 28–29.

15. Williams Service Records, Unknown to Williams, May 28, 1872.

16. Bancroft, *History of Arizona and New Mexico 1530–1888*, 725.

17. United States War Department, Records of United States Regular Army Mobile Units, 1821–1942 (Record Group 391), Returns of the Eighth Regiment of Cavalry, 1867–1873: Courtesy of Miller Library, Western New Mexico University, Silver City, New Mexico, Andrea Jaquez and Neta Pope, Fort Bayard Researchers, June 2007.

18. Personal Statement of J.M. Williams, an Applicant for Increase of Pension, March 22, 1890, Williams Service Records.

19. Phelps, "Memoirs," 35.

20. Ibid., 32.

21. Williams Service Records, Report of Retiring Board convened by Special Orders 194, Fort Leavenworth, Kansas December 14, 1870.

22. Blair to HQ, District of New Mexico, 16 September 1872. NARA, M1088, Letters Received, Headquarters, District of New Mexico, September 1865–August 1890, Roll 15, File B-46-1872, courtesy Andrea Jaquez and Neta Pope, Fort Bayard Researchers, Miller Library, Western New Mexico University.

23. Ibid.

24. Pope and Jaquez, *Fort Bayard Story*, 56–63, 68.

25. Williams to HQ, District of New Mexico, September 20, 1872. NARA, M1088, Letters Received, Headquarters, District of New Mexico, September 1865–August 1890, Roll 15, Gile B-46-1872, September 20, 1872, courtesy Andrea Jacquez and Neta Pope, Fort Bayard Researchers, Miller Library, Western New Mexico University.

26. Special Orders No. 143, Headquarters, Fort Bayard, NM, December 2,1872.

27. Devin to Judge Advocate of Department of Missouri, December 8, 1872.

28. Ibid.

29. Devin to Adjutant General, January 26, 1873.

30. Williams Service Records, Judge Advocate General to Secretary of War, February 11, 1873.

31. Williams Service Records, Williams to Post Adjutant, March 29, 1873.

Chapter 17

1. Eugene Parsons, *A Guidebook to Colorado* (Boston: Little, Brown, and Co., 1911), 206.

2. Susan Shelby Magoffin, *Down the Santa Fe Trail and into Mexico: The Diary of Susan Shelby Magoffin, 1846–1847*, ed. Stella M. Drumm (New Haven: Yale University Press, 1926; reprint, Lincoln: University of Nebraska Press, 1982), 76–77.

3. Magoffin, *Down the Santa Fe Trail and into Mexico*, 78–84.

4. Candy Moulton, *Roadside History of Colorado* (Missoula Montana: Mountain Press Publishing, 2006), pp?

5. Alexander. *Cavalry Wife*, 80–82.

6. Moulton, *Roadside History of Colorado*, 100.

7. Eugene Parsons, *A Guidebook to Colorado*, 202–204.

8. George S. Raper, "Cavalry Duty in the Southwest in the 1870s," in *Indian War Veterans: Memories of Army Life and Campaigns in the West, 1864–1898*, ed. Jerome A Greene (New York: Savas Beatie, 2007), 19.

9. Williams Letterhead, Kansas State Historical Society.

10. Thomas Jack, *The Gazetteer of the World: Prominence Being Given to Great Britain and Colonies, Indian Empire—United States of America*, Volume III (Edinburgh: Grange Publishing Works, 1885), 711.

11. Bancroft, *History of Arizona and New Mexico 1530–1888,* 736.

12. "Trinidad, Colorado: A Short History of the Early Days," accessed 9 June 2009, http://www.sangres.com/places /lasanimas/history.htm.

13. Parsons, *Guidebook to Colorado*, xvii–xviii.

14. Williams to Wood, January 15, 1878, Kansas State Historical Society.

15. Frank Hall, *History of the State of Colorado*, Vol. IV *(Chicago: Blakely Printing Co., 1895)*, 196.

16. Wilbur Stone, ed., *History of Colorado*, Vol. 1 (Chicago: S.J. Clarke Publishing Co., 1918), 351–358.

17. Ibid., 511–512.

18. Bill Shaw to Robert Lull, 11 August 2006. Mr. Shaw currently owns the house James Williams built. He conducted extensive research into its past and design. Ken Fletcher, a Trinidad historian, provided much of Shaw's historical information.

19. Parsons, *Guidebook to Colorado*, 204–205.

20. "From Conquistadors to Cougar Canyon: The History of Trinidad," accessed July 5, 2010, http://www.cougarcanyonliving.com/main/areahistory.

21. *Trinidad Daily Democrat*, November 1, 1882. The notation of "major" refers to Williams' regular army brevet rank.

22. *Trinidad Weekly News*, November 9, 1882.

23. Shaw to Lull; Personal Statement of J.M. Williams, an Applicant for Increase of Pension, March 22, 1890.

24. W.H. Whitney, *Directory of Trinidad, Colorado for 1888* (Trinidad: Advertiser Steam Job Print, 1888), 139.

25. Shaw to Lull, August 11, 2006.

26. Ibid.

27. *Directory of Trinidad*, 37.

28. William D. Kelly to Col. J. M. Williams, Washington, DC, June 16, 1890, Kansas State Historical Society.

29. *Leavenworth Times*, Leavenworth Kansas, October 8, 1890.

30. Ibid.

31. Ibid.

32. Ibid.

33. Ibid.

34. Gregg to Senate Committee on Military Affairs, January 9, 1890, included in Senate Committee on Military Affairs, *James M. Williams*, Report prepared by Senator C.K. Davis [To accompany S. 1037], 51st Cong., 1st sess., 1890, Committee Print 1002, 3–4. See the Appendix for full text of the report of the Senate Military Affairs Committee.

35. Ibid.

36. Senate Committee on Military Affairs, *James M. Williams*, Report prepared by Senator Davis [To accompany S. 1037], 51st Cong., 1st sess., 1890, Committee Print 1002, 2.

37. Ibid., 3. Presumably this reference is to Lieutenant Thomas Blair of the Fifteenth Infantry, who wrote the initial correspondence concerning Williams' unauthorized use of forage and building materials to construct and repair facilities for his troops.

38. Ibid.

39. President of the United States, "Commission of James M. Williams as Captain of Cavalry," January 12, 1891, Courtesy of Kansas State Historical Society.

40. Military Order of the Loyal Legion of the United States, *In Memoriam, Companion James Monroe Williams*, Circular No. 7, Series of 1907 (Commandery of the District of Columbia, February 16, 1907).

41. Williams to Alger, 16 April 1898, Williams Service Records.

42. District of Columbia, Certificate of Death, James M. Williams, Record No. 172072, February 15, 1907; Robert L. Williams to Military Secretary, February 15, 1907, Williams Service Records; "Gen. Williams Buried in Arlington Cemetery," *Washington Times*, February 18, 1907.

Conclusion

1. Edwin Bearss, letter to author, April 15, 2011.

2. Utley, *Frontier Regulars*, 172–173.

3. Thrapp, *Conquest of Apacheria*, 57.

4. Tabor, *Skirmish at Island Mound, Missouri: The First Battle Fought by an African-American Regiment during the Civil War*.

5. Spurgeon, *Man of Douglas, Man of Lincoln*, 235.

Bibliography

Primary Sources

Alexander, Eveline. *Cavalry Wife: The Diary of Eveline M. Alexander, 1866–1867*. Edited by Sandra Myres. College Station: Texas A&M University Press, 1977.

Arizona Gazette (Prescott, later Phoenix, renamed *Arizona Republic*). July 4, 1867.

Arizona Miner (Prescott). April 20, July 27, 1867.

Boyd, Mrs. Orsemus B. [Frances Anne Mullen Boyd]. *Cavalry Life in Tent and Field*. New York: J. Selwin Tait & Sons, 1894. Reprint, Lincoln: University of Nebraska Press, 1982.

Britton, Wiley. *The Civil War on the Border: A Narrative of Military Operations in Missouri, Kansas, Arkansas and the Indian Territory during the Years 1863–65, Based upon Official Reports and Observations of the Author*, Vol. II. New York: G. P. Putnam's Sons, 1899.

———. *Memoirs of the Rebellion on the Border, 1863*. Chicago: Cushing, Thomas & Co., 1882. Reprint, Lincoln: University of Nebraska Press, 1993.

Burke, W. S. *Official Military History of Kansas Regiments During the War for the Suppression of the Great Rebellion*. Leavenworth, Kansas: Heritage Press, n.d.

Carr, Camillo C. C. "The Days of Empire—Arizona, 1866–1869," in *The Struggle for Apacheria, Vol. 2, Eyewitnesses to the Indian Wars 1865–1890*. Edited by Peter Cozzens. Mechanicsburg: Stackpole Press, 2001.

Chipman, N. P. "Excerpt from Coln. N.P. Chipman to General [Samuel R. Curtis], 16 Oct. [1862], C-46, 1862, Letters Received, ser. 2593, Dept. of the MO, RG 393 Pt. 1 [C-104], in *Freedom, A Documentary History of Emancipation, 1861–1867, Series II, The Black Military Experience.* Edited by Ira Berlin. Cambridge: Cambridge University Press, 1982.

Creitz, William F. *Civil War Diary.* Topeka: Kansas State Historical Society. Accessed May 4, 2010. http://www.griffingweb.com/captain_creitz's_diary.htm.

Connecticut. *Lists and Returns of Connecticut Men in the Revolution.* Hartford: Connecticut Historical Society, 1909.

De Tocqueville, Alexis. *Democracy in America.* Translated by Henry Reeve. Vol. 1. New York: D. Appleton, 1904.

District of Columbia. Certificate of Death, James M. Williams. Record No. 172072, February 15, 1907.

Earle, Ethan. *Account Book of Ethan Earle* (Mss C 4911). R. Stanton Avery Special Collection Dept., New England Historic Genealogical Society.

Edwards, Whit. *The Prairie Was on Fire: Eyewitness Accounts of the Civil War in the Indian Territory.* Oklahoma City: Oklahoma Historical Society, 2001.

Emilio, Luis F. *A Brave Black Regiment: The History of the 54th Massachusetts, 1863–1865.* 1894. Reprinted with a new introduction by Gregory J. W. Urwin. New York: Da Capo Press, 1995.

Foreman, Grant. *Down the Texas Road: Historic Places along Highway 69 through Oklahoma.* Norman: University of Oklahoma Press, 1936.

Fort Selden State Monument General Management Plan. Appendix 4: "Historical Summary." Santa Fe: New Mexico Department of Cultural Affairs, 2004.

Gazetteer of the World: Prominence Being Given to Great Britain and Colonies, Indian Empire, United States of America, Volume III. Edinburgh: Grange Publishing Works, 1885.

Grayson, George W. *A Creek Warrior for the Confederacy: The Autobiography of Chief G. W. Grayson,* Civilization of the American Indian Series. Edited by W. David Baird. Norman: University of Oklahoma Press, 1988.

Hacker, John. "Jasper County Park to Commemorate Rader Farm Massacre," *Carthage* (Missouri) *Press,* November 16, 2009.

Higginson, Thomas W. *Army Life in a Black Regiment*. 1870. Reprint, New York: Dover Publications, 2002.

Home for Incurables. Drop Report—Pensioner, Mary E. Williams. Washington, DC: October 26, 1924.

House Bill No. 12: An Act to Divorce James M. Williams from the Bonds of Matrimony Heretofore Contracted with Lydia E. Williams, Late Lydia E. Francis. Fourth Arizona Territorial Legislative Assembly (September 23, 1867).

Hunt, Roger, ed. *Brevet Brigadier Generals in Blue*. Gaithersburg, Maryland: Olde Soldier Books, Inc., 1990.

Jack, Thomas. *The Gazetteer of the World: Prominence Being Given to Great Britain and Colonies, Indian Empire—United States of America*. Volume III. Edinburgh: Grange Publishing Works, 1885.

"Indian Outrages," *Arizona Miner*, July 27, 1867.

Kansas State Historical Society. James M. Williams Collection. Topeka, Kansas.

Leavenworth City Directory and Business Mirror for 1859–60. St. Louis: Sutherland and McEvoy, 1859.

Leavenworth City Directory and Business Mirror for 1859–60. St. Louis: Sutherland and McEvoy, 1860.

Leavenworth City Directory and Business Mirror for 1859–60. St. Louis: Sutherland and McEvoy, 1863.

Leavenworth City Directory and Business Mirror for 1859–60. St. Louis: Sutherland and McEvoy, 1865.

Leavenworth Land Record Index, Vols. 84–85. Leavenworth, Kansas.

Leavenworth Times. October 8, 1890.

Lewis County, New York. Grantee Index. Liber P, page 289–291; Grantor Index. Liber I, page 146; Liber S, page 330, 484; Liber U, page 72.

Magoffin, Susan H. *Down the Santa Fe Trail and into Mexico: The Diary of Susan Shelby Magoffin, 1846–1847*. Edited by Stella Drumm. 1926. Reprint, Lincoln: University of Nebraska Press, 1982

Mason, John. Quoted in Thomas E. Farish, *History of Arizona*, Vol. 5, 186. San Francisco: Filmer Brothers Electrotype Co., 1918.

"Military Art and Science," *The United States Service Magazine* (1865): 188.

Military Order of the Loyal Legion of the United States. *In Memoriam, Companion James Monroe Williams*. Commandery of the District of Columbia, Circular No. 7, Series of 1907. February 16, 1907.

Minges, Patrick, ed. *Black Indian Slave Narratives*. Winton-Salem: John F. Blair, 2004.

Moore, Frank, ed. *The Rebellion Record: A Diary of American Events*, Vol. 6. New York: G.P. Putnam, 1863.

Moulton, Candy. *Roadside History of Colorado*. Missoula: Mountain Press Publishing, 2006.

National Tribune. Washington, DC. November 1, 1883.

The New Era. "From the Front," (Fort Smith, Arkansas), May 7, 1864.

New York. "List of Claims to the State of New York for Arms and Clothing Provided by Individual Members of the State Militia, No. 15106," *Index of Awards on Claims of the Soldiers of the War of 1812*. Albany: New Adjutant General's Office, 1880.

New York. *State Census, 1825*.

New York Times. July 30, 1861, April 5, 1878.

"Old Kickapoo Cannon," Kansas State Historical Society. Accessed May 5, 2010. http://www.kshs.org/cool3/oldkickapoo.htm.

Ortiz, Alfonso ed., *Handbook of North American Indians, Vol. 10. Southwest*. General Editor William Sturtevant. Washington, DC.: Smithsonian Institution, 1983.

Phelps, Frederick. "Memoirs." Rio Grande Collection, New Mexico State University Library, Las Cruces, New Mexico, 2007.

Regimental Order Book, 79th United States Colored Infantry, Regimental and Company Books of Civil War Volunteer Union Organizations, compiled 1861–1865; Records of the Adjutant General's Office, Record Group 94; NARA, Washington, DC.

Report of the Adjutant General of the State of Kansas, 1861–1865. Vol.1. (Reprinted by Authority) Topeka, Kansas: The Kansas State Printing Company. 1896.

Rickey, Don. *Forty Miles a Day on Beans and Hay*. Norman: University of Oklahoma Press, 1963.

Robinson, Charles. *The Kansas Conflict*. New York: Harper & Brothers, 1892.

Robinson, Sara T.L. *Kansas: Its Interior and Exterior Life*. Boston: Crosby, Nichols and Company, 1856.

Sherman, William Tecumseh. *Memoirs of General William T. Sherman*. Bloomington: University of Indiana Press, 1957.

Smith, Sherry L. *The View from Officers' Row: Army Perceptions of Western Indians.* Tucson: University of Arizona Press, 1990.

Smoky Hill and Republican Union (Junction City, Kansas), September 6, 1862.

Stearns, John H. "Interesting Reminiscences of Colored Troops Who Probably Saved Mound City from the Fate of Lawrence," *Linn County Republic,* January 31, 1902.

Trego, Joseph. *Diary, 1861–63.* Microfilm MS 1008. Kansas State Historical Society.

Trinidad (Colorado) *Daily Democrat,* November 1, 1882.

Trinidad (Colorado) *Weekly News,* November 9, 1882.

United States Census Bureau. *1850 Census.* Accessed November 21, 2009. http://www.ancestry.com/?o_xid=21837& o_lid=21837&o_sch=Search.

United States Census Bureau. *1860 Census,* Leavenworth, Kansas; Family Search—Family History and Genealogy Records. Family Group Record: Parents and Siblings, Lydia Francis Williams. Accessed May 2, 2010. http://www.familysearch.org/eng/default.asp

United States Census Bureau. *1880 Census.* Accessed November 21, 2009. http://www.ancestry.com/?o_xid=21837& o_lid=21837&o_sch=Search.

United States. Congress. Senate. Committee on Claims. *Elkanah Huddleston.* Report prepared by Senator Willey. 41st Cong., 3d Sess., 1871, Report 332.

United States. Congress. Senate. Committee on Military Affairs. *James M. Williams.* Report prepared by Senator Davis to accompany S. 1037. 51st Cong., 1st Sess., 1890, Committee Print 1002.

United States. *Congressional Globe,* 37th Congress, 2nd Session, January 15, 1852, 334–336.

United States. National Archives and Records Administration. *Compiled Service Records, Records of the Adjutant General's Office, 1780–1917,* RG 94. Williams, James M. Washington. DC, n.d.

United States. National Archives and Records Administration. *Records of the Judge Advocate General (Army),* RG 153, *Records of the Proceedings of US Army General Courts-Martial.* Courtesy of Western New Mexico University Library, Neta Pope, Andrea Jaquez, Fort Bayard researchers.

United States. National Archives and Records Administration. *Letters Received, Headquarters, District of New Mexico, September 1865–August 1890,* M1088, Roll 15, File B-46, 1872.

United States. President (Benjamin Harrison). Commission. "James M. Williams as Captain of Cavalry," January 12, 1891.

United States. Secretary of War. Annual Report (1880): House Executive Document No. 1, Pt. 2, 46th Cong., 3d sess., Vol. 2 (Serial 1952), quoted in Utley, Robert. *Frontier Regulars: The United States Army and the Indian, 1866–1891. 1969.* Reprint, Lincoln: University of Nebraska Press, 1973.

United States. *US Constitution,* Article I, Section 6, Paragraph 2.

United States. War Department. General Order 97, May 26, 1865, J.M. Williams, Col, 1st Kan Colored Vols. Appointed to be Brigadier General by Brevet in the Volunteer Force, Army of the United States, effective February 15, 1865.

United States. War Department. Surgeon General's Office. *Circular No. 4: Barracks and Hospitals.* Washington, DC: December 5, 1870.

United States. War Department. Records of United States Regular Army Mobile Units, 1821–1942. RG 391. Returns of the Eighth Regiment of Cavalry, 1867–1873. Courtesy of Western New Mexico University, Neta Pope, Andrea Jaquez, Fort Bayard researchers.

United States. War Department. *The War of the Rebellion: A Compilation of the Official Records of the Union and Confederate Armies.* 128 Vols. Washington, DC: Government Printing Office, 1881–1900.

Ward, William H., ed. *Records of the Members of the Grand Army of the Republic with a Complete Account of the Twentieth National Encampment.* San Francisco: H.S. Crocker & Company, 1886.

Whitney, W. H. *Directory of Trinidad, Colorado for 1888.* Trinidad: Advertiser Steam Job Print, 1888.

Who Was Who in America. Vol. 1. Chicago: Marquis, 1950.

Williams, Charlean M. "The Battle of Poison Spring," in *The Old Town Speaks: Recollections of Washington, Hempstead County, Arkansas; Gateway to Texas 1833, Confederate Capital 1863.* Houston: Anson Jones Press, 1851.

Wisconsin. Wisconsin General Land Office Records, Southeastern Wisconsin. Accessed May 2, 2010. http://searches.rootsweb.com/cgi-bin/wisconsin/wisconsin.pl.

Washington (DC) *Times,* February 18, 1907.

Secondary Sources

Abel, Annie Heloise. *The American Indian in the Civil War 1862–1865.* 1919. Reprint, Lincoln: University of Nebraska Press, 1992.

Alexander, Bob. *Desert Desperados: The Banditti of Southwestern New Mexico.* Silver City, New Mexico: Gila Books, 2006.

———. *Sheriff Harvey Whitehill: Silver City Stalwart.* Silver City, New Mexico: High Lonesome Books, 2005.

Alexander, Bob, and Jan Devereaux. "Trumpeting Elephants & Kicking Asses: Republicans vs. Democrats, New Mexico Style," *True West* Vol. 57, No. 2 (January/February 2010): 26–31.

Alexander, David. *Arizona Frontier Military Place Names 1846–1912.* Revised Edition. Las Cruces, New Mexico: Yucca Tree Press, 2002.

Axelrod, Alan. *The Horrid Pit: The Battle of the Crater, the Civil War's Cruelest Mission.* New York: Carroll and Graf Publishers, 2007.

Baldwin, Gordon C. *The Warrior Apaches: A Story of the Chiricahua and Western Apache.* Tucson: Dale S. King, 1965.

Bancroft, Hubert. *The Works of Hubert Howe Bancroft, Volume XVII: History of Arizona and New Mexico 1530–1888.* San Francisco: The History Company, Publishers, 1889.

Beckwith, Albert. *History of Walworth County Wisconsin.* Vol. 1. Indianapolis: B.F. Bowen & Co., 1912.

Bearss, Edwin. C. *Steele's Retreat from Camden and The Battle of Jenkins' Ferry.* 1966. Reprint, Little Rock: Eagle Press, 1990.

Benedict, Bryce. *Jayhawkers: The Civil War Brigade of James Henry Lane.* Norman: University of Oklahoma Press, 2009.

———. "Kansas' Colored Btry Fought in Civil War." *Plains Guardian.* Vol. 43, No. 2, February 1998.

Berlin, Ira, ed. *Freedom, A Documentary History of Emancipation, 1861–1867, Series II, The Black Military Experience.* Cambridge: Cambridge University Press, 1982.

Bickley, Sally. Jornada Del Muerto—90 Miles of Hell. Accessed May 12, 2010. http://www.southernnewmexico.com /Articles/Southwest/Jornadadel Muerto-90mileso.html.

Blackmar, Frank W., ed. *Kansas: a Cyclopedia of State History, Embracing Events, Institutions, Industries, Counties, Cities, Towns, Prominent Persons, etc.* Vols. 2–3. Chicago: Standard Publishing Co., 1912.

Brandes, Ray. *Frontier Military Posts of Arizona.* Globe, Arizona: Dale Stuart King, Publisher, 1960.

Britton, Wiley. *The Union Indian Brigade in the Civil War.* Kansas City, Missouri: Franklin Hudson Publishing Company, 1922.

Burkhardt, George S. "No Quarter! Black Flag Warfare 1863–1865." *North and South.* Vol. 10, No. 1 (May 2007): 12–29.

Castel, Albert. "Civil War Kansas and the Negro," *The Journal of Negro History*, Vol. 51, No. 2 (Apr 1966): 126–127.

———. *Civil War Kansas: Reaping the Whirlwind.* Ithaca: 1958. Reprint, Lawrence: University Press of Kansas, 1997.

———. *General Sterling Price and the Civil War in the West.* Baton Rouge: Louisiana State University Press, 1996.

Christ, Mark K., ed. *"All Cut to Pieces and Gone to Hell:" The Civil War, Race Relations, and the Battle of Poison Spring.* Little Rock: August House Publishers, 2003.

———., ed. *Rugged and Sublime: The Civil War in Arkansas.* Fayetteville: University of Arkansas Press, 1994.

Church, John A. "Army Reduction," *The Galaxy.* Vol. 21, No.2 (February, 1876): 260.

Cohrs, Timothy. "Fort Selden, New Mexico." *Palacio.* Vol. 79, No. 4. 1973.

———, and Thomas Caperton. *Fort Selden, New Mexico: Fort Selden State Monument.* Santa Fe: Museum of New Mexico, 1983.

Collins, Robert. *General James G. Blunt: Tarnished Glory.* Gretna: Pelican Publishing, 2005.

Confer, Clarissa. *The Cherokee Nation in the Civil War.* Norman: University of Oklahoma Press, 2007.

Cornish, Dudley T. *Kansas Negro Regiments in the Civil War.* Topeka: Kansas Commission on Civil Rights, 1969.

———. *The Sable Arm: Black Troops in the Union Army, 1861–1865.* Lawrence: University Press of Kansas, 1987.

Cox, Jess. "Fort Bayard . . . Frontier Outpost." *New Mexico Magazine.* Albuquerque: New Mexico Department of Tourism, April 1964.

Cunningham, Roger D. "Douglas' Battery at Fort Leavenworth: The Issue of Black Officers During the Civil War." *Kansas History*, Vol. 23, No. 4 (Winter 2000–2001): 200–217.

Cutler, William G. *History of the State of Kansas.* Chicago: A.T. Andreas, 1883. Accessed May 12, 2010. http://www.kancoll.org/books/cutler/.

DeBlack, Thomas A. "An Overview of the Camden Expedition," in *"All Cut to Pieces and Gone to Hell:" The Civil War, Race Relations, and the Battle of Poison Spring,* ed. Mark K. Christ. Little Rock: August House Publishing, 2003.

Denny, James, and John Bradbury. *The Civil War's First Blood: Missouri, 1854–1861.* Boonville, Missouri: Missouri Life, 2007.

Duflo, Dorothy. *Lowville. Images of America.* With a foreword by Charlotte M. Beagle. Charleston: Arcadia, 2009.

Dobak, William. *Freedom by the Sword: The U.S. Colored Troops, 1862–1867.* Washington, DC: Center of Military History United States Army, 2011.

Edwards, Whit. Foreword to *Civil War in the Indian Territory*, by Steve Cottrell. Gretna: Pelican Publishing, 1998.

Eicher, John H., and David J. Eichner. *Civil War High Commands.* Stanford University Press, 2001.

Epple, Jess. *Honey Springs Depot: Elk Creek, Creek Nation, Indian Territory.* Muskogee, Hoffman Printing Co., 1964.

Etcheson, Nicole. *Bleeding Kansas: Contested Liberty in the Civil War Era.* Lawrence: University Press of Kansas, 2004.

Farish, Thomas E. *History of Arizona.* Vol. 3. San Francisco: Filmer Brothers Electrotype Co., 1918.

Forsyth, Michael J. *The Camden Expedition of 1864 and the Opportunity Lost by the Confederacy to Change the Civil War.* Jefferson, North Carolina: McFarland & Co., 2003.

Franks, Kenny A. *Stand Watie and the Agony of the Cherokee Nation.* Memphis: Memphis State University Press, 1979.

"From Conquistadors to Cougar Canyon: The History of Trinidad." Accessed July 5, 2010. http://www.cougarcanyonliving.com/main/areahistory.

Ganoe, William A. *The History of the United States Army.* 1942. Revised Edition, Cranbury, New Jersey: The Scholar's Bookshelf, 2006.

Glathaar, Joseph. *Forged in Battle: the Civil War Alliance of Black Soldiers and White Officers.* Baton Rouge: Louisiana State University Press, 2000.

Grady, John, and Bradford Felmly. *Suffering to Silence: 29th Texas Cavalry, CSA Regimental History.* Quanah, Texas: Nortex Press, 1975.

Grear, Charles D. "Cabin Creek: the One and a Half Million Dollar Raid," *North and South,* Volume 11, No. 6 (December, 2009): 30.

———. "Gano's Brigade: A History of the Fifth Texas Cavalry Brigade, 1863–1864." M.A. thesis, Texas Tech University, 2001.

———. "Red and White Fighting the Blue: Relations between Texans and Confederate Indians." In *The Seventh Star of the Confederacy: Texas during the Civil War,* War and the Southwest Series No. 10. Edited by Kenneth W. Howell, 167–188. Denton, Texas: University of North Texas Press, 2009.

Hall, Frank. *History of the State of Colorado, Volume IV.* Chicago: Blakely Printing Company, 1895.

Hart, Herbert M. *Old Forts of the Far West.* Seattle: Superior Publishing Company, 1965.

History of Vernon County, Missouri. St. Louis: Brown & Co., 1887.

Holmes, Alan. *Fort Selden 1965–1981: The Birth, Life, and Death of a Frontier Fort in New Mexico.* New Mexico Centennial History Series. Santa Fe: Sunstone Press, 2010.

Hough, Franklin B. *A History of Lewis County in the State of New York from the Beginning of Its Earliest Settlement to the Present Time.* Albany: Munsell & Rowland, 1860.

Hughes, Michael. "Western American Indians during the American Civil War, 1861–1865." Journal of the Indian Wars 1, No. 3 (2000): 69–114.

Jackman, Sidney. *Behind Enemy Lines: The Memoirs of Brigadier General Sidney Drake Jackman, CSA,* Richard L. Norton, ed. Springfield, Missouri: Oak Hills Publishing, 1997.

Joiner, Gary D. *One Damn Blunder from Beginning to End: The Red River Campaign of 1864.* Wilmington, Delaware: Scholarly Resources, 2003.

Jones, Ralph, and Mike Adkins. *The Battle of Honey Springs: A Clash of cultures in the Indian Territory.* Oklahoma City: Oklahoma Historical Society, 1993.

Josephy, Alvin M. Jr. *The Civil War in the American West.* New York: Random House, 1991.

Lanning, Michael L. *Defenders of Liberty: African-Americans in the Revolutionary War.* New York: Kensington Press, 2000.

Lindberg, Kip, and Matt Matthews, "'To Play a Bold Game:' The Battle of Honey Springs." *North and South* 6, No. 1 (December 2002): 61–62.

Livingston, John. *Such a Foe as Livingston: The Campaign of Confederate Major Thomas R. Livingston's First Missouri cavalry Battalion of Southwest Missouri.* Wyandotte, OK: Gregath Publishing Company, 2004.

Lusk, Don. "Fighting Post." *New Mexico Magazine.* Albuquerque: New Mexico Department of Tourism, June 1936.

Mann, Howard. *True Tales of the Tenth Kansas Infantry: Excitement at Alton Prison.* Accessed February 20, 2010. http://www.civilwarstlouis.com /Gratiot/tenthkansas2.htm.

Mason, John. Quoted in Thomas E. Farish, *History of Arizona*, Vol. 5, 186. San Francisco: Filmer Brothers Electrotype Co., 1918.

Matthews, Matt, and Kip Lindberg. "'Shot All To Pieces' The Battle of Lone Jack, Missouri, August 16, 1862," *North and South* 7, No. 1 (January 2004): 56–72.

Mays, Thomas D. *The Saltville Massacre.* Fort Worth: Ryan Place Publishers, 1995.

McKinney, Roger. "Battle of Island Mound marked first time blacks fought in Civil War combat," *Joplin Globe*, July 30, 2011.

Monaghan, Jay. *Civil War on the Western Border, 1854–1865.* 1955. Reprint, Lincoln: University of Nebraska Press, 2004.

Moneyhon, Carl. "1865: 'A State of Perfect Anarchy,'" in *Rugged and Sublime: The Civil War in Arkansas*, ed. Mark Christ. Fayetteville, Arkansas: University of Arkansas Press, 1994.

Moore, H. Miles. *An Early History of Leavenworth City and County.* Leavenworth: Sam'l Dodsworth Book Co., 1906.

Moore, John C., *Confederate Military History of Missouri.* Pensacola: eBooks OnDisk.com, 2004.

Northrup, A. Judd. "Slavery in New York: A Historical Sketch," *State Library Bulletin: History.* No. 4 (May 1900).

Nottage, Mary Ellen. "Cannons, Spinning Wheels, and a Train: A History of the Museum Collection," *Kansas History.* No. 7 (Spring 1984). Topeka: Kansas State Historical Society.

O'Conner, Charles M. "The Eighth Regiment of Cavalry," in *The Army of the United States: Historical Sketches of Staff and Line with Portraits of*

Generals-in-Chief, ed. Theophilus Rodenbough. New York: Maynard, Merrill, & Co., 1896.

Parrish, William Earl. *David Rice Atchison, Border Politician*. Columbia: University of Missouri Press, 1961.

Parsons, Eugene. *A Guidebook to Colorado*. Boston: Little Brown, and Co., 1911.

Pope, Neta and Andrea Jaquez. *The Fort Bayard Story: 1866–1899*. Silver City, New Mexico: Andrea Jaquez, 2011.

Quarles, Benjamin. *The Negro in the Civil War*. Boston: Little Brown, 1953. Reprint, New York: Da Capo Press, 1989.

Raper, George. "Cavalry Duty in the Southwest in the 1870s," in *Indian War Veterans: Memories of Army Life and Campaigns in the West, 1864–1898*, ed. Jerome Greene. New York: Savas Beatie, 2007.

Redkey, Edwin, ed. *A Grand Army of Black Men: Letters from African American Soldiers in the Union Army 1861–1865*. New York: Cambridge University Press, 1993.

Richards, Ira Don. "The Battle of Poison Spring," *Arkansas Historical Quarterly*, Vol. 18, No. 4. (Winter, 1959).

Schultz, Duane. *Quantrill's War: the Life and times of William Clarke Quantrill*. New York: St. Martin's Griffin, 1996.

Selig, Robert. "The Revolution's Black Soldiers," *American Revolution.org*. Accessed June 1, 2011. http://www.americanrevolution.org/blk.html.

Simmons, Marc. *The Last Conquistador: Juan de Onate and the Settling of the Far Southwest*. Oklahoma Western Biographies, Vol. 2. Ed. Richard Etulain, Norman: University of Oklahoma Press, 1991.

Smith, John David, ed. "Let Us All Be Grateful That We Have Colored Troops That Will Fight." In *Black Soldiers in Blue: African American Troops in the Civil War Er*a. Chapel Hill: University of North Carolina Press, 2002.

Spencer, John, ed. *Thunder on the Plains: 140th anniversary of the Battle of Mine Creek* Topeka: Kansas State Historical Society, 2004.

Spring, Leverett W. *Kansas: the Prelude to the War for the Union*. Boston: Houghton, Mifflin, 1885.

Spurgeon, Ian M. *Man of Douglas, Man of Lincoln: the Political Odyssey of James Henry Lane*. Columbia: University of Missouri Press, 2008.

Stone, Jayme M. "Brother against Brother: The Winter Skirmishes along the Arkansas River," in *Civil War Arkansas: Beyond Battles and Leaders*, eds. Anne J. Bailey and Daniel E. Sutherland. Fayetteville: University of Arkansas Press, 2000.

Stone, Wilbur F., ed. *History of Colorado.* Vol. I. Chicago: S.J. Clarke Publishing Company, 1918.

Sunderwirth, Richard, ed. *"The Burning" of Osceola, Missouri.* Independence, Missouri: Two Trails Publishing, 2009.

Sutherland, Daniel. "1864: 'A Strange, Wild Time,'" in *Rugged and Sublime: The Civil War in Arkansas,* ed. Mark K. Christ. Fayetteville: University of Arkansas Press, 1994.

Sylvester, Nathaniel B. *Historical Sketches of Northern New York and the Adirondack Wilderness.* Troy, New York: William H. Young. 1877.

Tabor, Chris. *The Skirmish at Island Mound, Mo.: the First Battle Fought by an African-American Regiment during the Civil War.* Butler, Missouri: Bates County Historical Society, 2001.

Tharp, Judy. "A Story from Platt County, Missouri: 'Old Kickapoo.'" *The Border Star,* Nov–Dec, 2007. Reprint, *The Missouri Unionist, Newsletter of the Department of Missouri—Sons of Union Veterans of the Civil War.* Vol. 2, No. 2 (December 2007).

Thrapp, Dan L. *The Conquest of Apacheria.* Norman: University of Oklahoma Press, 1967.

"Trinidad, Colorado: A Short History of the Early Days." Accessed June 9, 2009. http://www.sangres.com/places /lasanimas/history.htm.

Trudeau, Noah Andre. *Like Men of War: Black Troops in the Civil War 1862–1865.* New York: Little Brown, 1998. Reprint, Edison, New Jersey: Castle Books, 2002.

Urwin, J.W., ed. *Black Flag over Dixie: Racial Atrocities and Reprisals in the Civil War.* Carbondale: Southern Illinois University Press, 2004.

Utley, Robert. *Frontier Regulars: The United States Army and the Indian, 1866–1891.* New York: Macmillan Publishing, 1969. Reprint, Lincoln: University of Nebraska Press, 1973.

———. *The Indian Frontier of the American West 1846–1890.* Albuquerque: University of New Mexico Press, 1984.

Vaughn, Dale, *The Chance.* Leawood, Kansas: Leathers Publishing, 2004.

Walkes, Joseph A. "Captain William D. Matthews: Freemason, Leavenworth, Kansas," *The Phlaxis* 14 (4th Quarter, 1987): 3–8, 29.

Wallace, Ernest. *Charles DeMorse: Pioneer Statesman and Father of Texas Journalism*. Paris, Texas: Wright Press, 1985. First published 1943 by Texas Tech Press.

Ward, William H. ed., *Records of the Members of the Grand Army of the Republic with a Complete Account of the Twentieth National Encampment*. San Francisco: H.S. Crocker & Company, 1886.

Warren, Steven L. *Brilliant Victory: The Second Civil War Battle of Cabin Creek, Indian Territory*. Wyandotte, Oklahoma: Gregath Publishing, 2002.

Waugh, John C. *Sam Bell Maxey and the Confederate Indians*. Abilene, Texas: McWhiney Foundation Press, 1998.

Westwood, Howard C. "Captive Black Union Soldiers in Charleston: What to Do?" in *Black Flag Over Dixie: Racial Atrocities and Reprisals in the Civil War,* ed. Gregory J.W. Urwin. Carbondale, Illinois: Southern Illinois University Press, 2004.

"When Kansas Became a State." *Kansas Historical Quarterly*, Topeka: Kansas State Historical Society. Vol. 27, No. 1 (Spring 1961).

Woodworth, Steven E. *Manifest Destinies: America's Westward Expansion and the Road to the Civil War*. New York: Alfred A. Knopf Publisher, 2010.

Wooster, Robert. *The Military and United States Indian Policy 1865–1903*. Lincoln: University of Nebraska Press, 1988. Reprint, 1995.

Worcester, Donald. *The Apaches: Eagles of the Southwest*. Norman: University of Oklahoma Press, 1979.

Yenne, Bill. *Indian Wars: The Campaign for the American West*. Yardley, Pennsylvania: Westholme Publishing, 2006.

Zornow, William F. *Kansas: A History of the Jayhawk State*. Norman: University of Oklahoma Press, 1957.

Index